STUDY ABROAD

Recent Titles in
Contributions to the Study of Education

STUDY ABROAD

The Experience of American Undergraduates

Jerry S. Carlson, Barbara B. Burn,
John Useem, and David Yachimowicz

CONTRIBUTIONS TO THE STUDY OF EDUCATION,
NUMBER 37

GREENWOOD PRESS
New York · Westport, Connecticut · London

Library of Congress Cataloging-in-Publication Data

Study abroad : the experience of American undergraduates / Jerry S.
  Carlson . . . [et al.].
      p. cm.—(Contributions to the study of education, ISSN
  0196-707X ; no. 37)
    Includes bibliographical references.
    ISBN 0-313-27385-5 (alk. paper)
    1. Foreign study—Evaluation.   2. Language and languages—Study
  and teaching—Evaluation.   I. Carlson, Jerry S.   II. Series.
  LB2375.S78   1990
  370.19′6—dc20   89-49243

British Library Cataloguing in Publication Data is available.

Library of Congress Catalog Card Number: 89-49243
ISBN: 0-313-27385-5
ISSN: 0196-707X

First published in 1990

Greenwood Press, Inc., 88 Post Road West, Westport, Connecticut 06881
An imprint of Greenwood Publishing Group, Inc.

Printed in the United States of America

The paper used in this book complies with the
Permanent Paper Standard issued by the National
Information Standards Organization (Z39.48-1984).

10 9 8 7 6 5 4 3 2 1

CONTENTS

TABLES

PREFACE

PRELIMINARY COMMENT

The number of American undergraduates who study abroad has increased significantly in the last decade. More and more students believe that a study abroad experience will make an important difference in obtaining a job after completing their studies and in pursuing internationally related careers. Many seek an overseas experience for personal enrichment and development. Faculty members and senior administrators in American colleges and universities increasingly recognize that study abroad and exchanges can make a major contribution to students' knowledge of other countries and cultures and their foreign language proficiency.

In an interdependent world, study abroad is thought to be an important vehicle for producing an internationally aware and concerned citizenry. It may also develop the cross-cultural skills and knowledge that are needed to enhance the global competitiveness of American business and the effectiveness of the United States in its relations with other nations. In the widespread concern to reassess general education and liberal education, some institutions are giving priority to study abroad on the assumption that it may contribute to achieving such educational goals as expanded analytic abilities, awareness of cultural diversity, and the capacity to deal with ambiguity.

Despite widely held convictions and assumptions on study abroad, little hard data and comprehensive research have documented the actual contribution that it makes to students and their educational development. Little is known about the conditions under which students profit most from study abroad and in what ways. The Study Abroad Evaluation Project (SAEP), the subject of this volume, was launched in 1982 in order to undertake the kind of systematic and comprehensive research needed to document and give future guidance to the role of study abroad. The focus of the study is on what difference, if any, study abroad makes to students in their undergraduate careers and later lives, or, put differently, the outcomes for students of study abroad.

SOME PROJECT FINDINGS

The findings of the SAEP form the heart of this book. While some, not surprisingly, support the conventional wisdom about study abroad, others provide fresh insights. Among the findings, to mention only some, are the following:

- Study abroad students were more dependent on financial aid and received less parental support than the comparison group students (these "stay-at-home" students were chosen for their comparability to the study abroad students).
- Oral interview testing showed that most study abroad students in foreign language countries move from the intermediate to the advanced level in language proficiency based on the FSI/ACTFL rating system (Foreign Service Institute of the Department of State and the American Council on the Teaching of Foreign Languages).
- A low level of interaction with fellow American students correlated positively with international learning, lack of problems experienced abroad, integration into the host culture, and strong academic performance.
- The students who performed best academically also gained the most from their non-academic experiences abroad.
- In the group of students studied, which was overwhelmingly in an immersion situation, differences among host countries were far less important to the students' international education achievements than that they studied abroad.
- Students who studied abroad were more satisfied with their year abroad than were the comparison group students with their junior year at home.
- Close to half the study abroad students expected to have careers involving living and/or working abroad.

ORIGIN OF THE STUDY ABROAD EVALUATION PROJECT

The SAEP was initiated in part as a follow-up to the President's Commission on Foreign Language and International Studies (1980a, 1980b). The commission's report emphasized the contribution of study abroad and exchanges to international education. In 1981 the National Council on Foreign Language and International Studies, set up after the commission finished its work, joined with the European Cultural Foundation to sponsor a conference in Bellagio, Italy, to undertake a comparative assessment of foreign language and international studies in Europe and the United States. An important recommendation of the Bellagio conference was that the intra–European Community student and faculty exchange program, the Joint Study Program, should be assessed in terms of the outcomes of study abroad for students and their institutions.

A year after the Bellagio meeting, agreement was reached with the European Institute of Education and Social Policy (Paris) on a joint Europe–U.S. research project on study abroad, the SAEP. The U.S. institutions identified to participate in the project were chosen for their shared characteristics with European institutions active in study abroad and exchange programs: (1) their study abroad activities included Western Europe, (2) the U.S. institutions mostly integrated their students into the host institutions abroad, (3) the programs involved reciprocal exchanges of students, and (4) the U.S. institutions could access study abroad data going back at least a decade and preferably longer.

The U.S. institutions selected for participation on the basis of these criteria were the University of California (Berkeley, Los Angeles, and Santa Barbara), the University of Colorado at Boulder, the University of Massachusetts at Amherst (the coordinating institution on the U.S. side), and Kalamazoo College. Even though Kalamazoo's study abroad programs offer limited reciprocity and do not integrate all Kalamazoo students into host institutions, the college was included because it has maintained a very active role in study abroad and because—as a small, liberal arts, private midwestern institution—its inclusion would make the SAEP more broadly representative of study abroad in American higher education. (Appendix I discusses Kalamazoo's involvement in the SAEP.)

The agreed focus of the SAEP was on the role of study abroad in students' acquisition of foreign language proficiency, knowledge of and concern for other countries and cultures and international issues, knowledge of and attitudes toward their home country and its values, and career objectives and accomplishments. The participating European institutions, nearly thirty, are located in the United Kingdom, France, Sweden, and the Federal Republic of Germany. They include not only universities but a range of other postsecondary institutions. The total number of study abroad programs offered by the European institutions is over forty; by the U.S. institutions, twelve (counting all the programs of one U.S. institution in a given country as a single program).

LIMITATIONS OF THE PROJECT

The Study Abroad Evaluation Project is a landmark in its comprehensiveness and empirical findings on a number of pragmatic questions. There are, however, some limitations in its broad applicability to the entire field of study abroad by U.S. students (and Europeans as well), as explained below.

1. Because the U.S. participating institutions, with the exception of Kalamazoo College, were identified on the basis of the similarities among their study abroad programs and structures, including their centralized administration of programs, the relevance of the SAEP findings to study abroad programs not sharing these characteristics, while doubtless substantial, cannot be assumed.

2. A corollary to the foregoing is that, in large part, the SAEP could not document correlations between different study abroad program characteristics and students' in-

ternational learning not the extent to which particular program features are more or less conducive to various outcomes.

PROJECT TEAM AND PUBLICATIONS

In addition to the persons listed as co-authors of this book, the following persons were extremely important to the U.S. side of the project: William H. Allaway, University of California at Santa Barbara; Jean Delaney, University of Colorado at Boulder; Manfred Stassen at the German Academic Exchange Service (DAAD); Joe Fugate, Kalamazoo College; Maryelise Lamet, University of Massachusetts at Amherst; Elinor Barber, Institute of International Education; Patricia Martin, University of Pennsylvania; and Horst Hoffman, University of California at Riverside. The European team members are listed in Appendix II.

This book is one of several produced or planned as the product of the Study Abroad Evaluation Project. While this volume focuses on the U.S. experience, other SAEP publications will include a two-volume report dealing with all five countries involved in the project and presenting comparative findings and analyses on (1) study abroad programs and (2) student outcomes and impacts.

PROJECT FUNDING

U.S. participation in the SAEP would not have been possible without the generous grant of $70,400 provided by the United States Information Agency. The contributions of $3,500 each from the Council on International Educational Exchange, the Institute of International Education, and the National Association for Foreign Student Affairs (NAFSA) provided welcome additional funding for the SAEP. NAFSA's agreeing at an early stage to provide primary administrative oversight with no reimbursement for overhead costs was crucial not only in terms of financial support but especially in terms of commitment to the SAEP.

The total costs of the U.S. activities in the SAEP far exceeded the above-mentioned contributions. Each of the four participating institutions provided major support for the project through investment of staff time and coverage of substantial administrative and other costs.

The role of the European Institute of Education and Social Policy was indispensable in implementing the Study Abroad Evaluation Project. Its team of experts and consultants made a major contribution in helping to conceptualize the project, designing the instruments, collecting and analyzing data, and coordinating with the U.S. side. The Europeans also carried most of the burden for preparing the two-volume report on the project mentioned earlier, which will include all five countries.

CONCLUSION

The final chapter of this book focuses on (1) the significance of the issues and findings in the study in the context of our times and society; (2) policy implications for institutional decision-makers, funding organizations, and governments; and (3) implications for research. The SAEP proposes answers on some issues and, based on its extensive data base, suggests some directions for study abroad in the coming years. The Study Abroad Evaluation Project is exceptional in addressing a field, the growing importance of which far surpasses the pace of relevant research in documenting its role and contributions. The U.S. team for the project hopes that this study will stimulate a quickening of this pace.

INTRODUCTION

As universities and colleges throughout the United States renew and expand their interest in international educational exchange, study abroad programs will become a factor of increasing significance in the education of American college and university students. Although international educational exchange has a long history (Burn, 1985), the research literature (see, for example, Brislin, 1981; Church, 1982; Klineberg, 1981; Klineberg and Hull, 1979; Sell, 1983; Spaulding and Flack, 1976; Weaver et al., 1987, Yachimowicz, 1987) has not been systematic and few investigations have employed longitudinal, quasi-experimental designs. While pre-experimental designs, retrospective analyses, and noncontrolled cross-sectional studies can be informative, they can also be misleading and contribute only marginally to understanding the study abroad experience.

We realize that any single investigation can provide only a limited degree of knowledge on any given topic and make no claims for the present study that go beyond the research questions guiding the work, the instruments used, and the populations sampled. Nonetheless, we feel that the research to be presented in this book does make a significant contribution to our quest: understanding the meaning and significance of the study abroad experience.

Although the focus of the present volume is on the impacts of study abroad on American students, the Study Abroad Evaluation Project has, from the outset, had the complementary goals of in-depth and long-term analysis of the nature and impacts of study abroad programs. Through a seven-part series of instruments, the project has investigated the institutional context of each study abroad program, the experience of the student as participant, and the immediate and long-range impacts of study abroad on the student and the institution.

The development of the following series of instruments over the course of the project was a process of transatlantic cooperation. In the course of the study, the following instruments were used:

1. *Institutional Profile*. The institutional profile establishes the basic characteristics of each institution sponsoring a study abroad program in terms of student and faculty demographics and the environment of international activities in the broadest sense.

2. *Departmental Profile*. The departmental profile establishes the same framework of data as the institutional profile for the individual department sponsoring a specific study abroad program. This form of sponsorship is by far the most common in European institutions but is quite rare in the United States. Therefore, this instrument was little used by the U.S. team.

3. *Study Abroad Program Profile*. The program profile creates a detailed data base on each study abroad program. The major realms of inquiry are program characteristics, historical background, and experience and summary participant profile.

   Following the first stage of research in which institutional, departmental, and study abroad program profiles were completed, interviews were carried out at the institutions involved in the project. The goal of these interviews was to validate and bring to life the information gained in the earlier profiles. By discussing study abroad with a wide range of individuals (students, faculty, program directors, top-level administrators), the project sought to broaden the understanding of how and why study abroad programs find institutional support, accommodate the needs of the student and the institution, affect the institution, and so on.

4. *Student Questionnaires*. The premeasure student questionnaire gathers data on the students' background, motivation, learning style, language proficiency, knowledge and views of other countries, and career objectives prior to the sojourn abroad for the study abroad group and prior to the junior year on the home campus for the comparison group. Parts of the pre- and postmeasure questionnaires provide comparative data on student development in the above areas. In addition, the postmeasure administered to the study abroad students provides information specifically concerning the study experience.

5. *Long-Term Student Profile*. Inquiry into the long-term impacts of study abroad has been undertaken in two ways. The European institutions administered a questionnaire to individuals who participated in study abroad programs between five and fifteen years ago, assessing, primarily, the professional impacts that the study abroad experience had.

   The four U.S. institutions have followed an in-depth telephone interview approach to examine the long-term impacts of study abroad in areas such as career choice and experience; home and lifestyles; and social, cultural, and political points of view.

The book, which focuses on student questionnaires and long-term profiles, is divided into seven chapters. In Chapter 1, the research questions and the design of the study are presented. Chapter 2 describes similarities and differences between students who elect and who do not elect to study abroad. Chapter 3 explores experiences related to the sojourn of the study abroad students and changes in their foreign language proficiencies. Chapter 4 discusses the impacts of the study abroad experience, whereas Chapter 5 peruses analyses of personal and sojourn variables related to changes in study abroad students. The long-term effects of the study abroad experience are described and analyzed in Chapter 6. Finally, in Chapter 7 the significance of the study's findings are discussed as well as policy and research implications. When relevant to the chapter, a description of the sample used in the analyses as well as the methodological approaches employed to analyze and summarize the data precede the presentation of the results.

1

RESEARCH QUESTIONS AND
METHODOLOGY

A. RESEARCH QUESTIONS

As with any research endeavor, the quality and significance of the research questions asked are of paramount importance. The research questions guiding this study provide the framework for the design of the study, selection of the subjects, development of the instruments, and the approaches employed to analyze and interpret the data.

The research questions were:

1. Who chooses to study abroad? Or, How do the students who study abroad differ from those who remain on their home campuses?
2. What changes occur in the two groups of students over the time span of the junior year?
3. What aspects of the individual and/or the sojourn abroad contribute to variation in the changes observed?
4. What are the long-term effects of the study abroad experience? How pervasive and durable are they?

B. DESIGN

Overview

The most common approach employed to assess sojourn effects is to administer questionnaires and/or interview students subsequent to the sojourn abroad (Church, 1982). Whether questionnaires, interviews, or a combination of the two are employed, the student is most often asked to reflect on the experience abroad and through retrospection to provide an account of changes and developments in orientation and perspective that he or she attributes to the sojourn. While valuable information concerning sojourns abroad can be gained by employing a posttest-only design, the approach may result in misleading and incorrect results and conclusions. There are several reasons for this.

First, individuals' recall of circumstances, events, and their attitudes toward these is often inaccurate (Eagley and Himmelfarb, 1978). Second, perceived change in one's attitudes and perspectives may not accurately reflect the actual change that occurred (Pool, 1965; Zajonc, 1981). This may be particularly true for student sojourners, as students studying abroad are in a situation where significant changes in self and worldview are expected by themselves and by their contemporaries (Spaulding and Flack, 1976). If substantial change were not felt and/or reported, regardless of whether or not it occurred, many students may feel that they failed or were "shortchanged" in some way. Accordingly, study abroad participants may have a predisposition to perceive change in themselves and to attribute the change to the study abroad experience. Third, attributions students make to the factors involved in perceived change in their views, abilities, and perspectives may often be erroneous (Kelman, 1975). Fourth, since students change regardless of whether or not they participate in study abroad, observed change in one group is difficult to interpret (Carlson and Widaman, 1988; Smith, 1955), as changes similar to those observed in study abroad students might have occurred had the students remained on their home campus.

In order to address some of these issues, research approaches must be employed that control as many factors as possible that affect, or potentially affect, the internal and external validity of study abroad research designs. For research on the effects of study abroad on students, the optimal research design is a fully randomized, pretest-posttest control group design. In the case of undergraduate study abroad programs, such a design would require random selection of students and random assignment to the study abroad and control groups. Through random assignment and appropriately large sample sizes, the study abroad group and the group designated to remain on the home campus would, at least at the outset, constitute functionally equivalent groups; consequently, subsequent differences observed between the groups could be attributed to circumstances following the initial assignment. The challenge for the researcher is to discover the dimensions of sojourn change as well as the circumstances, singly or in combination, that are related to the change. In other words, changes at both the individual and group level need to be documented and the correlates of change discovered.

An additional caveat concerning assessment of the impacts of study abroad on students is that the usefulness of the comparison group is limited by the extent to which the measures and/or questions are equivalent for both groups. To the extent that equivalence is lost, an important element of control and comparability is sacrificed. On the other hand, strict equivalence of measures administered to the experimental and control groups would be inappropriately restrictive, requiring that specific questions be ignored that would be relevant to the study abroad group only.

Since for a variety of practical and ethical reasons random assignment to study abroad cannot be made, true experimental research designs are not feasible. Instead, research on study abroad must be limited to pre-experimental and quasi-experimental research designs. For reasons already outlined, pre-experimental designs are of questionable utility when addressing questions of change attributed to the study abroad experience. Quasi-experimental research designs, however, are viable alternatives with the primary advantage of providing an approximation of an experimental design when the researcher does not have full control over subject selection and assignment to condition and times of treatments and measurements (D. T. Campbell and Stanley, 1963).

Since students cannot be placed in study abroad programs in order to meet research requirements, quasi-experimental designs offer practical alternatives to a fully randomized, experimental research design. Furthermore, in some cases, they can be of greater utility than experimental designs, as the comparison group can be representative of a population of interest that originally may or may not have been the functional equivalent of the study abroad group. In the present study, for example, a nonequivalent control group design was employed; sophomores who generally met the academic criteria to study abroad but, for a variety of reasons, elected to remain on their home campuses during their junior year, composed the comparison group of interest. In addition, nonequivalent control group designs permit assessment of the same subject population over time, provide significant control over maturational effects and subject selection, and allow comparisons to be made between or among groups of specific interest (D. T. Campbell and Stanley, 1963). While these designs may not be unusual in the behavioral sciences, they are rarely employed in research assessing sojourn effects.

A caveat regarding sojourn research in general—and this study in particular—involves the potentially troublesome problem of primary reliance on opinions of the students being studied. By applying multimethod, multitrait approaches (D. T. Campbell and Fiske, 1959) and correlating a number of self-report measures with one another and with, where possible, behavioral indexes, the problem would be reduced. Unfortunately, it is not feasible to apply multimethod, multitrait approaches in studies of the scope and diversity of the present investigation, although we did make an attempt to do this in language proficiency assessment.

An additional problem that besets sojourn research is that opinions of individuals from one culture concerning peoples and institutions from other cultures often reflect the stereotypes that groups have of each other. As D. T. Campbell (1967, p. 827) has pointed out, "The most ubiquitous fallacious aspect of stereotypes is not so much the falsity of the descriptive content as it is in the several *causal misperceptions* [emphasis added] that accompany them." This suggests that one must exercise caution in interpreting the explanatory and attributional bases sojourners make concerning their observations of foreign people and their cultures and customs.

The Present Study

In order to address the research questions guiding this investigation, two subject cohorts were used: one cohort was surveyed in connection with the first three research questions; a second cohort was employed to address the fourth research question. For Cohort 1, a longitudinal, nonequivalent control group design was used. The study abroad group comprised students who had been chosen to participate in year-long study abroad programs, commencing autumn 1984. As mentioned earlier, they came from the four American institutions participating in the study—the University of California (UC), the University of Colorado (CU), the University of Masachusetts at Amherst (UMass), and Kalamazoo College—and were to study at universities in one of four European countries: France, the Federal Republic of Germany (FRG), the United Kingdom (UK), or Sweden. The comparison group comprised students from UC and UMass who, while not electing to participate in study abroad, did meet the general grade point average and academic standing criteria for such participation. The comparison sample was randomly selected from this population. Comparison group data were not obtained from CU or from Kalamazoo College.

Questionnaires were administered to Cohort 1 at two points in time: at the end of the sophomore year (spring 1984) and at the beginning of the senior year when all the study abroad students were back on their home campuses (autumn 1985).

Cohort 2, employed in order to evaluate the long-term effects of study abroad, comprised alumni and alumnae of the study abroad programs from the four U.S. institutions who had studied in one of the target European countries between five and twenty years ago. Information concerning the effects of study abroad on these individuals was obtained by means of a short questionnaire followed by a detailed telephone interview.

The design of the study as well as the times of assessment are depicted in Table 1.1.

C. THE SAMPLE

Cohort 1

As can be seen from inspection of Table 1.1, Cohort 1 was made up of two groups of students: students who studied abroad during their junior year and students who remained on their home campuses during their junior year. The latter is termed a *comparison group*, rather than a *control group*, inasmuch as

Table 1.1
Research Design

	Cohort 1	Cohort 2
Study Abroad	Pre-study abroad questionnaire spring 1984 Post-study abroad questionnaire fall 1985 (UC, UMass, CU, and Kalamazoo)	Post-study abroad Winter 1986-87
Comparison	Pre-junior year questionnaire spring 1984 Post-junior year questionnaire fall 1985 (UC, UMass)	

they were randomly selected from the sophomore (1984) class from the University of California and the University of Massachusetts at Amherst but not randomly assigned from the study abroad population at these two institutions. The University of California campuses from which the comparison group students were drawn were Berkeley, Los Angeles, and Santa Barbara. The reason for choosing the UC comparison group sample from these three campuses of the university is that the student bodies at these campuses are generally representative of UC as a whole, making sampling from each of the eight general campuses of the university unnecessary and inefficient. The comparison group was randomly selected from the population of students who met the general criteria for inclusion in study abroad programs (a 3.0 or better grade point average and sophomore status). Foreign language proficiency criteria were not used in selection of the comparison group.

Since the focus of the investigation was American students who study abroad, we have chosen to focus our efforts on deliberately chosen populations from selected institutions. This restriction is both a strength and a weakness of the study. The strength is that by sampling U.S. institutions that have year-long reciprocal exchanges in Western Europe and study abroad program records that go back at least ten years, we have obtained greater sample representativeness than any previous sojourn investigation with which we are familiar. The weak-

Table 1.2
Number of Pre–Junior Year Questionnaires Distributed and Number and Percentage Returned

	Distributed	Returned
France	291	192 (66%)
W. Germany	137	135 (99%)
Sweden	20	17 (85%)
U.K.	201	144 (72%)
Comparison	820	355 (43%)

ness is that the generalizability of results is necessarily limited; for the sample to have been fully representative of American study abroad students, an elaborate and comprehensive sampling approach would have been needed. Such an approach was well beyond the scope of the present investigation and, in fact, most likely beyond the scope of any sojourn research in the foreseeable future. Although our sample permits reasonably broad interpretations of the data, generalizations to "American" students who study in Europe can only be made with circumspection.

An additional restriction concerning the present investigation should be mentioned. While contrasts among host universities and national differences are of importance and dealt with in detail in other reports of the Study Abroad Evaluation Project, our focus is exclusively on American students who study at European universities. Although we present sampling information and some analyses and discussion categorized by host country, our primary emphasis is on data aggregated across host institutions.

The number of pre–junior year questionnaires distributed to and returned by the study abroad and comparison groups are reported in Table 1.2.

Inspection of Table 1.2 will show that the return rates for the study abroad groups ranged from 99 percent for the students who were to study in West Germany to 66 percent for the students who planned to study in France. These figures are not surprising, as one would expect that students on the eve of a study abroad year would be highly motivated to comply with requests from officials from their institutions to complete a predeparture questionnaire (Carlson and Yachimowicz, 1987). The return rate for the comparison group was, as one would also expect, much lower, with 43 percent of the comparison group students responding. Both study abroad and comparison group students

Table 1.3
Number of Fall 1985 Questionnaires Distributed and Percentage Returned

	Distributed	Returned
France	291	102 (35%)
W. Germany	137	69 (60%)
Sweden	18	5 (28%)
U.K.	201	75 (37%)
Comparison	310	157 (51%)

who did not complete and return the questionnaires from the first mailing were sent follow-up letters requesting their cooperation.

The numbers of students who completed the fall 1985 questionnaires are given in Table 1.3.

Examination of Table 1.3 will show that the return rates for the study abroad students after the sojourn averaged around 40 percent. While this figure is not as high as one would prefer, it is not unusually low for students asked to complete a questionnaire after study abroad experience (Carlson and Yachimowicz, 1987) and provides a suitable basis from which generalizations can be made (Rosenthal and Rosnow, 1975). At 51 percent, the response rate for the comparison group was somewhat higher than for the study abroad group. As with the spring 1984 questionnaire, nonrespondents were sent follow-up letters. Additionally, nonrespondents from the University of California were contacted by telephone. While a number of factors undoubtedly contributed to the moderate response rate, two seem to be particularly important: first, the questionnaire was lengthy, with many of the sixty-nine items requiring multiple responses; second, questionnaires were distributed at a time of the academic year when students were very busy with their studies.

The sample used for the statistical analyses comprised only those students who completed *both* the pre- and postquestionnaires. The number of students in the "matched" sample by home U.S. campus are reported in Table 1.4.

Cohort 2

Cohort 2 was made up of individuals who graduated from the four U.S. institutions between 1960 and 1981 and who, as juniors, spent a year abroad in one of the four target European countries. The group chosen was selected

Table 1.4
Number of Students Who Completed Both the Pre- and Postquestionnaires, by Home Campus

Students	N
Study Abroad	
Kalamazoo College	22
Univ. of California	115
Univ. of Colorado	32
Univ. of Mass.	35
Total Study Abroad	204
Comparison	
Univ. of California	143
Univ. of Mass.	10
Total Comparison	153

from alumni and alumnae for whom relatively currently addresses were available. Letters were sent out to these individuals informing them of the project and requesting their cooperation. The individuals contacted were asked to complete and return a short questionnaire and indicate when it would be convenient to be telephoned for an approximately thirty-minute interview (see Chapter 6). The number of letters sent out and returned as well as the number of persons interviewed are given in Table 1.5.

D. GENERAL DEMOGRAPHIC CHARACTERISTICS OF THE SAMPLE

Cohort 1: Study Abroad and Comparison Group Students

The average age of the study abroad group was 20.7 years; the average age of the comparison group was 20.7 years. The standard deviations (SDs), an index indicating degree of dispersion around the mean, were 1.76 and 1.38, respectively. The gender distribution for the study abroad group was 31 percent male and 69 percent female; for the comparison group the figures were 39

Table 1.5
Letters Sent, Letters Returned, and Number of Individuals Interviewed

	Sent	Returned	Interviewed
UC	51	25	15
CU	39	24	22
UMass	41	33	24
Kalamazoo	25	19	16

percent male and 61 percent female. Although approximately 16 percent of the comparison and study abroad students reported that either their mother or father had been born outside the United States, almost all the students themselves were born in the United States. Neither the comparison nor study abroad group students reported that they had had an earlier extensive foreign living experience abroad. Those students who reported that their family, or a member of their family, had previously lived abroad (approximately 30 percent of each group), indicated the overseas sojourn was of short duration and usually part of a military assignment, frequently in Western Europe.

Socioeconomic information was gathered by asking the respondents questions concerning parents' occupations and educational levels. The study abroad and comparison groups did not vary appreciably in either of these areas. The general level of education of the parents of both groups was high: 43 and 48 percent of the comparison and study abroad students, respectively, reported that their fathers had completed at least a master's degree. The educational levels of the students' mothers, while lower than those of the fathers, were also relatively high (the median educational level was a college B.A.) and approximately the same for the two groups.

The academic interests of the study abroad participants departed substantially from those of students who remained at their home campus, even though the evidence is that students, especially at the early stages of their university lives, often do not stay with an earlier declared major (Astin, 1985). The study abroad group (except for Kalamazoo) was made up largely of students majoring in the humanities and social sciences, business, and education (81 percent reported majors in one of these areas). Only 19 percent of the study abroad students majored in the sciences or mathematics. By contrast, and not surprisingly, the majors reported by the comparison group represented the range of majors found in the populations from which they were selected, with approximately 60 percent of the students majoring in the humanities, social sciences, business, and education and 40 percent majoring in the sciences, mathematics, and engineering.

The reasons that the students from both groups gave for choosing their majors were fairly similar. The most highly rated factor was interest and perceived ability to succeed in the subject matter. Although still rated highly, career- and job-related factors were somewhat less important, with the comparison sample tending to rank career-related reasons for choosing a major slightly higher than the study abroad group did. While an explanation of this finding might lie in the significant difference in the patterns of major areas of study of the two groups, data gathered as part of this investigation suggest that the study abroad students, at least prior to their foreign experience, tended to be less set in their career choices than their non–study abroad counterparts.

Since grade point average is a factor in the selection of study abroad students and the comparison group was randomly drawn from the population of students who also had grade point averages high enough to participate in study abroad (3.0 or better), both groups were made up of students who had good records of academic achievement. Furthermore, both groups tended to rate themselves as substantially above average in academic accomplishments and revealed themselves to be realistically confident in their ability to succeed in an academic environment.

Parental financial contributions did not constitute the sole source of support for either the study abroad or comparison group students. For the study abroad group, only 59 percent of the total university expenses were underwritten by the students' parents; income from the student's own work, grants, loans, and scholarships contributed the rest. The figures for the comparison group are similar except that these students tended to rely somewhat more on parental support (64 percent of the costs were borne by the parents) than on support from other sources. These results provide clear evidence that, on average, the study abroad students received less financial support from their parents than their counterparts who did not study abroad.

In summary, the background and demographic data reveal many more similarities than differences among the study abroad and comparison group students. Both groups were generally composed of high-achieving students, individuals who appeared confident in themselves and convinced that their chosen major area of study was right for them. The students from both groups had parents who were relatively highly educated. Furthermore, the data indicate that while the students' parents provided the majority of the financial support for their children's university education, it was heavily supplemented by income from the students' own work, grants, loans, and scholarships. While not statistically significant, there seems to be a tendency for the study abroad students to be somewhat more financially self-reliant than the comparison students.

The study abroad students were asked when they were informed about the study abroad programs at their college or university. Approximately 50 percent of the group reported that they had been informed about study abroad prior to entering college. Not surprisingly, this figure was substantially higher at Kalamazoo College, where 96 percent of the students reported that they knew about study abroad prior to enrolling. (The Kalamazoo College curriculum is designed to have the student participate in study abroad.) When queried if information about study abroad was part of general written information related to the field of study the student was interested in, 81 percent of the Kalamazoo College students responded positively to this question; less than 30 percent of the students from the other U.S. universities answered affirmatively, however. This suggests that few academic departments consider study abroad to be an important aspect of their curriculum. Written information from international services offices and study abroad programs and informal information from friends and acquaintances were noted as primary ways that students became informed about study abroad. Teaching staffs and student counselors appeared to play a minimal role in informing students about the possibility of studying abroad.

2

How Do Students Who Study Abroad Differ from Those Who Remain on Their Home Campus?

THE SAMPLE

The sample employed to address the first research question—How do students who study abroad differ from those who remain on their home campus?—included students from the University of California and the University of Massachusetts at Amherst only, since neither the University of Colorado nor Kalamazoo College was able to provide comparison groups. The sample comprised 303 students who completed both the pre- and postquestionnaires: 150 were in the study abroad group; 153 were in the comparison group (see Table 1.4).

METHODOLOGICAL APPROACHES

The methodological approaches utilized to examine the question of who studies abroad and how study abroad students differ from non–study abroad students are presented in each of the main sections of the chapter. The data were all taken from the premeasure administered in the spring of the students' sophomore year.

In Section A, the similarities and differences between the study abroad and comparison groups are presented as they pertain to (1) interests in other countries, (2) attitudes toward the United States and foreign countries, (3) career orientation, and (4) study abroad students' motivations to study abroad.

In Section B, the results of factor analyses of the multidimensional scales used in the premeasure questionnaire are given. The reason for subjecting the data from these scales to factor analysis was to determine the structure of the scales, thereby identifying dimensions to be used in subsequent statistical analysis. The scales analyzed include: (1) international understanding, (2) learning styles, and (3) personal self-efficacy.

In Section C, the results of discriminant analysis are outlined, showing which of the several variables derived from the premeasure are useful in describing differences between the study abroad and comparison group students.

In Section D, the salient descriptive and demographic characteristics of the groups are summarized and the results of the statistical analyses discussed.

A. SIMILARITIES AND DIFFERENCES BETWEEN THE STUDY ABROAD AND COMPARISON GROUPS

Knowledge and Interest in Other Countries

As would be expected from academically capable and confident college students, all respondents indicated high levels of interest in other countries, current events, and foreign affairs; student sojourners, however, had even higher levels of interest in these areas than the comparison group. This finding is not surprising, especially since the study abroad students had made the commitment to participate in foreign study.

The primary information sources students used to gain knowledge about other countries were television and domestic newspapers and magazines. In fact, about two-thirds of all respondents relied primarily on these media for their knowledge of other countries. Less than one-third of the students reported that their main sources of information were books published in the United States. Only 8 percent of the study abroad students indicated that foreign newspapers or books published in foreign countries were used as sources of information about those countries. This is similar to the comparison group, of which only about 3 percent reported using such materials.

Attitudes toward Other Countries and the United States

Attitudes toward other countries were assessed by asking the students to indicate their opinions concerning certain aspects of the country in which they were going to study (study abroad group) or the country that they knew best (comparison group—the most-often-named countries were Western European countries). In parallel fashion, the students were asked to express their opinions toward the United States on the same dimensions. The areas queried ranged from attitudes toward postsecondary education, to government foreign policy, to customs and traditions, to social structure. The scale employed was a 5-point scale, with 5 being highly negative and 1 being highly positive. The means and standard deviations for the comparison and study abroad groups concerning their attitudes toward the foreign country as well as toward the United States are presented in Table 2.1.

Inspection of Table 2.1 will reveal several interesting contrasts between the study abroad and comparison groups. For example, while the postsecondary education system of foreign countries was viewed equally highly by both groups,

Table 2.1
Means and Standard Deviations for Study Abroad and Comparison Groups
Concerning Attitudes toward a Foreign Country and the United States

	Foreign Country Mean (SD)	United States Mean (SD)
Post Secondary Education		
Study Abroad Group	2.18 (.73)	2.14 (.89)
Comparison Group	2.21 (.93)	1.83 (.74)
Government Foreign Policy		
Study Abroad Group	2.72 (.79)	3.42 (.98)
Comparison Group	3.01 (.98)	3.05 (1.05)
Cultural Life		
Study Abroad Group	1.71 (.73)	2.33 (.89)
Comparison Group	1.97 (.93)	2.05 (.87)
Media		
Study Abroad Group	2.52 (.87)	2.55 (1.09)
Comparison Group	2.69 (.97)	2.31 (1.03)
Customs, Traditions		
Study Abroad Group	2.00 (.76)	2.59 (.87)
Comparison Group	1.96 (.82)	2.58 (.90)
Social Structure		
Study Abroad Group	2.72 (.93)	2.74 (.92)
Comparison Group	2.59 (1.06)	2.66 (.95)

Scale:

1=Highly positive opinion	2=	3=	4=	5=Highly Negative Opinion

the comparison group valued the U.S. system of postsecondary education more highly than did the study abroad group. Interestingly, and related perhaps to their somewhat more critical attitude, the study abroad students seemed to be more critical of U.S. governmental foreign policy than they were of the foreign policy of the government of the country in which they were to study.

While the cultural life of the foreign country was ranked highly by both the study abroad and comparison group students, the prospective sojourners were significantly less positive than the comparison group students when asked about cultural life in the United States. In contrast, the students from both groups were about the same in their opinion concerning the customs and traditions of United States and the customs and traditions of the foreign country. Similarly, students from both groups were more favorably disposed to the customs and traditions of the foreign country that they knew best than to the customs and traditions of the United States. No significant differences were detected between the groups in views about any of the other areas queried: recent immigrant groups, the media, social structure, and the family.

The data concerning attitudes toward a foreign country and the United States provide several interesting contrasts between students who will and will not study abroad. While one can only speculate on the results, it seems as though study abroad students, even with little foreign experience and specific knowledge of the country in which they will study, have positive "mind-sets" toward their future host country and its institutions. The source of the general positive orientation toward the host country is unclear. It may be derived, at least partially, from somewhat critical perspectives of certain institutions in the United States, resulting, therefore, in positive attitudes toward corresponding institutions in a foreign country. If this is the case, it suggests the possibility of dynamic tensions between "pushes" away from the United States and "pulls" toward the foreign country. The bases of these dynamic tensions may lie in yet another dynamic interaction, the interplay between cognitive and affective factors as they influence an individual's perspective at any given time. It seems safe to assume that this interaction is particularly powerful in the sojourner, both prior to and during the period abroad. It suggests a theoretical model that could be useful in explaining the dynamics involved in students' changing perspectives concerning their home and host countries and sheds light on motivational variables that may be important in orienting students to want to participate in study abroad programs.

Career Perspectives

Study abroad and comparison group students were asked to indicate how likely they were to enter postgraduate studies. On a 5-point scale, with 1 being "most probably," the mean response for students from both groups was just over 2.0, indicating a fairly high level of commitment to enter graduate school. The students were also asked how set they were in their career goals. The results indicated that the comparison group students were moderately determined to pursue a particular career (mean of 2.5 on the 5-point scale); the study abroad group students, however, tended to be more open with regard to career choice (mean of 3.3).

Although students toward the end of their sophomore year tend not to be firmly fixed on a particular career choice, the students queried considered career factors to be highly important for choosing a major area of study. This was followed closely by interest and perceived ability in the subject area. A substantial number of study abroad students noted that career factors were significant to them in electing to study abroad. For example, between one-fifth and one-fourth of the study abroad students planned on careers in international business and viewed the upcoming experience abroad as almost essential to their career development. The perceived significance of the sojourn abroad for later career development is underscored by the fact that between 87 percent and 95 percent of the study abroad students felt that they would be able to utilize the general aspects of their international experience in their later professional life. Over 50 percent of these students indicated that their careers will most likely involve some sort of international contact; somewhat fewer than 50 percent of the study abroad students expected that their careers will involve living and working in foreign countries.

Motivation to Study Abroad

The reasons that the study abroad students ranked about equally as being most influential in their decision to want to study abroad included desire for foreign cross-cultural experience, improvement of foreign language ability, desire to live in/make acquaintances from another country, interest in gaining another perspective on their home country, desire for travel, and enhancement of understanding of a particular host country. Ranked just below these categories was the expectation that the study abroad experience would improve career prospects. Becoming acquainted with subject matter not offered at their home institution was of only moderate importance in the students' decision to study abroad. Of even less importance was that friends might be going on a study abroad program or that the study abroad experience would afford an opportunity to establish ties with one's own family or ethnic heritage.

The comparison group students were asked how interested they were in studying abroad. On a 5-point scale ranging from "extremely interested" (1) to "not at all interested" (5), 54 percent of the students marked either "1" or "2"; only 23 percent of the students marked "4" or "5." When asked to indicate if they would be willing to commit time and money by enrolling in study abroad, 66 percent of the comparison group indicated that they were at least moderately willing to do this. When queried further as to reasons for their nonparticipation in study abroad, 50 percent of the comparison group students indicated that it was unnecessary for their course of studies, 40 percent suggested that it would be inappropriate for their majors, and 46 percent thought that study abroad might delay their graduation.

In short, the primary reasons students gave for choosing to study abroad were related to their desire to experience new cultures and learn the language of the host country. Academic reasons seem to be of secondary importance for electing to study abroad unless the study abroad program is integrated into the academic curriculum of the home university or college. Although a good proportion of the comparison group students reported that they were interested in study abroad, they indicated a variety of reasons for not applying to participate in study abroad programs. Among these were perceived lack of curricular relevance of study abroad and the perception that study abroad may delay their graduation from college. This suggests that greater number of qualified and academically motivated students would participate in study abroad programs were they more clearly related to students' academic programs and the institution's curricula. This underscores the importance of integration of study abroad programs into the academic core of the university. We will have occasion to return to this issue in the concluding chapter of this volume.

B. RESULTS OF FACTOR ANALYSIS OF THE MULTIDIMENSIONAL SCALES

International Understanding

One of the often-stated goals of international education exchange is that it should lead to increased levels of global understanding (Abrams, 1960; Coelho, 1962; Stassen, 1985). While the goal is laudatory, heightened levels of international understanding resulting from a foreign sojourn remain difficult to document. One reason for this is that there is little theory to guide our conceptualization of what international understanding is. Accordingly, the measures used to assess the construct are varied and not representative of a defined set of behaviors and/or attitudes. In our view, one's level of international understanding is not static; rather, we see it as time and place dependent and the product of a complex set of dynamic interactions that involve one's orientation to changing circumstances and events. Hence, no single definition of international understanding can be made with confidence, and at least for the present time, the construct must be understood in terms of the specific operational definitions given to it by researchers in the field. (For a discussion of these issues, see Brislin [1981] and Carlson and Widaman [1988].)

Consistent with these caveats, we make no claim to assess international understanding beyond the meaning ascribed to it by the measures used in the present study: two independent scales based on the Education Testing Service's 1981 survey, *College Students' Knowledge and Beliefs: A Survey of Global Understanding* (Barrows et al., 1981). There were two primary reasons for relying on the Educational Testing Service scales. First, they have been used in other investigations that have assessed global awareness (Carlson and Widaman, 1988, Carlson and Yachimowicz, 1986, 1987). Second, they are multidimensional, representing a higher degree of complexity than unidimensional scales would. This is important because any meaningful definition of international understanding must be multidimensional.

The first scale employed assesses cognitive aspects of international understanding. It asks the respondent to describe his or her position, ranging from "extensive" (1), to "considerable" (2 and 3), to "fair" (4), to "slight (5 and 6), to "nonexistent" (7), on 17 items. Examples of the items are: "Awareness of problems common to many nations," "Critical views of your own country," and "Interest in learning more languages."

The second scale employed assesses affective aspects of international understanding. It also utilizes a 7-point response format. On this 13-item scale, the respondent is asked to indicate how strongly he or she agrees or disagrees with the statement presented. The choices, ranging from "strongly disagree" (1), to "moderately disagree" (2), to "slightly disagree" (3), to "indifferent" (4), to "slightly agree" (5), to "moderately agree" (6), to "strongly agree" (7), include "Pacific [peaceful] demonstrations [picketing missile bases, peace walks, etc.] are harmful to the best interests of my home country," "Patriotism and loyalty are the first and most important requirements of a good citizen," "It is none of our business if other governments restrict the personal freedom of their citizens," and "I prefer to be a citizen of the world than of any country."

The procedures for analyzing and presenting the data from both international understanding scales, as well as the results for the other multidimensional scales subjected to factor analysis, will be first to give the results of the principal factor analyses. Then the mean factor scores and standard deviations for the factor scores for both the comparison and study abroad groups will be given. Promax rotation was employed in each of the factor analyses, with the number of factors extracted based on their Eigenvalues, Scree plots, and examination of the percentage of variance each factor contributed to the total variance. The minimum factor loading for an item to be considered to mark a factor was .30. Factors that had Eigenvalues of less than unity were not considered. Since the scales subjected to factor analysis were given as pre- and postmeasures, that is, prior to the junior year and subsequent to the junior year, only those items were retained that contributed significantly to the dimensions isolated at both times of testing. Thus, if a particular item loaded significantly on a given factor on a premeasure but did not load significantly on a postmeasure, that item was eliminated from consideration. In this way, equivalency of items on the pre- and postmeasures was established. The sample employed for the factor analyses consisted of the University of California and University of Massachusetts study abroad and comparison group (N = 355).

International Understanding Cognitive Scale. Principal factor analysis of the 17 items on the first International Understanding scale identified 15 items that were useful in defining the significant dimensions of the scale. As can be seen from inspection of Table 2.2, the three extracted factors account for 100 percent of the total variance. The intercorrelations among the factors were moderately high, all around the .45 level.

The first factor, contributing 69 percent of the variance, was composed of 7 items, involving attitudes toward global issues and international peace and cooperation. Factor 1 was labeled "Peace and Cooperation." The second factor, contributing 17 percent of the variance, was defined by 4 items that tend to tap social and cultural dimensions. Factor 2 was defined as "Cultural Interest." The third factor, explaining 14 percent of the variance, was defined by 4 items involving cultural relativism and respect for others. Factor 3 was termed "Cultural Respect." The means and standard deviations of the factor scores for the study abroad and comparison groups are presented in Table 2.3.

International Understanding Affective Scale. Principal factor analysis of the

Table 2.2
Rotated Factor Pattern, Communality Estimates, and Eigenvalues for International Understanding Cognitive Scale (premeasure)

Factor 1: PEACE AND COOPERATION (7 items)	1	2	3	h^2
1. Awareness of Problem Common to Many Nations	.58	.02	-.08	.31
2. Concern with Problems of Third World Countries	.65	.04	-.01	.45
3. Desire for International Peace	.67	-.07	.05	.44
4. Wish to Find Solutions to Global Problems	.77	-.02	-.05	.54
5. Need for Closer Cooperation among Nations	.58	.14	.09	.50
6. Critical Views of Your Own Country	.37	-.10	.17	.18
7. Memberships in Organizations Concerned with Peace	.33	.25	-.24	.18
Factor 2: CULTURAL INTEREST (4 items)				
1. Desire to Meet and Interact with Foreigners	.02	.81	.04	.71
2. Actual or Desired Travel to Foreign Nations	-.10	.81	.01	.60
3. Actual Participation in Activities Aimed at	.30	.40	-.16	.28
4. Interest in Learning More Languages	.03	.61	.05	.39
Factor 3: CULTURAL RESPECT (4 items)				
1. Respect for Historical, Cultural Traditions and Achievements of Nations Other than Your Own	.27	.28	.32	.50
2. Negative Feelings About Foreigners	.18	-.01	-.33	.09
3. Views that Values of Your Own Society Are Not Universal and that Values of Other Societies are Just as Valid	.08	-.06	.69	.49
4. Respect for Traditions, Culture, Way of Life	.05	.09	.80	.76
Unrotated Eigenvalues of the Correlation Matrix	8.38	2.09	1.67	
Proportion of Variance	.69	.17	.14	

13 items composing the second International Understanding scale resulted in two factors marked by 6 items each. The factors are relatively independent, with the intercorrelation between Factor 1 and Factor 2 being .19. Factor 1, which contributed 67 percent of the total variance, was marked by items that appear to be related to the students' attitudes toward their home country. Factor 2, contributing 35 percent of the total variance, was marked by items that involve attitudes toward international issues. Factor 1 was labeled "Domestic Orientation"; Factor 2 was termed "International Concern."

Table 2.3
Factor Means and Standard Deviations of the International Understanding
Cognitive Scale

	"Peace and Cooperation"	"Cultural Interest"	"Cultural Respect"
Study Abroad	2.73 (.80)	1.85 (.55)	2.6 (.69)
Comparison	3.17 (.93)	2.78 (1.19)	3.0 (.81)

Scale: 1 = "extensive"; 7 = "nonexistent"

The rotated factor pattern, communality estimates, and Eigenvalues for the second international understanding scale are reported in Table 2.4. The means and standard deviations of the factor scores for the study abroad and comparison groups are presented in Table 2.5.

Learning Styles

Academic learning styles were assessed by a question asking the student to respond to several subparts of the general question: "How would you assess your current academic/learning abilities and accomplishments?" The student was to indicate on a 5-point scale whether or not he or she was "very strong" (1) or "very weak" (5) on each of the 24 items queried. Examples of the items are: "Working consistently," "Working under time pressure," "Formulating hypotheses and using them in analysis," "Coping with ambiguity," and "Understanding approaches from several disciplines."

Principal factor analysis was once again employed in order to determine the dimensionality of the Learning Styles Scale. Using the previously described criteria for factor extraction and determination of the items marking a factor, 4 factors were extracted that were defined by a total of 14 items. The factors were labeled "Intellectuality" (Factor 1; 3 items), "Academic Style" (Factor 2; 6 items), "Work Habits" (Factor 3; 3 items), and "Persistence" (Factor 4; 2 items).

The factors, the items defining the factors, and their factor loadings are reported in Table 2.6. Factor means and standard deviations for both groups in Cohort 1 are reported in Table 2.7.

Table 2.4
Rotated Factor Pattern, Communality Estimates, and Eigenvalues for
International Understanding Affective Scale (premeasure)

	1	2	h^2
Factor 1: DOMESTIC ORIENTATION (6 items)			
1. Pacific Demonstrations are Harmful to the Best Interests of My Home Country.	.46	-.26	.33
2. The Immigration of Foreigners to My Country Should be Kept Down so that We Can Provide for Our Own People First.	.46	-.10	.24
3. Patriotism and Loyalty are the First and Most Important Requirements of a Good Citizen.	.77	.01	.60
4. Immigrants Should Not be Permitted to Come into Our Country if they Compete with Our Own Workers.	.59	.00	.34
5. No Duties are More Important than Duties Towards One's Country.	.67	.01	.45
6. We Should Not Allow Foreign Business Enterprises to Have Substantial Holdings in Our Country.	.45	.17	.20
Factor 2: INTERNATIONAL CONCERN (6 items)			
1. I Believe My Country Should Send Food and Materials to any Country that Needs them.	-.14	.26	.10
2. The Mining and Distribution of Mineral Resources Should be Controlled by an International Authority.	.13	-.63	.38
3. We Should Have a World Government with the Powers to Make Laws that Would be Binding to All its Member Nations.	.02	.60	.35
4. An International Authority Should be Established and Given Direct Control Over the Production of Nuclear Energy in All Countries.	.07	.72	.18
5. I Prefer to be a Citizen of the World than of any Country.	-.30	.48	.37
6. It is Our Responsibility to do Everything Possible to Prevent People from Starving Anywhere in the World.	-.12	.38	.18
Unrotated Eigenvalues of the Correlation Matrix	3.97	2.09	
Proportion of Variance	.67	.35	

Table 2.5
Factor Means and Standard Deviations of the Second International
Understanding Affective Scale

	"Domestic Orientation"	"International Concern"
Study Abroad	2.90 (.97)	4.13 (1.23)
Comparison	3.56 (1.24)	4.00 (1.24)

Scale: 1 = "strongly disagree"; 7 = "strongly agree"

Personal Self-Efficacy

It has been repeatedly asserted that an extended sojourn abroad can be instrumental in offering the individual challenges and opportunities that result in intellectual growth (Abrams, 1960), international understanding (Coelho, 1962; Deutsch, 1970), expansion of one's worldview (Sanford, 1962), more positive attitudes toward foreigners (Sell, 1983), enhanced self-concept (Carsello and Greiser, 1976), and greater sociability (McGuigan, 1984). While not made explicit, the external source of both cognitive and emotional development is based on "disequilibrating" experiences that an individual encounters (see, for example, Allport, 1955; Block, 1982; Festinger, 1957; Luria, 1976; Piaget, 1950). In order for an event to be disequilibrating, there must be a "mismatch" between the individual's level of mental organization (cognitive and affective) and the external event(s) (Hunt, 1961). If the mismatch is not too great, the external event or events can be incorporated into existing cognitive and affective structures or levels and catalyze change as the individual seeks to accommodate to the new information. Fundamentally important to this process is the question of how one perceives and reacts to particular environmental circumstances and challenges. The interaction is both subtle and complex and mediated by a number of cognitive and noncognitive variables. One of the noncognitive variables of interest to us in the context of study abroad is an individual's personal self-efficacy. Our interest in personal self-efficacy is based on the view that (1) an extended sojourn abroad will positively affect the sojourner's self-concept and (2) one's self-concept is likely to mediate change in several important areas that are affected by the study abroad experience.

The personal self-efficacy scale used in the investigation is based on Susan Harter's work on effectance motivation (Harter, 1978). In her general theoret-

Table 2.6
Principal Factor Analysis of Learning Styles (study abroad and comparison groups)

Factor 1: INTELLECTUALITY (3 items)	1	2	3	4	h²
1. Apply Theories, Abstract Knowledge to Practical Issues	.78	.01	.03	-.09	.57
2. Abstract Problem Solving	.88	-.13	-.03	.05	.71
3. Formulating Hypotheses and Using Them in Analysis	.45	.15	.17	.07	.40
Factor 2: ACADEMIC STYLE (6 items)					
1. Cooperating With Others in Academic Work	.00	.38	.03	-.07	.13
2. Motivating Other People	-.14	.49	.08	.02	.23
3. Articulating Own Thoughts/Views	.03	.53	.05	.02	.32
4. Imagination	.09	.31	-.08	-.02	.12
5. Choosing Tasks Commensurate With Abilities	-.04	.43	.09	.03	.21
6. Developing Own Point of View	.13	.58	-.16	.02	.41
Factor 3: WORK HABITS (3 items)					
1. Working Consistently	-.04	-.01	.97	-.19	.85
2. Discipline in Learning	.07	-.10	.72	.16	.59
3. Planning and Following Through	-.08	.27	.55	.11	.50
Factor 4: PERSISTENCE (2 items)					
1. Assuming a Heavy Workload	-.07	.11	.20	.87	.78
2. Working Under Time Pressure	.08	.07	-.17	.60	.40
Unrotated Eigenvalues of the Correlation Matrix	6.3	4.2	2.5	1.7	
Proportion of Variance	.52	.31	.20	.09	

ical model, Harter considers the individual's sense of self and *perceived* competence as mediating the interactions that one has with one's environment. Since individuals are not equally competent in all areas, Harter has developed a differentiated set of scales that assess cognitive competence, social competence, and physical competence. Each of these domains can be divided into specific subdomains. In the present study, we chose to focus on social competence, or what we term *personal self-efficacy*. The reason for this is that we consider this dimension of one's perception of self to be particularly relevant for study abroad students (Adler, 1975), relating perhaps to the degree of success that a student has on the sojourn abroad.

The social competence scale used in the study is a modification of a scale

Table 2.7
Factor Means and Standard Deviations for Academic Learning Styles

	"Intellect-uality"	"Academic Style"	"Work Habits"	"Persistence"
Study Abroad	2.36 (.82)	2.07 (.53)	2.35 (.82)	1.94 (.70)
Comparison	2.60 (.83)	2.28 (.61)	2.31 (.96)	2.10 (.89)

Scale: 1 = "very strong"; 5 = "very weak"

developed by Harter for use with children and adolescents. Since with college-age students we found the adapted scale to yield the expected factor patterns, the scale appears to be suitable for use with the population sampled in the present study.

Factor analysis of the Self-Efficacy Scale was achieved by employing the same criteria for analysis and item retention as used in the previous factor analyses. Two interpretable factors were extracted: "Attitude toward Self," Factor 1, defined by 9 items, accounting for 78 percent of the total variance; and "Sociability," Factor 2, marked by 5 items, explaining 22 percent of the total variance. The intercorrelation between Factor 1 and Factor 2 was .43.

The factors identified, the items that define them, and their communalities are presented in Table 2.8. The means and standard deviations for the study abroad and comparison groups for the two factors of the Self-Efficacy Scale are reported in Table 2.9.

C. DISCRIMINANT FUNCTION ANALYSIS

In order to determine the characteristics of undergraduates who are likely to participate in study abroad, a statistical technique known as discriminant analysis was employed. This approach is used to classify individuals into one of two or more groups on the basis of a set of measurements (Affifi and Clark, 1984). In the present study, the procedure was employed to identify the relevant variables for defining differences between the study abroad and comparison groups. This was accomplished by a stepwise discriminant procedure and a linear discriminant function, which determine the accuracy of classification into each group (study abroad versus comparison). The primary advantage of discriminant analysis techniques over univariate techniques (t-tests and univariate analysis of variance) is that it provides estimates of the *independent* contribution that each variable makes in separating and defining the populations of interest.

Table 2.8
Rotated Factor Pattern, Communality Estimates, and Eigenvalues for the Harter Self-Efficacy Scale (premeasure)

FACTOR 1: ATTITUDE TOWARD SELF (9 items)	1	2	h^2
1. Some students find it hard to make friends.	.41	-.27	-.31
2. Some students feel there are a lot of things about themselves they would change if they could.	.59	.02	.34
3. Some students don't think they are a very important member of their group.	.57	-.08	.36
4. Some students feel good about the way they act.	-.40	.24	.28
5. Some students think maybe they are not a very good person.	.74	.18	.48
6. Some students wish more people liked them.	.63	-.07	.43
7. Some people are very happy being the way they are.	-.44	.21	.31
8. Some people aren't very happy with the way they do a lot of things.	.72	.17	.46
9. Some people are sure that what they are doing is the right thing.	.31	.27	.23
FACTOR 2: SOCIABILITY (5 items)			
1. Some students have a lot of friends.	-.02	.66	.45
2. Some students are always doing things with a lot of other students.	.21	.53	.25
3. Some people are really easy to like.	-.02	.46	.22
4. Some students are pretty sure of themselves.	-.32	.37	.32
5. Some students are popular with their classmates.	-.09	.69	.51
Unrotated Eigenvalues of the Correlation Matrix	5.69	1.84	
Proportion of Variance	.78	.22	

Correlational analysis of factor scores of the various attitude domains from the premeasure revealed that several of the variables were highly correlated. To cite one perhaps obvious example, students' attitudes toward international issues correlate positively with their having lived abroad as well as with their knowledge of foreign and host countries. Since intercorrelations among the variables could potentially lead to confounded results and misleading interpretations of the data, an approach that allows each variable to be analyzed independently of all other variables is preferred. Thus, a multivariate analysis was employed so that the independent contribution of each variable (partial correlation) could be estimated in the identification and differentiation of students who participate in study abroad and those who remain at their home campus.

Table 2.9
Factor Means and Standard Deviations for the Self-Efficacy Scale

	"Attitude Toward Self"	"Sociability"
Study Abroad	2.58 (.42)	2.14 (.52)
Comparison	2.53 (.47)	2.12 (.59)

Scale: For Factor 1, "Attitude Toward Self", 1 indicates a "low" score; 4 indicates a "high" score. For Factor 2, "Sociability," 1 indicates a "high" score; 4 indicates a "low" score.

The original sample used for the stepwise discriminant analysis comprised UC and UMass study abroad and comparison group students of Cohort 1 who completed both the pre- and postquestionnaires (N = 301). In order for a subject to be included in the analysis, data on that subject had to have been complete. Those students who failed to answer any part of the measures entered into the discriminant analysis were dropped from consideration. This procedure reduced the sample size from 301 to 269 students: 135 from the study abroad group and 134 from the comparison group.

Twenty variables representing identical individual items and groupings of items from the questionnaire administered to both the study abroad and comparison groups at the end of the students' sophomore year were entered into the stepwise discriminant analysis. Item groupings were based on the results of factor analysis of the multidimensional scales previously mentioned: International Understanding, Learning Styles, and Self-Efficacy. The 20 variables entered into the analysis are listed in Table 2.10.

The variables that were identified by means of analysis of variance as separating the study abroad from the comparison group are presented in Table 2.11. It should be kept in mind that many of these variables are intercorrelated and do *not* necessarily make an *independent* contribution toward defining the groups. Nonetheless, it is of interest to compare the list presented in Table 2.11 with the variables defined through discriminant analysis (see Table 2.12), which *do* make *independent* contributions to group definition.

The most significant variable emerging from the discriminant analysis (see Table 2.12) was "Cultural Interest." This 4-item variable was derived from the scale designed to measure cognitive aspects of International Understanding

Table 2.10
Variables Entered into the Stepwise Discriminant Function Analysis

1. "Peace and Cooperation," Factor 1 from the
    International Understanding Cognitive Scale
2. "Cultural Interest," Factor 2 from the
    International Understanding Cognitive Scale
3. "Cultural Respect," Factor 3 from the
    International Understanding Cognitive Scale
4. "Domestic Orientation," Factor 1 from the
    International Understanding Affective Scale
5. "International Concern," Factor 2 from the
    International Understanding Affective Scale
6. "Intellectuality," Factor 1 from the
    Learning Styles Scale
7. "Academic Style," Factor 2 from the
    Learning Styles Scale
8. "Work Habits," Factor 3 from the
    Learning Styles Scale
9. "Persistence," Factor 4 from the
    Learning Styles Scale
10. "Attitude Toward Self," Factor 1 from the
    Personal Self-Efficacy Scale
11. "Sociability," Factor 2 from the
    Personal Self-Efficacy Scale
12. Self-estimate of Grade Point Average
13. Self-rating of Academic Achievement
14. Experience Abroad
15. Contact with Foreigners
16. Participation in International Clubs
17. Level of Education of the Father
18. Level of Education of the Mother
19. Interest in Current Events, Other Countries,
    European and/or International Affairs
20. Commitment to Specific Career Goals

Table 2.11
Summary of Variables Determined by Analysis[1] Variance to Differentiate the Study Abroad and Comparison Group Students

Variable	F Value	p
"Peace and Cooperation"*	21.9	<.0001
"Cultural Interest"*	56.1	<.0001
"Domestic Orientation"**	21.2	<.0001
"Intellectuality"*	6.8	<.009
"Academic Style"*	11.9	<.0006
Self-estimate, GPA*	18.3	<.0001
Self-estimate, Academic Achievement*	11.8	<.0007
Contact with Foreigners*	10.4	<.0014
International Clubs*	13.0	<.0004
Interest in Current Events, International Affairs*	21.2	<.0001

1 - degrees of freedom 1, 167

*Indicates that the Study Abroad Group was Higher than the Comparison Group; **Indicates that the Comparison Group was Higher than the Study Abroad Group.

and accounted for 17 percent of the total variance. As one might expect, study abroad participants have a significantly greater interest in other cultures than those who choose not to study overseas. The next variable identified by the stepwise discriminant procedure was "Domestic Orientation," a 6-item variable obtained from the scale measuring affective dimensions of International Understanding. Study abroad participants scored lower on this domain than the comparison group. It was further determined that students who participate in study abroad programs are more likely to have participated in international clubs on their home campus, to have a somewhat higher self-rating of their

Table 2.12
Summary of Stepwise Discriminant Analysis, F and *p* Values, and Canonical R^2

Variable	F	p	R^2
"Cultural Interest"*	56.1	<.0001	.17
"Domestic Orientation"**	12.2	<.0006	.20
International Clubs*	9.7	<.002	.24
Self-estimate, Academic Achievement*	7.4	<.007	.26
Interest in Current Events, International Affairs*	3.4	<.06	.27

*Indicates that the Study Abroad Group was Higher than the Comparison Group; **Indicates that the Comparison Group was Higher than the Study Abroad Group.

academic achievement, and to be generally more interested in current events and international affairs than non–study abroad students.

A summary of the results of the stepwise discriminant analysis and the independent contribution of each variable is presented in Table 2.12.

In order to determine the accuracy of predicting if students are likely to study abroad, the data for each participant were entered into the discriminant function model to determine the probability of the model yielding a correct classification of individuals, that is, correct assignment of individuals either to the study abroad group or to the comparison group. The results of this procedure revealed that 76 percent of the study abroad group were classified correctly; 70 percent of the comparison group were classified appropriately. The accuracy of prediction reflects the efficacy of the variables used for predicting which students will participate in international studies during their undergraduate education.

D. SUMMARY AND CONCLUSIONS

The first research question asked, "Who chooses to study abroad?" Its corollary was, "How do students who study abroad differ from those who remain on their home campuses?'' The findings related to these questions are interesting for a number of reasons, as they are both supportive of and contradictory to views commonly held concerning study abroad students.

Descriptive and Demographic Characteristics

The background and demographic characteristics of the study abroad and comparison group students were similar in two respects: the relatively high levels of education of the parents and the relatively high social status of the father (defined by job classification). The groups differed only slightly in amount of parental support given for college education, with the study abroad group being somewhat less dependent on parental funding and more dependent on their own resources (work, scholarships, grants, loans, etc.) than the comparison group. The percentage of females and numbers of students majoring in the humanities, languages, and social sciences were, except for Kalamazoo, substantially higher in the study abroad group than in the comparison group.

While generally positive toward the United States, the study abroad students were less enthusiastic than the comparison group students concerning U.S. postsecondary education, U.S. government foreign policy, and American cultural life. Both groups rated the customs and traditions of European countries more highly than the customs and traditions of the United States and were similar in their perspectives concerning American media, social structure in the United States, and the American family. Although the study abroad students were positively oriented to the culture of their future host country, they were no more knowledgeable about the host country culture and institutions than the students composing the comparison group.

Although somewhat less certain than the comparison group of their career goals, the study abroad students were keenly interested in applying their foreign study experience to future career opportunities. Even if these students did not envision that their careers would be directly related to the skills and abilities that they hoped to gain while abroad, they felt that the foreign experience would generally aid them in their careers.

The primary motivation for most students to study abroad seemed to stem from the cultural and living experiences that they expected to have while abroad. Language development was also a significant reason for wanting to participate in a study abroad program. Although academic reasons tended not to be a primary motivation to participate in a study abroad program, it did play a role in choice of program, especially if the home institution had integrated study abroad into its general and/or departmental curricula. A significant proportion of the comparison group students were interested in participating in a study abroad program, but the perception of the lack of relevance of study abroad to their academic programs as well as the possibility that study abroad might delay graduation were seen as major deterrents.

Summary and Interpretation of the Discriminant Analysis

Discriminant analysis was the primary technique used to determine the statistical and practical significance of the variables that differentiated the study abroad group from the comaprison group. The statistics derived from the discriminant analysis that provide information concerning the statistical and practical significance of a variable or composite set of variables that differentiate the study abroad group from the comparison group were F and R statistics, respectively. The multiple correlation coefficient squared (R^2) provides an estimate of the amount of variance explained by the measure, indicating its practical utility. If two completely reliable variables were perfectly correlated, that is, $r = 1.00$, an individual's performance on one measure would predict with 100 percent accuracy his or her performance on another measure. Correlations less than unity are, of course, more difficult to interpret. That is why effect size (r^2 for bivariate and binomial correlations; R^2 for multiple correlations), rather than simple statistical significance, is important to consider for the interpretation of the relationship between two or more variables.

Understanding of the practical utility of r^2 and R^2 values can perhaps be facilitated by use of an example employing what Rosenthal and Rubin (1982) have called the "Binomial Effect Size Display." In order to illustrate the meaning of effect size—that is, the practical significance of r and r^2 values—Rosenthal and Rubin use a dramatic example: life and death rates related to a hypothetical medical treatment or intervention. The model they use is illustrated in Table 2.13. The effect sizes (r and r^2 derived from binomial or bivariate distributions) can be interpreted as analogous to multivariate R and R^2 values.

In the first example illustrated in Table 2.13, the treatment apparently did not result in decreased mortality rates, and "improvement" (living versus dying) was unrelated to the treatment. In the second example, the treatment seemed to have some effect, as mortality rates were decreased. Even though the treatment condition explained just 6 percent of the variance ($r = .25$; $r^2 = .06$), it is very meaningful if one considers the significance of the outcome. In the third example, the treatment was even more effective, resulting in substantially reduced mortality rates and accounting for 25 percent of the variance ($r = .50$; $r^2 = .25$). Appreciation of the meaning of effect size should help provide a meaningful context for interpretation of the results of the discriminant as well as the regression (see Chapter 5) analyses.

Twenty variables from the premeasure questionnaires distributed to the study abroad and comparison groups were entered into stepwise discriminant analysis. The variables included single-question variables such as previous experience abroad, level of education of the father, participation in international clubs, and so on, as well as composite variables that were identified from the results of the factor analyses of the multidimensional scales, that is, the two International Understanding scales, the Learning Styles Scale, and the personal Self-Efficacy Scale. Initial analysis, which did not take into account the intercorre-

Table 2.13
Binomial Effect Size Displays for r's of .00, .25, and .50 ($r^2 = 0$, .06, and .25, respectively)

Effect Size	Condition	Treatment Results Alive	Dead	Total
$r = .00$	Treatment	50	50	100
$r^2 = .00$	Control	50	50	100
	Total	100	100	200
$r = .25$	Treatment	63	37	100
$r^2 = .06$	Control	37	63	100
	Total	100	100	200
$r = .50$	Treatment	75	25	100
$r^2 = .25$	Control	25	75	100
	Total	100	100	200

lations among the variables, resulted in 10 dimensions or areas that differentiated the study abroad group from the comparison group. Further analysis provided results that showed the *independent* contribution that each of the variables made in differentiating the groups of interest. The 5 remaining variables that contributed to the differentiation were:

1. "Cultural Interest," a composite variable from the first International Understanding scale. The variable is defined by the students' awareness of problems of many nations, concern for problems of the Third World, need for closer cooperation among nations, and so on.
2. "Domestic Orientation," a composite variable from the second International Understanding scale, defined by attitudes involving restriction of immigration of foreigners to the United States, the importance of duty toward the United States, the significance of patriotism and loyalty to being a good citizen, and the like.
3. Participation in International Clubs
4. Self-rating of Academic Achievement
5. Interest in Current Events and International Affairs

The study abroad group was significantly higher than the comparison group in their "Cultural Interest" ($R^2 = .17$), their participation in international clubs

($R^2 = .04$), self-estimate of academic achievement ($R^2 = .02$), and interest in current events and international affairs ($R^2 = .01$). The comparison group was significantly higher than the study abroad group in "Domestic Orientation" ($R^2 = .03$). The 5 variables taken together account for a very impressive 27 percent of the variance ($R^2 = .27$) in separating the comparison group from the study abroad group.

The findings from the discriminant analysis show that students who are going to study abroad differ from students who do not study abroad in important and definable ways. As was suggested earlier in this chapter, students who do not study abroad tend to have the general perception that their academic goals would not be realized as well through study at a foreign university as by continued study at their home institution. Furthermore, a significant percentage of these students believe that study abroad would extend the time required to earn the baccalaureate degree. Both of these factors are important in what they imply about study abroad programs and what they tell us about students' perceptions of the programs. Beyond this, however, the results of the discriminant analysis suggest that additional factors seem to be involved in the self-selection process that determines which students aspire to study abroad. These factors seem to go beyond issues related to perceptions of the academic integrity of study abroad programs and reflect fundamental differences in the students themselves.

The most salient factor differentiating the study abroad students from the comparison group students was "Cultural Interest." This single variable accounted for an impressive 17 percent of the explained variance. The second most salient variable accounting for differences between the groups is "Domestic Orientation." The study abroad students were higher in their "Cultural Interest" scores and lower in their "Domestic Orientation" scores than the comparison group. The combination of just these two composite variables provides a relatively powerful model ($R^2 = .20$) for predicting who is and who is not likely to study abroad.

Although we have no data on *how* differences develop between the study abroad students and students who remain on their home campuses during their junior year, we do have strong indications that the students differ in predictable ways. Further research is needed to address questions such as (1) how students' interests in other cultures develop, (2) how curricular integration of study abroad programs can be achieved, and (3) how students' perceptions concerning study abroad are shaped.

3

EXPERIENCES RELATED TO THE SOJOURN OF STUDY ABROAD STUDENTS AND CHANGES IN THEIR LANGUAGE PROFICIENCY

THE SAMPLE

The sample employed to describe the experiences abroad of the student sojourners comprised all study abroad students from the University of California, the University of Colorado, Kalamazoo College, and the University of Massachusetts at Amherst who completed the post–study abroad questionnaire. The number of respondents per country in which the students studied was as follows: France, 102; the Federal Republic of Germany, 69; Sweden, 5; the United Kingdom, 75. The sample used to examine changes in foreign language proficiency comprised those students who completed both the pre- and postmeasures with the exception of students who studied in the UK or Sweden. The reason for excluding UK students from the sample is obvious as few took a foreign language and the language of the country is English. The reason for excluding the students who studied in Sweden was because of the small sample size and the resulting instability in the data.

METHODOLOGICAL APPROACHES

Data from the post–study abroad questionnaire utilized to describe student experiences abroad are presented in Section A of this chapter. In Section B, change in language proficiency is described. Although contrasts between the study abroad and comparison groups are not made in this chapter, when relevant, differences among students who studied in the four European host countries will be pointed out.

A. DESCRIPTIVE ASPECTS OF THE STUDY ABROAD EXPERIENCE

Accommodations

The American undergraduates who studied in Europe tended to have a variety of different living situations, depending on the country in which they studied. In Sweden, West Germany, and the United Kingdom, the majority of the students (upward of 75 percent) lived in university dormitories. In France, on the other hand, half of the students (50 percent) resided in apartments or in private homes. Only 13 percent of the students studying in France lived in university dormitories. Most of the students, regardless of country, lived primarily with students who were nationals of the host country. The percentages ranged from 94 percent for Sweden to 61 percent for France. In France, 21 percent of the students lived with other Americans. In the UK, West Germany, and Sweden the figures were substantially lower, ranging from 11 percent, to 9 percent, to 2 percent, respectively.

Academic Aspects

The students appeared to feel confident in their abilities to perform well and in the general academic and linguistic preparation that their home institutions gave them. While abroad, the majority of the students (66 percent) took at least a few courses that they could not or would not have taken on their home campuses, developed new areas of interest (57 percent), and took courses to broaden their academic and cultural backgrounds (68 percent). These data strongly suggest that the experience abroad enabled the students to expand their academic and intellectual horizons beyond what they would or could have obtained, had they remained at their home institutions.

As was indicated previously, the duration of the U.S. programs involved in this investigation was one academic year. The average length of time the students spent abroad was approximately ten months. The majority of the students (60 percent) felt that the ten-month period was just about right. A sizable minority of students (38 percent) felt that the sojourn abroad was too short, however. Only 2 percent of the students felt that the period of study abroad was too long.

Analysis of the quality of the academic experience overseas was obtained by a series of questions. These ranged from comparisons of the academic standards of the home and host institutions to perceptions of the academic standards expected of the American students as contrasted with the standards expected of host country students to open-ended questions concerning aspects of their home institution that the students learned to appreciate or to be critical of as a result of the study abroad experience.

When asked to compare the academic standards expected of the American student abroad with the academic standards expected by his or her home institution, the average response on a 5-point scale (1 = much lower; 5 = much greater) was 2.55. West Germany and France were rated the lowest, with means of 2.25 and 2.37, respectively. Sweden and the UK were rated "about the same," with means of 3.00 and 3.03, respectively.

Comparing the academic standards expected of the American student with those expected of host country students, the respondents indicated that somewhat less was expected of them than of the host country nationals. The overall mean on the 5-point scale was 2.52.

These results, plus the finding that the American students who studied in continental Europe (the UK was an exception) felt that they were graded more leniently than host country nationals, suggest that the students perceive that the academic standards in France and West Germany are lower than the academic standards of their U.S. campuses. This perception may be explained in part by (1) the apparent differential—that is, less rigorous—treatment accorded American students by French and German faculty and (2) by lack of integration of the American students into the academic life of the host institution.

When commenting on those aspects of their *home* institution that the American students learned to appreciate or appreciate more as a result of their sojourn abroad, the most common comments centered around the organization of lectures and classes as well as the use of frequent assignments and evaluations. A few representative comments follow.

"Basically, I like the relationship between the student and the teacher at my home institution."

"I knew specifically what I was supposed to study each night. Yet in Bordeaux it was left up to the student."

"The involvement of the teachers; the texts used; atmosphere in the classroom."

"Written tests given throughout the semester/quarter. Use of textbooks augmented by supplemental reading."

"I learned to appreciate the grading system and diversity of material at my home institution. I like having my work evaluated throughout the year rather than having everything ride on a final exam."

Comparison group students were asked to comment on those aspects of the junior year that they especially liked or appreciated about their home institution. The comments the students made tended to focus specifically on the quality of the instructors and organization of classes. The following comments are representative and illustrate this point.

"The high level of the teaching staff."

"Professors are usually very interesting, and the teaching assistants I have had have all been committed to helping me to get as much as possible out of the course."

"One in which the teacher tries to be in tune with how fast the students are absorbing the material."

Comments concerning those aspects of the home institution that the students became more critical of as a result of study abroad often focused on the perception that the students were "spoon-fed," treated as though they were not mature, independent learners, and forced to work under the artificial pressure of external rewards such as grades. A few representative comments follow.

"I don't feel that the instructors are able to adequately evaluate a student's performance from one or two midterms and a final, especially if the tests are multiple choice."

"Emphasis on grades."

"The rigorous structure, inflexibility, and rate at which information is transmitted to students. There is very little time for contemplation or development of individual thoughts regarding a subject."

"Mostly the emphasis on the textbook as a teaching utensil rather than a guideline."

"Spoon-feeding students with what to do, what to read, what to memorize, rather than making students think for themselves."

The critical comments made by the comparison group students generally focused on problems such as the ten-week quarter, big classes, and too much emphasis on factual information. The responses, although critical, are clearly and obviously not informed by the perspectives gained by the students who went abroad. A few selected comments follow.

"The size of most classes (too large). The large amount of material to be learned every quarter."

"Administration, size of classes."

"Some professors should spend less time worrying about research and more time worrying about students."

"Some of the classes are too big. Not being able to get all the classes I wanted."

While the study abroad students were somewhat critical of the academic aspects of some of the universities that they attended, they tended to rate their *general* intellectual development during the study abroad period higher than had they remained on their home campuses for their junior year. This conclusion is supported by data from a question that asked the students to rate their intellectual/academic achievements in comparison with what they would have expected to have obtained at home. The average rating on a 5-point scale (1 = abroad much less; 5 = abroad much greater) was 3.72. The means for each of the host countries were very similar, with the UK being highest (3.96) and France the lowest (3.59). Examination of comments made by the students provides insight into some of the reasons for the students' positive evaluation of their intellectual accomplishments while abroad.

France

"It is difficult to say because it was so different. The material was less overall, but the material covered was in a foreign language (French), which I was constantly improving. Had I had to do the same amount of work (e.g., reading especially) that I do at home in a foreign language, I would not have been able to do it at all. Much of my intellectual development came through experiences outside the classroom while I was abroad. The opposite would be true at home. I've learned to accomplish more intellectually (to be more critical) in everyday activities."

France

"It wasn't so much that I learned more in the classes I took over there, but there was a different bias on the information. It was quite interesting to learn about U.S. history from a foreign view. Also, just being in another culture and another country you learn a lot."

West Germany

"Although less was expected of me, I learned a lot about myself academically and intellectually—it was just a different way of learning."

West Germany

"Academic accomplishment: much less abroad. Classes met once a week; no reading classes were usually required. Intellectual development: there, much more. My horizons broadened considerably; my mind opened to new ideas."

United Kingdom

"Not only did I really learn to improve my writing (which was already good) due to so much emphasis on papers in England, but associating with so many Europeans tremendously broadened my interest in the European community, their role in world affairs and history."

United Kingdom

"I was constantly intellectually stimulated inside and outside of class. I also studied subjects that I probably wouldn't have at home."

United Kingdom

"I was tested less but had to do more private research and write more essays; so although I may have learned fewer 'facts,' I learned to research and write better, and study what I choose."

In summary, the study abroad period was a time when the students took courses and participated in events that were academically and intellectually enriching as well as personally broadening. A sizable minority of the students wished to extend their European studies beyond the single academic year. On average, students who studied in the Federal Republic of Germany and France felt that the academic standards of the host country universities were somewhat lower than at their home institutions, a perception that has been corroborated by other evaluations of study abroad programs (Carlson and Yachimowicz, 1986, 1987). The students also reported that they were treated by their professors differently from host country students, with French and German professors requiring less of the Americans than they did of their own students. In the UK, the students felt highly integrated into the general academic life of the host university and indicated that the academic standards in the UK were similar to or somewhat more rigorous than those of their home institutions. (See Carlson and Yachimowicz [1986, 1987] for corroboration of this general finding.)

Personal Aspects

While the academic aspects of the sojourn abroad are of substantial importance to the study abroad experience and to the integrity of study abroad programs, it must be kept in mind that "academics" constitutes just one dimension of the experience that the student has; this point is underscored by some of the comments included in the previous section.

Several aspects of the students' lives abroad contribute to the richness of their overall experience. For example, extracurricular activities such as clubs, athletics, social and cultural events, travel, reading, "people watching," and discussions with students and host country nationals are important elements that help involve the student with the foreign culture and provide insight into the culture.

One of the most valuable extracurricular activities that the American students engage in while in Europe is traveling. After the period of foreign study has begun, the average time spent traveling is well over thirty days. The amount of travel done by the students is fairly consistent regardless of host European country. The richness of the experiences that the students gain from travel and the significant role that travel plays in their general development are exemplified in the following comments.

France

"Fifteen days in Israel at Passover time. I saw a culture and a religion even more apart from that of my own country or host country. Very enlightening and educational."

France

"A French-affiliated trip to the Soviet Union was a highlight of my total year abroad. The cliché 'My eyes were finally opened to reality' applies here—being able to meet Soviet citizens, talk to them in private about their insights on their government, etc., provided me with much to think about, especially re-evaluating my feelings of my own country—realizing how extremely lucky I am to be a U.S. citizen."

Sweden

"Visiting all countries and experiencing their cultures, but especially Eastern bloc countries. It was important to see both the realities and the Western myths."

West Germany

"Traveling in my host country was very rewarding because I understood the customs and was able to speak the language and felt very comfortable in German-speaking countries."

United Kingdom

"I learned to make decisions and live with mistakes. I met lots of people. Learned a lot about art."

United Kingdom

"I proved that I could be independent."

In addition to travel, personal interaction with a variety of people plays an important part in shaping the study abroad experience. The American students reported that the contacts they had with host country students as well as with other nationals of the host country contributed greatly and about equally to their experience abroad. Contacts with the teaching staff of the host country as well as contacts with fellow American students were considered to be important but of substantially lesser significance. Contacts with administrative representatives of the home country or with home country faculty were not seen as being important in contributing to the students' overall experience while abroad.

A few representative comments provide the flavor of the sort of personal relationships that contribute positively to the students' overall experience while abroad.

France

"The students of the SAP [Study Abroad Program] host country. They gave me the fullest opportunity to learn about France and the French."

France

"My host family, because I felt I could get from them the feelings, reactions, etc., of the average French person."

West Germany

"Students from host and home countries: . . . . It is important to talk and learn from them and verbalize my own thoughts."

United Kingdom

"Students and people of the host country—I totally immersed myself with them—they showed me a portion of their culture I never would have otherwise seen."

As friends and acquaintances are fundamentally important in helping the American students develop insight into and appreciation of the study abroad experience, the students reported that the most significant forum for becoming familiar with their host country was through group discussions and talking with host nationals. Host country nonfiction, journals, television programs, and lectures were viewed as contributing only marginally to the students' general understanding and appreciation of the culture and society in which they lived.

In conclusion, the academic aspects of the study abroad year constitute only one dimension, albeit a very important dimension, of the study abroad experience. Development of personal knowledge, self-confidence, independence, cultural awareness, and social abilities constitute other factors that contribute substantially to the study abroad experience. Participation in discussion groups, personal relations with host country nationals, clubs, and travel were considered by the study abroad students to be extremely important for their personal and intellectual growth.

A number of questions remain open concerning the integration of the students into the academic life of the host institutions. Language undoubtedly plays a significant role in this as well as some major differences between the American system of higher education and the systems of higher education in the Federal Republic of Germany and in France. Since integration into the academic life of the host institution is a stated goal of many, if not most, American study abroad programs, the issue should be given considerable attention.

Reintegration and Satisfaction with the Junior Year

Although only a small minority of the students who studied abroad changed their majors during the year abroad (9 percent as opposed to 22 percent for the comparison group), a sizable minority (26 percent) indicated that they had become interested in courses or areas of study that they had not considered before. Although their academic horizons had broadened as a result of studying and living abroad, the study abroad students reported that about the only thing that they did at their home institution when they returned that was related to the international education was to complete questionnaires. The overwhelming majority of the respondents (72 percent) indicated that they had not informed or been involved with their home institution in any special way since their return from their sojourn and had not participated in reintegration activities.

The students who completed the postsojourn questionnaire were in the first quarter or semester of the senior year and not necessarily fully informed about the number of course unit credits they would receive as a result of their foreign study; nonetheless, 57 percent of them felt that the year abroad was not likely to prolong the total duration of undergraduate studies. The question of whether or not study abroad participants take more time to graduate than do students who do not participate in study abroad is complicated by the fact that in addition to the possibility that not all courses will be credited, study abroad students seem to be very interested in pursuing a variety of academic opportunities and less interested in graduating "on time" than their non–study abroad counterparts.

When asked to indicate their overall satisfaction with their junior year, the study abroad students indicated that they were very satisfied. The mean value on a 5-point scale was 1.48 (1 = very satisfied; 5 = very dissatisfied), with no appreciable differences in satisfaction across the four European host countries. The comparison group's mean was 2.18 on the same scale.

The students felt that it was worthwhile to study abroad for a variety of reasons, the most significant (means close to 1 on a 5-point scale) being foreign language proficiency (the UK was, of course, an exception), perspectives gained on the United States, perspectives gained and knowledge acquired about the host country and its peoples, perspectives gained on the students' own lives, the opportunity to travel, and a break from the previous routine. Of secondary importance (means around 2) were exposure to new teaching methods and subjects not offered at the home institution, career prospects, and exposure to other intellectual perspectives in their fields. Of tertiary importance (means around 3) were acquaintances with the students' family or ethnic heritage. The reasons given for the study abroad period being worthwhile are very similar to the reasons that they gave for wanting to participate in study abroad in the first place.

In short, the study abroad participants were very satisfied with their year abroad. They felt that it enriched them culturally, linguistically, academically, and personally. The sojourners indicated that the perspectives gained from the year abroad would be useful in their future lives and in the careers that they wished to pursue.

Although the returned study abroad students were enthusiastic and clearly felt "different" as a result of having been abroad, the home institutions seemed to ignore the experiences that they had, and reintegration into the daily academic and social life of the home institution remains problematic. Ideally, reintegration would not be equated with "reabsorption"; rather, it should mean that the intellectual, academic, personal, and linguistic gains made by the students would be taken into account by their home institution so that the returnees could apply their newly gained proficiencies to the intellectual and social life of their home campuses.

B. LANGUAGE DEVELOPMENT DURING STUDY ABROAD

One of the primary objectives of study abroad programs is the improvement of students' foreign language skills. To provide an example to illustrate this point, the regents of the University of California, in establishing the university's Education Abroad Program in 1961, noted that among other goals the "improvement of the students' communication with all aspects of a foreign society by developing their skills in the use of a foreign language" was of primary importance. Consistent with this emphasis, the majority of students who study abroad, with the exception of those who study in English-speaking countries of course, rank development and refinement of foreign language skills as their top-priority goal (Carlson and Yachimowicz, 1987; Prater et al., 1980). The significance of study abroad to the development of foreign language competence was underscored further by the President's Commission on Foreign Language and International Studies—under the Carter administration—when it noted in its 1980 report entitled *Strength through Wisdom* that "a priority concern [is] the failure of schools and colleges to teach languages so that students can communicate in them" (p. 20).

Approaches to Assessment

Two measurement approaches were used to assess foreign language proficiency: (1) a self-appraisal method developed by the Educational Testing Service (ETS) and (2) the language proficiency oral interview (OI) developed by the American Council on the Teaching of Foreign Languages (ACTFL) and the ETS. The ETS scale, developed by ETS for Education and the World View, a two-year project of the Council on Learning (1978–80), consists of "can do" statements assessing language ability in four areas: speaking proficiency, listening comprehension, reading ability, and writing ability. The items are arranged in a Guttman-like scale, that is, in an ascending order of difficulty. The task of the individual completing the scale is to indicate those items that he or she can do quite easily in the foreign language that he or she knows best. In the case of the study abroad students, this was defined a priori as the language of the country in which the student would be studying.

Descriptions of the self-appraisal statements for the four domains are as follows.

Speaking Proficiency has 14 items representing levels of proficiency of increasing complexity ranging from "Count to ten in the language," to "Buy clothes in a department store," to "Describe your present job, studies, or other major life activities accurately and in detail," to "Describe the system of government of your country."

Listening Comprehension has 11 levels, ranging from "Understand very simple statements or questions in the language," to "In face-to-face conversation with a native speaker who is speaking slowly and carefully, tell whether the speaker is referring to past, present, or future events," to "On the telephone, understand a native speaker who is talking as quickly and as colloquially as he or she would to another native speaker."

Reading Ability has 8 levels. These range from "Read personal letters or notes written to you in which the writer has deliberately used simple words and construction," to "Read and understand magazine articles at a level similar to those found in *Time* or *Newsweek,* without using a dictionary," to "Read newspaper 'want ads' with comprehension, even when many abbreviations are used."

Writing Ability has 6 levels ranging from "I cannot really communicate any information in the language of the SAP host country through writing" to "My writing, in all situations, cannot be distinguished from that of an educated native speaker of the SAP host country."

The oral interview accurately assesses speaking abilities that range from novice to the language competence of a native speaker. The interview is carried out by one or two trained testers who have native-speaker proficiency and who have had extensive training in the use of the approach. The individual being tested converses with the interviewer(s) for ten to forty minutes, depending on his or her level of proficiency. The speech sample is recorded and analyzed according to a 9-point scale. The lowest level of proficiency is defined as "no practical ability to function in the language"; the highest level of proficiency is marked by "ability equivalent to that of a well-educated native speaker." Oral interviews were conducted in German with thirty-three University of California and University of Colorado students who were to study in the Federal Republic of Germany. Restrictions related to cost and travel time did not permit interviews to be carried out with study abroad students from the University of Massachusetts or Kalamazoo College. For financial reasons, oral interviews were not done in French.

Self-Appraisal and Oral Interview Results Prior to Study Abroad

The results of the self-appraisal scales for speaking proficiency, listening comprehension, reading ability, and writing ability for the students who studied in France and the Federal Republic of Germany are given in Tables 3.1 through 3.4. The "prior" level of ability reflects the student's evaluation of his or her ability in the domain indicated *before* going abroad. Students who studied in Sweden were excluded from this analysis because of the very small sample size.

Examination of the self-evaluations indicates that the students considered themselves to be quite proficient in the language of the host country in which they were to study. The oral interview results (see Table 3.5) as well as other language proficiency data (Carlson and Yachimowicz, 1986, 1987) suggest that confidence in the validity of students' self-evaluations prior to an extended sojourn abroad may be misplaced. The data indicate that students' assessments of their language abilities prior to the experience of living abroad are significantly higher than their own post–study abroad retrospective evaluations of their language abilities before the study abroad experience.

The results of the oral interviews are reported in Table 3.5.

Of the 37 sojourners assessed, the majority (15) were considered to be at the

Table 3.1
Self-Appraisal of Speaking Proficiency Prior to and After Study Abroad

	French		German	
Speaking Skill:	Prior	After	Prior	After
Count to ten in the language	100%	100%	100%	100%
Say the days of the week	99%	100%	100%	100%
Give the current date (month, day, year)	99%	100%	100%	100%
Order a simple meal in a restaurant	96%	100%	93%	100%
Ask for directions on the street	95%	100%	95%	100%
Buy clothes in a department store	91%	99%	84%	100%
Introduce yourself in social situations and use appropriate greetings and leave-taking expressions	88%	98%	86%	100%
Give simple biographical information about yourself (place of birth, composition of family, early schooling, etc.)	96%	100%	98%	100%
Talk about your favorite hobby at some length, using appropriate vocabulary	63%	93%	67%	96%
Describe your present job, studies, or other major life activities accurately and in detail	76%	97%	52%	97%
Tell what you plan to be doing five years from now, using appropriate vocabulary	56%	95%	46%	93%
Describe your country's educational system in some detail	49%	87%	46%	86%
State and support with examples and reasons a position on a controversial topic (for example, birth control, nuclear safety, environmental pollution)	36%	78%	25%	73%
Describe the system of government of your country	35%	81%	29%	67%
Mean percent across skill categories	77%	95%	73%	94%

Intermediate level. The specific definition of this category is that the individual is "Able to satisfy some survival needs and some limited social demands. [The individual exhibits] some evidence of grammatical accuracy in basic construction, e.g., subject-verb agreement, noun-adjective agreement, some notion of inflection. Vocabulary permits discussion of topics beyond basic survival needs, e.g., personal history, leisure time activities. [The individual is] able to formulate some questions when asked to do so."

Table 3.2
Self-Appraisal of Listening Comprehension Prior to and After Study Abroad

	French		German	
Listening Skill	Prior	After	Prior	After
Understand very simple statements or questions in the language ("Hello, how are you?", "What is your name?", "Where do you live?", etc..)	100%	100%	100%	100%
In face-to-face conversation, understand a native speaker who is speaking slowly and carefully (deliberately adapting his or her speech to suit you)	100%	100%	98%	100%
On the telephone, understand a native speaker who is speaking to you slowly and carefully (deliberately adapting his or her speech to suit you)	96%	100%	97%	100%
In face-to-face conversation with a native speaker who is speaking slowly and carefully, tell whether the speaker is referring to past, present, or future events	95%	99%	98%	99%
In face-to-face conversation understand a native speaker who is speaking as quickly and as colloquially as he or she would to another native speaker	35%	89%	38%	75%
Understand movies without subtitles	34%	87%	26%	84%
Understand news broadcasts on the radio	24%	82%	22%	87%
From the radio, understand the words of a popular song you have not heard before	10%	38%	18%	45%
Understand play-by-play descriptions of sports events (for example, a soccer match) on the radio	10%	39%	11%	48%
Understand two native speakers when they are talking rapidly to one another	23%	81%	27%	68%
On the telephone, understand a native speaker who is talking as quickly and as colloquially as he or she would to another native speaker	11%	74%	15%	57%
Mean percent across skill categories	49%	78%	50%	74%

Summaries of the basic proficiencies of the other levels indicated are as follows:

Intermediate minus. "Able to satisfy basic survival needs and minimum courtesy requirements."

Intermediate plus. "Able to satisfy most survival needs and limited social demands."

Table 3.3
Self-Appraisal of Reading Ability Prior to and After Study Abroad

Reading Skill:	French		German	
	Prior	After	Prior	After
Read personal letters or notes written to you in which the writer has deliberately used simple words and constructions	99%	99%	98%	99%
Read on store fronts the type of store or the services provided (for example, "dry cleaning," "book store," or "butcher")	96%	99%	98%	99%
Understand newspaper headlines	99%	99%	91%	99%
Read personal letters and notes written as they would be to a native speaker	75%	99%	64%	99%
Read and understand magazine articles at a level similar to those found in _Time_ or _Newsweek_, without using a dictionary	51%	97%	30%	97%
Read popular novels without using a dictionary	13%	95%	6%	95%
Read newspaper "want ads" with comprehension, even when many abbreviations are used	31%	91%	23%	91%
Read highly technical material in a particular academic or professional field with no use or very infrequent use of a dictionary	15%	80%	16%	80%
Mean percent across skill categories	60%	95%	53%	95%

Advanced. "Able to satisfy routine social demands and limited work requirements."

Advanced plus. "Able to satisfy most work requirements and show some ability to communicate on concrete topics relating to particular interests and special fields of competence."

Superior. "All performance above advanced plus."

The results of the ACTFL/ETS oral interviews and the ETS self-appraisal verbal proficiency scales given prior to the sojourn abroad offer some interesting contrasts. First, as already noted, it appears that when students use self-rating procedures to evaluate their verbal proficiency, they give themselves excessively high marks. The majority of the students indicated, for example, that using the language of the country in which they will study they can rather easily describe the system of government in their own country. This is, of course, a difficult task, requiring control over a range of vocabulary and grammatical constructions. Yet the oral proficiency interviews show that a majority of the students were classified only at the intermediate level, that is, being able to satisfy some survival needs and some limited social demands. Since all the

Table 3.4
Self-Appraisal of Writing Ability Prior to and After Study Abroad

Skill	French		German	
	Prior	After	Prior	After
I cannot really communicate any information in the language of the SAP host country though writing	---	---	---	---
I can write a few sentences in the language of the SAP host country, using very basic vocabulary and structures	---	---	1%	---
I can write relatively simple items (such as a short note to a friend) that communicate basic messages but usually contain a considerable number of misspellings and/or grammatical errors	18%	5%	34%	12%
I can write fairly long personal letters as well as uncomplicated business letters, which convey meaning accurately and which contain relatively few errors, although they are not completely idiomatic in expression	55%	80%	62%	76%
I can write complex personal and business letters, as well as many other kind of documents (for example, a "letter to the editor" of the local newspaper) using in each case the particular vocabulary and style of expression appropriate to the particular writing situation. There is only an occasional hint that I am not a native writer of the language	6%	15%	3%	11%
My writing, in all situations, cannot be distinguished from that of an educated native speaker of the SAP host country	---	3%	---	1%

students who were rated higher than the intermediate level on the oral interview had extensive experience in Germany and with German-speaking people, it would appear that the "normal" language proficiency of those who will study abroad probably does not exceed the intermediate levels of the OI and that students' self-evaluations of their own oral proficiency are substantially inflated. One probable reason for the apparently inflated self-evaluation of verbal

Table 3.5
ACTFL/ETS Oral Interview Scale Levels and Frequencies Prior to Study Abroad

Superior	Advncd+	Advncd	Advncd-	Intermed+	Intermed	Intermed-
5	3	4	4	4	15	2

Table 3.6
Correlations* among the Oral Interview and "Can Do" Scale and among the "Can Do" Scales
(German above the diagonal; French below the diagonal)

	OI	Speaking	Listening	Reading	Writing
OI	--	.62(N=33)	.60(N=33)	.51(N=33)	.51(N=33)
Speak.	--	--	.62(N=132)	.57(N=132)	.54(N=132
Listen.	--	.42(N=186)	--	.65(N=132)	.42(N=130)
Read.	--	.41(N=184)	.61(N=185)	--	.54(N=130)
Writ.	--	.41(N=184)	.41(N=185)	.31(N=183)	--

*All correlations are statistically significant (p < .05)

proficiency scores is that students who are selected to study abroad have had only limited experience in using the language of the host country and have not had the types of foreign language and cultural experiences that would allow them to place their own language proficiency in the context of living and studying in a foreign culture. Inflation of assessment of language proficiency may also be a way for students to cope with insecurities stemming from concern about communicating with people in the host country.

Self-Appraisal and Oral Interview Correlations

The correlations between the OI and various "can do" scales for German are reported in Table 3.6. reported in Table 3.6 are the correlations among the various "can do" scales for German and French. Although moderate in magnitude, the correlations among all the variables are statistically significant ($p < .05$). For German, OI performance correlates about as well with performance on the various "can do" scales as the "can do" scales correlate among themselves. Similar results were obtained for the French data, although the correlations among the various "can do" scales tended to be somewhat lower than for German. The magnitude of the correlations, especially among the OI and "can do" scales, is reduced owing to restriction of range, particularly in the OI data.

The correlations presented in Table 3.6 suggest that the OI and self-appraisal scales, though related statistically, tap somewhat different abilities. Thus, in order to obtain a relatively differentiated perspective of language proficiency

Table 3.7
Number of Students Who Completed the Pre- and Post–Study Abroad Language
Measures

Scale	Pre-Measure N	Post-Measure N
Self-Appraisal		
French	190	102
German	135	69
Swedish	35	5
Oral Interview		
German	34	20

and how language proficiency changes over time, measurement should be made
by employing more than one instrument.

Self-Appraisal and Oral Interview Results
Subsequent to Study Abroad

For each language area, the numbers of students who completed the pre–
study abroad and post–study abroad self-appraisal scales and oral interviews
are presented in Table 3.7. As discussed in Chapter 1, the return rate for the
study abroad students was approximately 50 percent, as is reflected in Table
3.7. Difficulty in scheduling was the primary reason that only twenty of the
original thirty-four students could be given the German oral interviews.

The results of the self-appraisal scales for the various domains assessed and
for each of the languages can be seen in Tables 3.1 through 3.4. Inspection of
these tables will show substantial increases in language proficiency for each
language category. The areas in which the students indicated the highest level
of proficiency were in listening, speaking, and reading. Writing continued to
provide the students with the greatest difficulty. One reason for this is that
although the students have a good deal of experience speaking, listening to the
language, and reading the language while abroad, many students report that the
amount of writing (especially evaluated writing) they do in the language of the
host country is quite limited. Another reason for the modest gains in writing is
probably due to the simple fact that writing is the most difficult of the various
areas of language acquisition. Yet another factor contributing to the relative
lack of improvement in writing scores may be the fact that the self-appraisal

Table 3.8
ACTFL/ETS Post–Study Abroad Oral Interview Levels and Frequencies

Superior	Advncd+	Advncd	Advncd-	Intermed+	Intermed	Intermed-
10	1	6	1	0	2	0

writing scale is rather restricted. The amount of gain required to move from one level of proficiency to another is more substantial than for the other self-appraisal scales.

The increases from the pre–study abroad to post–study abroad oral interviews ranged from 0 in one instance to 1.50. The majority of the students moved from the intermediate level (''able to satisfy most survival needs and limited social demands'') to the advanced (''able to satisfy most work requirements and show some ability to communicate on concrete topics relating to particular interests and special fields of competence'') or superior categories. The distributions of students for each of the oral proficiency levels are given in Table 3.8.

Contrasting the results reported in Table 3.8 with those found in Table 3.5 reveals very significant gains in oral proficiency for the students who studied abroad. In fact, if one ''averages'' out the level of oral proficiency before the sojourn and compares it with oral proficiency subsequent to the sojourn, it becomes clear that the students moved from rather poor control of the German language to levels of proficiency that are outstanding. Indeed, to our knowledge, gains in language proficiency of this magnitude have not been documented in courses of language study that do not involve a sojourn abroad.

In conclusion, significant gains in language proficiency were found for the study abroad students who studied in France, Germany, and Sweden. The language areas in which the students became most proficient were listening, speaking, and reading. The students' ability to write the language of the host country lagged substantially behind their gains and abilities in the other areas assessed. The oral interview results, based on a somewhat restricted sample, offer supportive evidence for the conclusions drawn from the self-appraisal scales: that very substantial gains in foreign language proficiency resulted from the sojourn abroad. These results are impressive and encouraging. Nonetheless, it is well to keep in mind that gains made in language proficiency should be understood in terms of their duration, that is, their maintenance over time (R. Campbell and Schnell, 1987). We were unable to address this issue in the present investigation; it should, however, be included in future work in the area. Another caveat that should be mentioned concerns the generalizability of the results to languages other than those assessed in the present study. While the magnitude of change documented in this study may be general for students who study in

French-, German-, Spanish-, or Swedish-speaking countries, they may be more modest for students who study in countries whose languages are substantially more difficult for English-speaking persons to learn, for example, Japanese, Korean, or Chinese.

4

IMPACTS OF THE STUDY ABROAD EXPERIENCE

Chapter 4 documents changes in the study abroad students and comparison group students that occurred between administration of the pre- and postmeasures. When relevant, contrasts among the students who sojourned in different European host countries are pointed out.

The chapter is divided into five major sections. In Section A, the sojourners' interest in and knowledge of the host country, their attitudes toward the host country and the United States, and their expectations of the study abroad experience are presented. In Section B, changes in international understanding are explored. Section C discusses academic issues. And Section D presents the results of the personal self-efficacy measure. In Section E, the students' professional goals and satisfaction with the study abroad experience are discussed.

THE SAMPLE

The sample comprised study abroad and comparison group students who completed both the pre–junior year and post–junior year questionnaires. Accordingly, statistical analyses of change between and within the study abroad and comparison groups could be made. The details of this sample are reported in Table 1.4. The sample is the same as that used to address the first research question and comprises 153 comparison group students and 148 study abroad students from the Universities of California and Massachusetts.

A. INTERNATIONAL AFFAIRS, KNOWLEDGE, AND VIEWS OF OTHER COUNTRIES AND THE UNITED STATES

Interest and Knowledge

Prior to their junior years, most students, regardless of whether or not they were to study abroad, indicated a moderate interest in other countries and international affairs. When asked to evaluate the extent to which they were interested in other countries, European affairs, and/or international affairs, the overall mean for the future study abroad participants was 2.66 on a 5-point scale (1 = extremely interested; 5 = not at all interested). The comparison group's level of interest was 2.71. The most extreme difference in level of interest for the study abroad students was for those who were to study in France and West Germany. Prior to foreign study, the former seemed to have the least interest in international affairs (mean = 3.45), whereas the latter appeared to have the greatest interest (mean = 2.55).

As one might expect, the study abroad group's interest in international affairs was significantly greater after the sojourn (mean = 2.07) than before (mean = 2.66). The students who remained in the United States also indicated higher interest in international affairs after the junior year than prior to it (means 2.71 and 2.20), although the degree of change was not as great as for the study abroad students. This result is consistent with the expectation that college students tend to develop deeper interests in foreign affairs regardless of whether or not they study abroad (Sell, 1983).

Although the students' level of knowledge about their host country prior to the sojourn abroad was poor to moderate, it increased dramatically as a result of having lived and studied in that country. The areas of greatest gain were those that touched the students' lives most directly and were most interesting and salient to them. These areas included the host country's system of postsecondary education, its cultural life, its customs and traditions, its social structure, and the social issues dominant in the host country. Changes of level of knowledge in areas that were somewhat more distant from the students' personal experience, such as the host country's economic system and its foreign policy, were impressive but of lesser magnitude.

While the students' level of *knowledge* about the host country was not great prior to study abroad, their opinions about the same aspects of the country were quite positive. For example, and in apparent contrast to their level of knowledge, the students' *attitudes* toward postsecondary education in the country in which they were to study were very favorable. The same was the case for their attitudes toward the host country's social structure, its customs and traditions, and its governmental foreign policies.

When asked to indicate how they valued these same aspects and/or institutions of the host country *after* their return from study abroad, the study abroad students indicated that they continued to have favorable opinions concerning the host country's cultural life and its customs and traditions. Somewhat lower, but still consistent with the attitudes expressed prior to study abroad, were the students' opinions of the host country's media, social structure, and civic life.

A significant contrast to these results was the finding that the study abroad students had clearly lower opinions of the system of postsecondary education in their host country than they had prior to the sojourn abroad. The country for which the change was greatest was France (mean shift on a 5-point scale from 2.36 to 3.20). This was followed by the Federal Republic of Germany (mean shift from 2.14 to 2.75) and the UK (mean shift from 2.03 to 2.39).

Prior to the junior year, students from both the study abroad group and the comparison group viewed postsecondary education in the United States quite positively. For the two groups, the means on a 5-point scale were 2.14 and 1.83, respectively. Although not statistically significant, the study abroad group tended to view American postsecondary education slightly higher after than before the sojourn abroad (mean = 2.06). The comparison group also continued to value American postsecondary education highly (mean = 1.92).

While several aspects of the United States came to be viewed less favorably than comparable ones in the host country, the study abroad students tended to regard the media, social structure, and customs and traditions in the United States about the same as they did previous to the foreign sojourn.

An area that the returned study abroad students tended to view less favorably than they did prior to the sojourn abroad—and the opinions were not very favorable in the first place—was U.S. governmental foreign policies (mean shift from 3.42 to 3.75). The comparison group, while somewhat more favorable toward U.S. foreign policy than the study abroad group on both the pre- and postmeasures, showed only a slight and statistically nonsignificant tendency toward greater negativism on the postmeasure (mean shift from 3.05 to 3.14).

Expectations of the Study Abroad Experience

On the pre–study abroad measure, the student sojourners were asked to indicate briefly, and in order of significance, the main areas in which they hoped to gain significant knowledge about their host country. A parallel query was made on the post–study abroad questionnaire as the students were asked to indicate the main areas in which they actually gained significant knowledge about the host country. A few representative pre- and postmeasure paired responses are given below. As will be seen, there is general consistency between what the students hoped to learn about the host country and what they actually did learn.

France

(Before) "Language, culture, living modes, history, politics."

(After) "The language, social trends, general culture, system of education, values and beliefs."

(Before) "Language, culture, literature, customs, economics, political system, government, television, radio, newspapers, etc."

(After) "The French people themselves, watching television each night, traveling, my courses, living with a French family."

West Germany

(Before) "Language, culture, history."

After) "Language, cultural life, political issues, foreign policy, attitudes."

(Before) "The German people and the culture, traditions, and attitudes. Government and foreign policy (extensively)."

(After) "Government and political parties, regional diversity in the country, religion, and social life/culture."

United Kingdom

(Before) "English literature, social structure, institutions, national attitudes toward economy, foreigners, other countries."

(After) "Social/political issues, especially students' social and class structure (including higher education), modes of behavior and 'personality,' geography, climate, Britain's relationship with France and The Netherlands—historically, culturally."

(Before) "Social structure, governmental polities (foreign and domestic), customs, economic system, cultural life."

(After) "Political system, role of Queen/royalty, education in England, life-styles."

In conclusion, the study abroad and comparison groups were moderately interested in foreign affairs prior to the junior year. After the junior year, interest in foreign affairs increased for both groups, with the change in interest being greatest for the study abroad students. Although positively oriented toward a number of institutions and aspects of the host country—for example, system of postsecondary education, the social structure, and governmental foreign policy—the study abroad students did not have a great deal of knowledge about these areas. Subsequent to the study abroad experience, dramatic changes in level of knowledge were found. With one notable exception, the study abroad students' overall positive evaluation of the institutions and characteristics of the host country did not change as a result of the sojourn abroad. The exception was the host country's system of postsecondary education, with the study abroad students tending to become more critical of postsecondary education in their host country.

B. INTERNATIONAL UNDERSTANDING

The International Understanding scales employed on the premeasures were administered again to the study abroad and comparison groups on the postmeasure. The dimensionality of the postmeasure scales was determined by principal factor analysis with promax rotation. Comparisons were made using the matched sample of 153 comparison group students and 202 study abroad group students who completed and returned both the pre- and postquestionnaires.

Cognitive Dimensions

The results of the factor analysis of the first International Understanding scale are given in Table 4.1. Of the 17 items assessing cognitive aspects of international understanding, 15 items were found to be useful in defining the dimensions of the scale. The factor patterns extracted on the postmeasure of the scale were somewhat different from those extracted from the premeasure. On the postmeasure, the first factor, which accounted for 72 percent of the variance, was made up of 8 items and labeled "Cultural Interest and Respect." This factor contains the same 8 items as Factors 2 and 3 of the premeasure. The second factor extracted was labeled "Peace and Cooperation" and accounted for 13 percent of the variance. This 4-item factor is very similar to the first factor of the premeasure. Factor 3, termed "International Activities," has 3 items and does not correspond closely with any of the factors identified on the premeasure. Since Factor 3 accounted for only 12 percent of the total variance and since it was made up of only 3 items, it was eliminated from further consideration.

The mean factor scores and standard deviations were derived from the items common to the pre- and postmeasures that defined the dimensions "Peace and Cooperation" and "Cultural Interest and Respect." They are reported in Table 4.2.

As can be inferred from inspection of Table 4.2, the means for the study abroad group on both factors seem to be somewhat higher than the means on the same factors for the comparison group. In order to test for the statistical significance of the differences between groups over time, repeated measures analysis of variance was performed. The results revealed nonsignificant within-subject F values, indicating no statistically significant differences between the before and after data for either the study abroad or comparison groups. Significant between-subject F's were found, however, indicating that the study abroad group was higher than the comparison group on both the "Peace and Cooperation" ($F_{1,347} = 26.1$, $p < .001$) and the "Cultural Interest and Respect" factors ($F_{1,347} = 88.6$, $p < .001$) both prior to and after the junior year.

These results suggest that the differences detected between the study abroad and the comparison groups prior to the junior year continued to exist after the junior year. They indicate further that neither group increased significantly in cognitive aspects of international understanding between administrations of the pre- and postmeasures, although there was a nonsignificant trend for the study abroad group to score higher on "Peace and Cooperation" as well as on "Cultural Interest and Respect" subsequent to the year abroad. Two reasons for the

Table 4.1
Rotated Factor Pattern, Communality Estimates, and Eigenvalues for Cognitive International Understanding Scale (postmeasure)

Factor 1: CULTURAL INTEREST AND RESPECT (8 items)	1	2	3	h^2
1. Respect for Historical, Cultural Traditions Achievements of Nations Other than Your Own	.51	.25	-.00	.34
2. Desire to Meet and Interact with Persons Not From Your Home Country	.53	.26	.16	.66
3. Actual or Desired Travel to Foreign Nations	.56	.05	.20	.56
4. Negative Feelings About Foreigners	-.34	.04	.14	.45
5. Critical Views of Your Own Country	.32	.12	.05	.55
6. Views that Values of Your Own Society are Not Universal and that Values of Other Societies are Just as Valid	.66	-.04	-.03	.47
7. Respect for Traditions, Culture, Way of Life of Other Cultures	.75	-.05	-.08	.55
8. Interest in Learning More Languages	.56	-.06	.25	.60
Factor 2: PEACE AND COOPERATION (4 items)				
1. Desire for International Peace	-.08	.94	-.07	.61
2. Wish to Find Solutions to Global Problems	-.03	.65	.10	.55
3. Need for Closer Cooperation among Nations	.06	.75	.02	.72
4. Concern with Problems of Third World Countries	.16	.30	.14	.40
Factor 3: INTERNATIONAL ACTIVITIES (3 items)				
1. Awareness of Problems Common to Many Nations	.13	-.01	.32	.87
2. Actual Participation in Activities Aimed at	.01	-.04	.85	.68
3. Memberships in Organizations Concerned with International Issues and Problems	-.19	.04	.83	.86
Unrotated Eigenvalues of the Correlation Matrix	10.68	1.89	1.81	
Proportion of Variance	.72	.13	.12	

trend not quite reaching statistical significance suggest themselves. First, the factors upon which the analyses are based are defined by relatively few items, reducing the reliability of the index; second, since the study abroad group tended to score toward the top of the scales of both factors, ceiling effects undoubtedly limited the change that could be observed.

Table 4.2
Means* and Standard Deviations of the Factor Scores of the International
Understanding Cognitive Scale

Group	Factors	
	"Peace & Cooperation"	"Cultural Interest"
Study Abroad		
Pre-measure	2.13 (.86)	1.89 (.64)
Post-measure	2.07 (.79)	1.92 (.59)
Comparison		
Pre-measure	2.59 (.97)	2.54 (.96)
Post-measure	2.54 (.98)	2.48 (.81)

*Scale: 1 = "extensive"; 7 = "nonexistent"

Affective Dimensions

The results of the factor analysis of the second International Understanding scale are shown in Table 4.3. While the dimensions of the pre– and post–junior year analyses of the scales are identical and marked by the same items, the factors themselves are reversed: Factor 1 in the premeasure ("Domestic Orientation") became the second factor in the postmeasure, and Factor 2 in the premeasure ("International Concern") became the first factor in the postmeasure. The change in importance of the factors suggests that over the time between when the pre- and postmeasures were given, the range (variability) of opinion concerning the items that define the "Domestic Orientation" dimension was reduced. The opposite seems to be the case for "International Concern," where greater variability was detected on the post- than on the premeasure.

The means and standard deviations of the factor scores for the study abroad and comparison groups for "Domestic Orientation" and "International Concern" are reported in Table 4.4.

Examination of Table 4.4 will reveal apparent divergencies between the comparison and study abroad groups in "Domestic Orientation," both prior and subsequent to the junior year. There appears to be a trend for the comparison group to be higher in "Domestic Orientation" on the postmeasure than on the premeasure. The opposite trend can be inferred for the study abroad group, as they appear to become somewhat less "domestically oriented." No such trends can be inferred for the "International Concern" factor, although the

Table 4.3
Rotated Factor Pattern, Communality Estimates, and Eigenvalues for Affective International Understanding Scale (postmeasure)

	1	2	h^2
Factor 1: <u>INTERNATIONAL CONCERN</u> (6 items)			
1. I Believe My Country Should Send Food and Materials to any Country that Needs them.	<u>.36</u>	-.12	.17
2. The Mining and Distribution of Mineral Resources Should be Controlled by an International Authority	<u>.56</u>	.05	.30
3. We Should Have a World Government with the Powers to Make Laws That Would be Binding to All its Member Nations.	<u>.71</u>	.11	.47
4. An International Authority Should be Established and Given Direct Control Over the Production of Nuclear Energy in All Countries.	<u>.78</u>	.07	.59
5. I Prefer to be a Citizen of the World Rather than of any Country.	<u>.54</u>	-.27	.46
6. It is Our Responsibility to do Everything Possible to Prevent People from Starving Anywhere in the World.	<u>.33</u>	-.16	.16
Factor 2: <u>DOMESTIC ORIENTATION</u> (6 items)			
1. Pacific Demonstrations are Harmful to the Best Interests of My Home Country.	-.24	<u>.50</u>	.38
2. The Immigration of Foreigners to My Country Should be Kept Down so that We Can Provide for Our Own People First.	-.08	<u>.45</u>	.23
3. We Should Not Allow Foreign Business Enterprises to have Substantial Holdings in Our Country.	.03	<u>.28</u>	.08
4. Patriotism and Loyalty are the First and Most Important Requirements of a Good Citizen.	.04	<u>.74</u>	.54
5. Immigrants Should Not be Permitted to Come into Our Country if they Compete with Our Own Workers.	.00	<u>.50</u>	.25
6. No Duties are More Important than Duties Towards One's Country.	.03	<u>.70</u>	.47
Unrotated Eigenvalues of the Correlation Matrix	4.38	1.83	
Proportion of Variance	.76	.32	

Table 4.4
Means* and Standard Deviations of the Factor Scores on the International
Understanding Affective Scale

Group	Factors	
	"Domestic Orientation"	"Int. Concern"
Study Abroad		
Before	2.94 (.82)	4.19 (1.23)
After	2.71 (1.05)	4.25 (1.44)
Comparison		
Before	3.55 (1.24)	4.01 (1.23)
After	3.28 (1.31)	3.93 (1.13)

*Scale: 1 = "strongly disagree" (low score)

7 = "strongly agree" (high score)

comparison group appears to have a lower score on this dimension after the junior year than prior to it.

Once again, repeated measures analysis of variance was used in order to test for the statistical significance of the trends mentioned. This analysis revealed significant between-subject and within-subject F values for "Domestic Orientation," $F_{1,347} = 31.4$, $p < .001$ and $F_{1,347} = 26.3$, $p < .001$, respectively. No significant between- or within-subject F values were calculated for the "International Concern" factor.

The results of the repeated measures analysis of variance (ANOVA) indicate that the study abroad group was significantly less (higher numerical score) "domestically oriented" than the comparison group prior to the study abroad year. Subsequent to the junior year, both the study abroad and comparison group students tended to exhibit somewhat less domestic orientation than prior to the junior year.

C. ACADEMIC ISSUES

Three areas are dealt with under the general rubric "academic issues." These are (1) problems that the students may have had during the academic year abroad, (2) learning styles and abilities, and (3) students' perspectives of the importance of different ways of thinking and learning. These topics will be dealt with in order.

Problems during Study Abroad

Problems that student sojourners have while abroad have been the focus of a number of investigations (Church, 1982; Hull, 1978; Spaulding and Flack, 1976). An implicit assumption of the approach taken in most of the research has been that problems that foreign students may experience in a new culture stem from or are related to modes of adaptation to the new culture. While most of the studies have focused on the experience of foreign students in the United States, it may be that the foreign student is more "student" than "foreign" (Coelho-Oudegeest, 1971; Walton, 1968), and problems related to the sojourn may be more general than specific in nature.

In their extensive cross-national study of over 2,500 students in eleven countries, Klineberg and Hull (1979) found that the most significant problems that sojourners have are related to language, finances, adjusting to a new educational system, and coping with the customs and social norms of the host country. It has been suggested that students who study in countries whose cultures stand in marked contrast to their own will be more likely to experience problems than students who come from countries more similar to the host culture (David, 1971; Furnham and Bochner, 1982; Hull, 1978; Morris, 1960; Smith, 1955).

In the present investigation, the study abroad and comparison group students were asked to indicate on a 5-point scale (1 = very serious problems; 5 = no problem at all) the extent to which they had problems during their sojourn abroad or during their junior year, as the case may be. The areas (18 matched items administered by both groups) tapped primarily, but not exclusively, academic dimensions. These included taking courses and/or examinations in a foreign language, academic level of the courses, teaching methods, financial matters, counseling, and so on.

The "problems" scale was submitted to principal factor analysis with promax rotation. The results of the factor analysis are presented in Table 4.5. Inspection of Table 4.5 will show that two factors were extracted that are marked by 10 items. The first and second factors accounted for 84 percent and 16 percent of the variance, respectively. The first factor was labeled "Academic Problems" and was marked by academic level of courses, teaching and/or learning methods, and so on. The second factor was called "Integration/Lifestyle Problems" and was defined by interaction with host country students, guidance concerning academic and nonacademic areas, and climate. The high correlation between the two factors (r = .57) indicates that the dimensions are not independent.

As can also be seen from Table 4.5, the means for all items are around 4.0, suggesting that the study abroad students, on average, did not tend to have

Table 4.5
Principal Factor Analysis of Problems during the Year: Study Abroad Group

Factor 1: ACADEMIC PROBLEMS (6 items)	1	2	Mean	S.D.
1. Academic Level of Courses too Easy	.44	-.09	3.96	1.13
2. Differences in Teaching/Learning Methods	.53	.03	3.50	1.12
3. Readiness on Part of Teaching Staff to Meet and/or Help Foreign Students	.65	.00	3.85	1.17
4. Differences in Class or Student Project Group Size	.65	-.03	4.11	1.11
5. Administrative Matters	.41	.24	3.67	1.23
6. Financial Matters	.40	-.06	4.07	1.10
Factor 2: INTEGRATION/LIFESTYLE PROBLEMS (4 items)				
1. Interaction Among/With Host Country Students	-.19	.66	3.99	1.10
2. Guidance Concerning non-Academic Matters	.12	.59	4.15	1.05
3. Guidance Concerning Academic Matters	.35	.47	3.72	1.23
4. Climate, Food, Health, etc.	-.08	.37	3.94	1.11
Unrotated Eigenvalues of Correlation Matrix	3.85	0.88		
Proportion of Variance	.84	.16		

Scale:
1=Very serious problems   2=   3=   4=   5=No Problem at all

significant problems in the areas queried. The means and standard deviations for the student sojourners were remarkably similar regardless of the country in which they studied. The only exceptions were that the students who studied in France indicated that they had too much contact with other American students (mean = 2.83) and that at French universities administrative matters tended to be somewhat problematic (mean = 2.93). Independent analyses of variance performed on the two extracted factors revealed no group (study abroad–comparison group) difference on "Academic Problems" ($p > .25$). A main effect group difference ($F_{1,342} = 13.2$, $p < .01$) was detected for the "Integration/Lifestyle Problems" dimension, however, with the student sojourners experiencing more problems (mean = 3.83) than the comparison group (mean = 4.21).

Learning Styles and Abilities

The "learning styles" question given to the study abroad and comparison groups in the premeasure was administered again in the postmeasure. The premeasure results showed that the scale has four relatively independent dimensions: "Intellectuality," "Academic Style," "Work Habits," and "Persis-

Table 4.6
Principal Factor Analysis of Learning Styles: Study Abroad and Comparison Groups (postmeasure)

Factor 1: INTELLECTUALITY (3 items)	1	2	3	4	h^2
1. Apply Theories, Abstract Knowledge to Practical Issues	.48	.10	-.02	.17	.40
2. Abstract Problem Solving	.49	.04	.03	.22	.44
3. Formulating Hypotheses and Using Them in Analysis	.39	.18	.01	.23	.42
Factor 2: ACADEMIC STYLE (6 items)					
1. Cooperating With Others in Academic Work	.09	.35	.07	-.05	.17
2. Motivating Other People	-.03	.52	.03	-.05	.24
3. Articulating Own Thoughts/Views	.00	.45	.13	.15	.35
4. Imagination	.23	.54	-.08	-.22	.36
5. Choosing Tasks Commensurate With Abilities	-.02	.32	.20	.22	.30
6. Developing Own Point of View	.23	.35	-.09	.18	.34
Factor 3: WORK HABITS (3 items)					
1. Working Consistently	.11	-.05	.87	-.12	.72
2. Discipline in Learning	.00	-.04	.82	.08	.72
3. Planning and Following Through	-.14	.25	.62	-.02	.48
Factor 4: PERSISTENCE (2 items)					
1. Assuming a Heavy Workload	.09	.19	.26	.53	.43
2. Working Under Time Pressure	.04	-.07	.13	.90	.66
Unrotated Eigenvalues of the Correlation Matrix	6.14	3.51	2.01	1.61	
Proportion of Variance	.56	.21	.11	.08	

Scale:
1=Very strong   2=   3=   4=   5=Very weak

tence.'' On the premeasure the study abroad group was higher than the comparison group on the first two of these dimensions.

The results of principal factor analysis of the postmeasure "learning styles" question are depicted in Table 4.6. Comparison of Table 4.6 with Table 2.6 will show that the same factors emerged in both analyses. On the postmeasure, Factor 1, "Intellectuality," accounted for 56 percent of the total variance; Factor 2, "Academic Style," accounted for 21 percent of the variance; Factor 3, labeled "Work Habits," accounted for 11 percent of the variance; and Factor 4, "Persistence," accounted for 8 percent of the variance.

Table 4.7
Means* and Standard Deviations of the Factor Scores from the Learning Styles Scale

Group	Factors			
	"Intell."	"Ac. Style"	"Work Hab."	"Persis."
	Mean (SD)	Mean (SD)	Mean (SD)	Mean (SD)
Study Abroad				
Pre-measure	2.36(.82)	2.07(.53)	2.35(.83)	1.94(.70)
Post-measure	2.25(.81)	1.99(.59)	2.35(.97)	1.88(.88)
Comparison				
Pre-measure	2.60(.83)	2.28(.60)	2.32(.96)	2.10(.89)
Post-measure	2.39(.80)	2.20(.59)	2.30(.88)	1.96(.79)

*Scale: 1 = "very strong"; 5 = "very weak"

The means and standard deviations for these factors for both the pre- and postmeasures are reported in Table 4.7.

Examination of the means presented in Table 4.7 will indicate that there may be a slight trend for the study abroad group to be higher than the comparison group on the first two factors, "Intellectuality" and "Academic Style." There appear to be no other trends in the data.

Repeated measures analysis of variance was again employed to determine the statistical significance of changes within and between the study abroad and comparison groups over time. The results showed significant between-subject and within-subject F values for "Intellectuality." The F's were $F_{1,343} = 8.68$, $p < .01$ and $F_{1,343} = 7.86$, $p < .01$, respectively. This shows that the initial difference favoring the study abroad group was consistent over time and that both groups scored higher on the "Intellectuality" factor over time. The results of the repeated measures analysis of variance for Factor 2 revealed the same pattern of significant differences found on the premeasure between the study abroad and comparison groups (between-subject: $F_{1,347} = 13.60$, $p < .001$). Neither group increased in their "Academic Style" score over time, however. No significant between-group-over-time differences were detected for Factors 3 and 4, although the usefulness of the latter two factors is questionable owing to the few items defining them as well as the relatively small amount of variance they contribute to the overall variance in the scale.

The results of the analyses of the learning styles data indicate quite clearly that prior to the junior year the study abroad students viewed themselves to be somewhat more capable than the comparison group in abstract and hypothetical thinking abilities. Both groups perceived themselves to have increased significantly in these abilities in the time span between administration of the pre- and postmeasures.

Ways of Thinking and Learning

The importance that the students attribute to a variety of ways of thinking and learning was measured by a 19-item scale administered to the study abroad participants only. The format of the question was to ask the students to reflect back to before their junior year and to consider now, in their senior year, how important the various areas queried are (were) for their own learning and intellectual development. The areas included "learning facts," "understanding theories," "regular class attendance," and so on. Since longitudinal data were not gathered on this question—that is, there was no premeasure—the data were not subjected to multivariate statistical analysis. Rather, means and standard deviations of the more meaningful items of the question are reported in Table 4.8.

Although statistical tests of significance were not employed, and there are methodological problems in comparing perceptions of retrospective views with views reported to be held now, examination of Table 4.8 will reveal several interesting contrasts. For example, areas considered to be more important *after* than *before* the study abroad experience for the students' learning and intellectual development appear to be: "Systematic thinking," "Familiarity with different schools of thought," "Developing one's own point of view," "Obtaining knowledge from different disciplines," and "Independent work." Areas that the students appeared to consider to be less important subsequent to the sojourn abroad were "Learning facts" and "Studying to get good grades on examinations."

D. SELF-EFFICACY

The Self-Efficacy Scale administered on the premeasure was readministered on the postmeasure to the study abroad and comparison groups. As was discussed in Chapter 2, the purposes for using the scale were (1) to determine if students who plan to study abroad differ from those who do not study abroad in their perceptions of their social competence and self-confidence and (2) to examine the impact that study abroad may have on personal self-efficacy.

As with the other multidimensional scales used in the study, the Self-Efficacy Scale was again subjected to principal factor analysis.

Two factors were extracted. These factors, and the factor loadings of the items marking them, are essentially the same as found from the factor analysis of the scale given as a premeasure (see Table 2.8). As on the premeasure, Factor 1 was labeled "Attitude toward Self"; Factor 2 was called "Sociability."

The means and standard deviations for the factor scores derived from the items marking the factors that were common to in the pre- and postmeasures are reported in Table 4.9.

Inspection of Table 4.9 will reveal that the means for the study abroad and comparison groups were very similar both prior to and after the junior year. The lack of statistically significant differences between or within groups over time was confirmed by the repeated measures multivariate analysis of variance performed on the data. Accordingly, the expectation that the study abroad experience would result in increased levels of self-confidence and sociability was not supported. Although the findings seem to cast doubt on the hypothesis that self-efficacy can be enhanced through study abroad, further research is required before this conclusion can be reached with confidence. The primary reason for this is that there is a substantial body of evidence (Lachman, 1986) that suggests that interventions can and do affect individuals' perceptions of personal control and that enhanced levels of personal control lead to improved and more effective performance in a number of areas. Since personal control, which is closely related to perceived self-efficacy, mediates behavior (Bandura, 1982), it remains likely that the study abroad experience and students' reactions to the experience are not independent of dimensions of personality related to personal causation. Future research in this area should incorporate a variety of measures of personal control and self-efficacy to examine in detail the significance of this area for study abroad students.

E. PROFESSIONAL GOALS AND SATISFACTION WITH STUDY ABROAD

The majority of the student sojourners, regardless of the country in which they studied, anticipated that after receiving the baccalaureate degree they would enter graduate school. While both the study abroad and comparison groups were more determined or set in their career goals after the junior year than before it, the comparison students were more set in their future career aspirations than were the study abroad students. This is consistent with the pre–study abroad questionnaire finding that study abroad students tend to be somewhat less committed to specific, clearly defined career goals than students who do not participate in study abroad.

In order to gain insight into the range of career choices that study abroad and comparison group students considered, an open-ended question was asked on the postmeasure requesting the students to indicate as specifically as possible their present career plans. Examination of these responses indicates that while a minority of the study abroad students were interested in using their study abroad experience directly, a majority planned on careers that could be sub-

Table 4.8
Means and Standard Deviations for the Importance of Ways of Thinking and
Learning: Study Abroad Group

	Before Mean	Before (S.D.)	After Mean	After (S.D.)
1. Understanding Theories	2.07	(.91)	1.78	(.84)
2. Applying Knowledge to Practical Areas	2.21	(.96)	1.72	(.81)
3. Systematic Thinking	2.35	(.93)	1.72	(.81)
4. Methodology (Research Methodology, Computer Programming, Etc.)	3.01	(1.11)	2.67	(1.20)
5. Familiarity with Different Schools of Thought	2.52	(.91)	1.72	(.72)
6. Examining Relations Between Observations/ Hypotheses/Facts/Concepts	2.51	(.83)	2.06	(.92)
7. Obtaining Comparative (e.g., International/ European, Intercultural Perspectives	2.74	(.91)	1.43	(.62)
8. Developing One's Own Point of View	1.95	(.93)	1.43	(.61)
9. Utilizing Publications In a Foreign Language	3.50	(1.15)	2.47	(.93)
10. Obtaining Knowledge From Different Disciplines (Interdisciplinary Approach)	2.62	(1.00)	2.14	(1.00)

11. Out-of-Class Communication Between Students and Teaching Staff	2.60 (1.04)	1.80 (.94)
12. Independent Work (e.g., Writing Papers), Project Work	2.58 (1.11)	1.88 (.99)
13. Obtaining Regular Feedback From Teachers	2.32 (1.01)	1.95 (1.01)
14. Learning Facts	2.18 (.86)	2.35 (.96)
15. Regular Class Attendance	1.82 (.93)	1.88 (.94)
16. Studying to Get Good Grades on Examinations	1.81 (.93)	2.04 (.96)
17. Regarding the Teachers as the Main Source of Information	2.60 (.96)	3.05 (.95)
18. Taking on a Heavy Workload	2.29 (1.06)	2.51 (1.11)
19. Selecting Demanding Courses	2.16 (.96)	1.99 (.96)

Scale:
1=Very Important   2=   3=   4=   5=Not important at all

Table 4.9
Means and Standard Deviations of the Factor Scores on the Self-Efficacy Scale

Group	"Self-Attitude"	"Sociability"
Study Abroad	Mean (SD)	Mean (SD)
Before	2.58 (.42)	2.14 (.53)
After	2.62 (.51)	2.13 (.61)
Comparison		
Before	2.53 (.47)	2.12 (.59)
After	2.60 (.45)	2.18 (.55)

Scale: "1" reflects poor self-esteem and low
sociability; "4" reflects high self-esteem and
high sociability.

stantially, although indirectly, enhanced by the knowledge and perspectives that the sojourn abroad offered. The UK students seemed to be an exception to this, as, apparently, the foreign language skills that the students gained were of direct relevance to the importance that the study abroad year was perceived to have on future professional and/or career opportunities. When asked specifically the extent to which they thought that their study abroad experience would help them in achieving their professional and/or work-related goals, the returnees tended to feel that it most probably would be highly valuable.

A few examples of career interests specifically mentioned by the study abroad students are:

France

"I would like to work in the field of international education or international exchange programs."

"I want to be a French professor eventually."

West Germany

"To be a professor of economics (international finance, trade)."

"I would like to get a Ph.D. and teach comparative literature."

United Kingdom

"Law/academic."

"Sales or managerial position."

Career aspirations of the students in the comparison group were remarkably similar to the career aspirations of the sojourners who studied in the UK. Academically related career goals were mentioned most often.

The degree to which study abroad students were satisfied with their sojourn has been dealt with in other parts of the book. Nonetheless, it is informative to consider some representative comments that students made when asked on the post–study abroad questionnaire for "additional comments." As can be seen from the comments, the students were very thoughtful and reflective in their responses, indicating, for the most part, that the study abroad year was clearly of great significance to them academically and personally.

France

"I'll reiterate: The program was not the most academically enriching experience, but my personal growth and experience is a benefit that far outweighs any education I've ever received. I'd love to do it again!"

"I feel that I've grown tremendously from my experience abroad. I think this will help me in all areas of my life, my professional life as well."

"Before going abroad my career goals appeared to be set. After my year abroad I decided to pursue a new major in addition to the old one. I am happy with this decision; had I not gone abroad I might have perhaps haphazardly entered the Foreign Service. Regardless of a future career, if in international law/diplomacy/government or in an unrelated field, I am sure my year abroad helped me grow in some ways years in advance and the experience will help me deal with all situations in the future."

Sweden

"I found that I'm much more adaptable than I might have thought. By the end of the year abroad I really felt like I belonged in Sweden."

West Germany

"I have really been sorting through things in these last weeks, so this survey will give you perhaps the most objective picture. I think the most important thing I learned from my year abroad is that NOTHING, NOBODY, and NO PLACE is perfect. It seemed I was always searching for perfection, and it really struck home that life is a mixed bag when I was abroad. I realized that people were people all over the world—and we all have our quirks. Systems of government stink and shine on every continent—well, you get the idea. It cracked my 'happily ever after' complex and it's making my life now a lot more productive for it. Thanks."

"It was the best thing I've ever done. I grew in every way. Seeing the world has widened my knowledge in many areas—from geography to world affairs."

United Kingdom

"I think this will stand out as the best experience of my college years. I just wish there was a resource (or liaison) to help me get back for graduate school."

"I feel I gained as an individual through my participation. Despite the weather, homesickness, etc., I would go through the program again, as it proved to be a most rewarding experience."

5

ANALYSES OF PERSONAL AND SOJOURN VARIABLES RELATED TO IMPACTS OF STUDY ABROAD

METHODOLOGICAL APPROACHES

The third research question guiding the investigation asked, What aspects of the individual and/or the sojourn contribute to variation in the changes observed? In order to answer this question, variables that represent aspects of the individual and of the sojourn that were hypothesized to be related to changes in selected study abroad outcomes were isolated. Stepwise regression analysis was employed to analyze the data, as this procedure establishes a general predictive model from a single independent variable or some linear combination of independent variables to account for the variability in the dependent (outcome) variables of interest. Most significantly, the technique yields estimates of the *independent* contribution that each predictor variable makes to the dependent variable.

Differentiations between what we term "individual" and "sojourn" variables were made in order to create two classes of independent variables. Although the distinction between these two types of variables, as well as between the independent and dependent variables used in the analysis, is not unambiguous, the differentiation is useful in providing a framework for distinguishing and clarifying the correlates of change that occurred in the sample of sojourners.

Fifteen variables deemed to reflect characteristics of the sojourner were isolated. They were termed "individual" or sojourner variables and are listed in Table 5.1.

Six variables were selected that relate to or reflect some aspect of the environment or situation that the sojourners encountered during the study abroad year. They were termed "sojourn" variables and are listed in Table 5.2.

Table 5.1
"Individual" or Sojourner Variables

---

1. Gender

2. Academic Accomplishment and Intellectual
   Development While Abroad

3. Travel While Abroad

4. Academic and Other Problems While Abroad

5. Satisfaction with Study Abroad

6. Opinions Concerning the Host Country

7. Change in Knowledge about the Host Country

8. International Understanding - "Peace and
   Cooperation"

9. International Understanding - "Cultural and Social
   Interest"

10. International Understanding - "International
    Concern"

11. Learning Style - "Intellectuality"

12. Learning Style - "Academic Style"

13. Learning Style - "Work Habits"

14. Self-Efficacy - "Attitude Toward Self"

15. Self-Efficacy - "Sociability"

As can be seen from examination of Tables 5.1 and 5.2, the predictor variables were derived from scores from individual and/or composite questionnaire items or factor scores that represent identified dimensions of selected scales.

In this chapter the outcome (dependent) variable of interest will be first described. Analyses of the predictive relationship between the individual and sojourn variables and the selected dependent variable will then be presented. In a concluding section the general results will be summarized. The first dependent variable analyzed was change in language proficiency.

Table 5.2
Variables Related to the Sojourn

---

1. **Where the Student Lived While Abroad**

2. **Percent of Time Spent with Americans**

3. **Percent of Time Spent with Host Country Nationals**

4. **Percent of Time Spent with Other Country Nationals**

5. **Level of Integration into the Host University**

6. **Level of "Worthwhileness" to Study Abroad**

A. CHANGE IN LANGUAGE PROFICIENCY

It was thought that the best single index of host country language proficiency would be the combination of listening, speaking, reading, and writing scores taken from the self-appraisal scales. Accordingly, change (improvement) in language proficiency was created as a dependent variable by summing the individual change scores from the pre- and postquestionnaires across the four language competency self-appraisal scales: listening, speaking, reading, and writing.

The Sample

The sample employed for the statistical analyses of the language data comprises study abroad students from the four American institutions who completed the pre- and postquestionnaires and who studied in the Federal Republic of Germany or in France. The samples used for any specific statistical analysis comprised only those subjects for whom complete data were available on the variables of interest. Since the focus is exclusively on correlates of change related to the study abroad year, the comparison group was not included in any of the analyses.

Individual Correlates of Language Change

Of the 15 predictor variables entered into the stepwise regression analyses, 7 variables were significantly related to improvement in language proficiency. The general predictive model was highly significant ($F_{7,122} = 5.93$, $p < .001$). The linear combination of the independent variables accounted for just under 27 percent of the variance in the dependent variable.

The 7 statistically significant variables were "Gender," "Academic accom-

Table 5.3
Summary of Stepwise Regression Analysis of "Individual" Variables on
Language Change

Variable	R^2	F	p	df
Gender	.07	8.72	.01	1,122
Accomplish.	.13	4.44	.04	2,122
Opinion	.16	5.86	.02	3,122
Knowledge	.21	6.95	.01	4,122
Peace & Coop.	.23	3.30	.07	5,122
Self-Attitude	.25	4.25	.04	6,122
Academ. Style	.27	2.76	.09	7,122

plishment and intellectual development while abroad," "Opinions concerning the host country," "Change [increase] in knowledge about the host country," "International understanding" as measured by the "Peace and Cooperation" dimension of the Cognitive International Understanding Scale, level of personal "Self-efficacy" as reflected by the "Attitude toward Self" factor of the Self-Efficacy Scale, and "Academic Style," a dimension of the Learning Styles Scale assessing cooperative attitudes toward academic work.

As will be noted from examination of Table 5.3, the single most powerful predictor of language change was gender, accounting for just over 7 percent of the variance in the dependent variable. Examination of the means of the males and females both before and after study abroad showed that the greatest gain in language proficiency was made by the males. Prior to the study abroad year, the males were substantially lower than the females in foreign language proficiency. By the end of the sojourn, however, the males made gains that brought them up to the level of the females.

The summary statistics for the stepwise regression analysis are reported in Table 5.3. The multiple correlation coefficient squared (R^2) represents the amount of variance shared between the independent and dependent variables.

Sojourn Correlates of Language Change

Of the 6 sojourn variables entered into the regression analysis, 4 were statistically significant predictors of language improvement. The general model was

Table 5.4
Summary of Stepwise Regression Analysis of Sojourn Variables on Language Change

Variable	R^2	F	p	df
Academ. Integr.	.10	14.04	.001	1,129
Living	.14	5.53	.001	2,129
Worthwhileness	.16	4.19	.04	3,129
Not with Amer.	.19	4.35	.04	4,129

highly significant ($F_{4,129} = 7.45$, $p < .001$), with the linear combination of the statistically significant sojourn variables accounting for 19 percent of the variance in language change.

The variables contributing significantly to language change were: "Level of integration into the host university," "Percent of time spent with host country nationals," "Worthwhileness to study abroad," and "Percent of time spent with Americans."

The summary of the stepwise regression analysis is reported in Table 5.4.

Summary of Factors Leading to Improvement in Language Proficiency

Improvements in the study abroad students' language proficiency were significantly related to variables that were deemed to reflect aspects of the individual sojourner as well as variables considered to reflect elements of the sojourn. The best linear combination of variables from the former category making statistically significant contributions to change in language proficiency accounted for a very impressive 27 percent of the variance in the language change score. An only somewhat less impressive 19 percent of the variance in language change score was attributable to sojourn variables. The magnitude of these relationships is all the more impressive because of the general restriction of range in the language proficiency change scores and the necessary reduction in correlation between the independent variables and the dependent variable that results from restriction in range.

The results suggest that improvements in foreign language proficiency can be enhanced in a number of ways. For example, approaches taken by administrators of study abroad programs to increase students' language competencies might focus on the students' knowledge of the host country, facilitating the students' integration into the host country university, providing support to develop the students' self-confidence in meeting the challenges of studying and living in a foreign environment, and facilitating contact among the American students and students from the host country.

B. SATISFACTION WITH STUDY ABROAD

The Sample

The sample used for this analysis as well as for all subsequent analyses concerning the relationship between sojourn experiences and selected outcome variables comprises *all* matched study abroad group students (i.e., students from UC, UMass, CU, and Kalamazoo College) who responded to the pre- and postmeasures.

The satisfaction with study abroad variable was created from responses to a postsojourn question that asked the students to indicate their overall satisfaction (1 = very satisfied; 5 = very dissatisfied) with the study abroad. The mean on this question was 1.48 (SD = 0.79), suggesting that the sojourners were almost uniformly pleased with their experience abroad. No significant difference among the host countries was detected on level of satisfaction.

Individual Correlates of Satisfaction

The 15 predictor variables used in the language analysis were also used as independent variables in the stepwise regression analysis, with "satisfaction" as the dependent variable. A regression model with three independent variables was found to be statistically significant ($F_{3,126} = 11.81$, $p < .001$). This model accounted for a substantial 22 percent of the variance in the level of satisfaction with the study abroad year. Once again, the magnitude of the relationship is particularly impressive inasmuch as the variance on the "satisfaction" question was highly restricted.

The statistically significant independent variables were: "Academic accomplishment and intellectual development while abroad," "Change in knowledge about the host country," and "Academic and other problems while abroad."

The summary of the stepwise regression is given in Table 5.5.

Sojourn Correlates of Satisfaction

Of the 6 sojourn variables entered into the analysis, 2 were statistically significant predictors of satisfaction with the study abroad experience. The general model was statistically significant ($F_{2,192} = 13.2$, $p < .001$) and accounted for 12 percent of the total variance. While 12 percent of the variance accounted for in the dependent variable may not appear to be large, one should keep in

Table 5.5
Summary of Stepwise Regression Analysis of "Individual" Variables on
Satisfaction with Study Abroad

Variable	R^2	F	p	df
Academ. Growth.	.09	13.54	.001	1,192
Knowledge	.16	9.28	.001	2,192
Lack of Problems	.22	9.98	.001	3,192

mind that the sojourners tended to be highly satisfied with their year abroad
and there was little variability in their responses.

The statistically significant independent variables were: "Level of integration
into the host university" and "Level of 'worthwhileness' to study abroad."

The summary of this regression analysis is presented in Table 5.6.

Summary of Factors Leading to Positive Evaluation of the Study Abroad Experience

Students who felt that their year abroad was marked by academic accomplishment and growth, increased knowledge of the host country, lack of academic and personal problems, and a sense of integration into the university of
the host country tended to be most satisfied with the study abroad experience.
Although the statistical contributions made by each of these variables to satisfaction with study abroad are independent, they suggest a composite picture of
the student who views the study abroad experience as being highly positive.

Table 5.6
Summary of Stepwise Regression Analysis of Sojourn Variables on Satisfaction
with Study Abroad

Variable	R^2	F	p	df
Academic Integra.	.07	16.34	.001	1/192
Worthwhileness	.12	9.31	.001	2/192

Table 5.7
Summary of Stepwise Regression Analysis of "Individual" Variables on Integration into the Host University

Variable	R^2	F	p	df
Academic Growth	.12	16.55	.001	1/120
Language Change	.18	9.04	.001	2/122
"Academic Style"	.21	5.31	.02	3/122
Travel	.24	4.03	.05	4/122

C. INTEGRATION INTO THE HOST INSTITUTION

One of the main objectives of most American study abroad programs is that the students be integrated into the general academic and cultural life of the host university and society. As was suggested earlier, achievement of this goal is not often fully accomplished.

Individual Correlates of Integration

The 15 "individual" or sojourner variables plus a newly created variable of change (improvement) in language proficiency were entered into the stepwise regression equations with "Level of integration into the host university" as the dependent variable. The general model was defined by four independent variables and was highly significant ($F_{4,126} = 12.1$, $p < .001$), accounting for an impressive 24 percent of the variance.

The significant sojourner variables were: "Academic accomplishment and intellectual development while abroad," "Change (improvement) in language proficiency," "Academic Style" (Factor 2 from the Learning Styles Scale, which reflected primarily the students' desire to work cooperatively in group settings), and "Travel while abroad." Change (increase) in the "Cultural Interest and Respect" factor from the Cognitive International Understanding Scale was only marginally significant and was not considered further.

The statistically significant variables and their cumulative contribution to the variance of the academic integration measure are presented in Table 5.7.

Sojourn Correlates of Integration

Of the 5 sojourn variables entered into the regression analysis, only 1 independent variable contributed significantly to the general model ($F_{1,194} = 15.27$,

Table 5.8
Summary of Stepwise Regression Analysis of Sojourn Variables on Integration into the Host University

Variable	R^2	F	p	df
Living in Dorms	.07	15.27	.001	1/175

$p < .001$). The variable was "Where the student lived while abroad." It accounted for 7 percent of the variance. This result suggests that living in dormitory situations while abroad contributes significantly to the sojourners' integration into the host university and culture.

The results of the regression analysis are reported in Table 5.8.

Factors Related to Integration into the Academic Life of the Host Institution

The primary factors related to integration into the academic life of the host institution involve the students' general level of academic accomplishment, their improvement in proficiency in the language of the host country, a learning style that involves working and cooperating with others, travel while abroad, and living in an integrated dormitory situation.

While academic accomplishment constitutes only one dimension of the study abroad experience, the data suggest that it, along with language accomplishment, is perhaps the most important dimension of the students' sojourn abroad, exercising a powerful effect on the students' general evaluation of the study abroad experience. In addition, integration into the academic life of the host institution is facilitated by academic and linguistic success as well as integrated living arrangements. Accordingly, emphasis on academic accomplishment as well as on social and living situations designed to maximize contact with host national students could contribute significantly to the sense of integration that American students gain while abroad.

D. CHANGE IN KNOWLEDGE ABOUT THE HOST COUNTRY

The change in knowledge about the host country variable was created by summing the change scores across all items of the pre- and postmeasure questionnaires' "Change in knowledge about the host country" question. The items included knowledge about the host country's political system and institutions,

Table 5.9
Summary of Stepwise Regression Analysis of "Individual" Variables on Change in Knowledge about the Host Country

Variable	R^2	F	p	df
Language Change	.08	11.58	.001	1/126
Positive Opinion	.15	8.72	.001	2/126
Satisfaction	.18	6.19	.001	3/126
"Intellectuality"	.22	5.04	.001	4/126

dominant political issues, government foreign policy, cultural life, dominant social issues, and so on.

Individual Correlates of Knowledge Change

Of the 15 independent sojourner variables entered into the stepwise regression equation, four variables combined to yield a highly significant ($F_{4,126} = 5.64$, $p < .001$) model of change in knowledge about the host country. The predictors of knowledge change accounted for a substantial 26 percent of the variance. They were change (improvement) in language proficiency, positive opinions concerning the host country, general satisfaction with the year abroad, and the students' level of "Intellectuality" (Factor 1 of the Learning Styles Scale involving primarily the ability to reason abstractly, formulate hypotheses, etc.).

These results are summarized in Table 5.9.

Sojourn Correlates of Knowledge Change

None of the 6 sojourn variables entered into the stepwise regression analysis were significantly related to change in knowledge about the host country.

E. WORTHWHILENESS OF STUDY ABROAD

The extent to which the study abroad students found the sojourn abroad to be worthwhile was assessed by a 13-item omnibus question that asked the sojourners to indicate on a 5-point scale whether the experience was "extremely worthwhile" (1) or "not at all worthwhile" (5). Examples of the items include: "Exposure to other teaching methods other than those adopted at your home institution," "Career prospects," "Foreign language proficiency," "Perspec-

Table 5.10
Summary of Stepwise Regression Analysis of the "Individual" Variables That Contribute to Worthwhileness of the Study Abroad Year

Variable	R^2	F	p	df
"Academic Style"	.09	12.21	.001	1/125
Opinion	.15	8.05	.001	2/125
"Intellectuality"	.19	6.75	.01	3/125
"Intern. Concern"	.23	6.39	.01	4/125
Satisfaction	.26	3.37	.06	5/125

tive on your home country," and "Perspectives gained on your own future life." The "worthwhileness" variable was created by combining the scores on each of the items to obtain a total "worthwhileness" score.

Individual Correlates of Worthwhileness of Study Abroad

Of the 15 individual variables entered into the regression analysis, 5 were statistically significant predictors of the dependent variable. The general model was highly significant ($F_{5,125} = 8.21$, $p < .001$), accounting for a very impressive 26 percent of the total variance. The significant independent variables were: "Academic Style" (Factor 2 of the Learning Styles Scale, reflecting cooperative learning styles, working with others, etc.), "Opinions concerning the host country," "Intellectuality" (Factor 1 of the Learning Styles Scale, involving ability to think abstractly, formulate and apply hypotheses, etc.), "International Concern" (Factor 1 of the Affective International Understanding Scale, reflecting the importance of international cooperation), and "Overall satisfaction with the study abroad period."

The statistically significant independent variables and their cumulative contribution to the dependent variable reflecting the general worthwhileness of the study abroad year are presented in Table 5.10.

Sojourn Correlates of Worthwhileness of Study Abroad

Regression analysis involving the 5 sojourn independent variables did not yield a statistically significant predictive model of worthwhileness of study abroad.

Table 5.11
Summary of Stepwise Regression Analysis of "Individual" Variables on Academic Problems

Variable	R^2	F	p	df
"Domestic Orient."	.11	15.7	.001	1/126
Pos. Opin. Host Ctn.	.14	4.5	.03	2/126
Pos. Self-Image	.16	3.2	.05	3/126
Intellectuality	.18	3.2	.05	4/126
Knowledge	.21	3.3	.05	5/126

F. ACADEMIC AND INTEGRATION/LIFESTYLE PROBLEMS

Problems that the study abroad and comparison group students had, or perceived to have had, during their junior year were assessed by means of a multi-item scale that was described in Chapter 4, Section C, "Problems during Study Abroad." Factor analysis of the scale resulted in two factors: "Academic Problems" and "Integration/Lifestyle Problems." In order to determine which of the individual and/or sojourn variables were significantly related to the "problem" scales, regression analyses were employed using the entire sample of study abroad students who responded to the postmeasure. As will be recalled from Chapter 4, "Academic Problems" were defined by: "Academic level of courses too easy," "Differences in teaching/learning methods," "Readiness on part of teaching staff to meet and/or help foreign students," and so on. "Integration/Lifestyle Problems" were defined by: "Interaction among/with host country students," "Guidance concerning academic matters," and the like.

Individual Correlates of Problems While Abroad

Academic Problems. Using the 6-item "Academic Problems" scale as a dependent variable and the 15 "individual" variables as independent variables, regression analysis revealed a highly significant predictive model ($F_{5,126} = 5.84$, $p < .001$) with 5 predictor variables making statistically significant contributions. The variables and the cumulative R^2 values are reported in Table 5.11. As will be noted from examination of Table 5.11, 21 percent of the variance in the "Academic Problems" scale was accounted for by the predictor variables.

Table 5.12
**Summary of Stepwise Regression Analysis of "Individual" Variables on
Integration/Lifestyle Problems**

Variable	R^2	F	p	df
"Domestic Orient."	.08	11.1	.001	1/125
"Academic Style"	.12	5.9	.02	2/125
Travel	.17	6.6	.01	3/125

The results indicate that sojourners who have fewer or less pronounced academic problems while abroad tend to be those individuals who are lower in "Domestic Orientation" (Factor 1 of the Affective International Understanding Scale), have a positive opinion of their host country, have a positive self-image (Factor 1 of the Self-Efficacy Scale), consider themselves to be highly intellectual (Factor 1 of the Learning Styles Scale), and during the sojourn have shown considerable gain in knowledge about their host country.

Integration/Lifestyle Problems. Three of the 15 "individual" independent variables formed a statistically significant model to predict the dependent variable, "Integration/Lifestyle Problems" ($F_{3,125} = 6.93$, $p < .001$). These variables, as well as their cumulative R^2 values, are depicted in Table 5.12.

Once again, the most important predictor for *not* having integration and/or lifestyle problems while abroad was a low score on the "Domestic Orientation" factor of the Affective International Understanding Scale. Of less importance were (1) an "Academic Style" (Factor 2 of the Learning Styles Scale) that reflected the ability to engage in cooperative work with others, motivate others, and so on, and (2) a substantial amount of travel while abroad.

Sojourn Correlates of Problems While Abroad

Academic Problems. Only 1 of the 6 sojourn variables was significantly related to academic problems while abroad ($F_{1,126} = 9.88$, $p < .001$). The variable, accounting for 5 percent of the variance ($R^2 = .05$), assessed the degree to which the student felt integrated into the academic life of the host institution. Thus, perhaps somewhat of a tautology, sojourners who tend not to feel highly integrated into the host university's academic life also tend to have academic problems.

Integration/Lifestyle Problems. Of the 6 sojourn variables entered into the regression analysis to predict integration and/or lifestyle problems of the so-

Table 5.13
Summary of Stepwise Regression Analysis of Sojourn Variables on Integration/ Lifestyle Problems

Variable	R^2	F	p	df
Academic Integration	.07	14.9	.001	1/191
Living Arrangement w.				
Too Few Host Nationals	.09	3.3	.05	2/191

journer, only 2 were statistically significant ($F_{2,191} = 5.84$, $p < .001$). Once again, lack of integration into the academic life of the host institution was perceived by the sojourners to be an important factor contributing to their problems in adjustment abroad. The second variable to be related to integration and/or lifestyle problems of the study abroad students was *not* having sufficient contact with host country nationals in the sojourners' dormitory or other living arrangement. The significant independent variables and their cumulative R^2 values are shown in Table 5.13.

6

LONG-TERM EFFECTS: A FOLLOW-UP OF STUDY ABROAD ALUMNI/AE

The creative developmental psychologist and transcultural psychoanalyst Erik H. Erikson (1975) summarized the unifying perspective of his influential studies in the simple phrase: "Life histories are inextricably interwoven with history" (p. 20). It is this point of view that we use to explore the meaning of a study abroad experience in the subsequent life history of the alumni/ae.

Our organizing theme is the interconnections between the biographies of a small sample of study abroad alumni/ae and the changing context of American national society in a complexly interdependent world in the second half of the twentieth century.

METHODOLOGICAL APPROACHES

Addressing the fourth and final research question—What are the long-term effects of the study abroad experience?—involved gathering biographical information from a sample of study abroad alumni/ae and selecting appropriate demographic data and sociocultural studies on American life. The latter materials are referenced in the discussions throughout the chapter.

To gather the biographical information required: (1) identification of the pool of former students, (2) collecting background data through a questionnaire (see Appendix III) on such things as date of graduation, major, year and city/country of study abroad, approximate family income, jobs held since graduation, marital status, volunteer activities and experience overseas, if any, since their study abroad period, and (3) a telephone interview. The interview followed a specific format aimed at obtaining a picture of the individual and the meaning of his or her study abroad experience in various aspects of his or her life. (The interview schedule can be seen in Appendix III.) All interviews were conducted by one individual in order to enhance the reliability of the results across subjects. The interviewer was given special tutelage on telephone-interviewing techniques. Interviews were recorded and later transcribed.

THE SAMPLE

Selecting alumni/ae of study abroad programs for interviewing began with our consciously, albeit reluctantly, limiting the sample to those residing in the United States at the time of the interview. We could neither afford nor manage an authentic empirical study of those regularly residing and/or working outside their country of citizenship. None of the four institutions keep up-to-date records about their study abroad alumni/ae who more or less regularly reside and/ or work abroad. We would expect that the life course and perspectives of those study abroad alumni/ae who are expatriate Americans and who are in the United States only for "home leave," visits to the "home office," or attendance at family gatherings would differ considerably.

This early self-imposed constraint in our global outreach does not imply that the lives of those interviewed have been confined to the United States. Seven out of ten of the men and nine out of ten of the women reported at least episodic international mobility, and some have had extensive periods abroad. It does mean that the observations developed in this chapter can be generalized only to those study abroad alumni/ae who are residing in the United States.

The sample comprised a subset of randomly selected individuals who had participated in an education abroad program in one of the target Western European countries at intervals of five, ten, fifteen, and twenty years ago. Initially, 158 alumni/ae were selected from the four American institutions combined. Under the aegis of their undergraduate college or university, letters were sent to each of the selected sample, informing them of the project and requesting their cooperation. If they agreed, they were asked to provide a telephone number at which they could be reached for setting up a half-hour interview and to return the one-page profile questionnaire mentioned above.

At the outset, 101 individuals agreed to participate. Owing to disparate circumstances on both our side and theirs, the final number for whom we have both the profile and the telephone interview lessened to seventy-six: Kalamazoo College, sixteen; University of Massachusetts at Amherst, twenty-three; University of Colorado, twenty-two; and University of California, fifteen. Although the institutional variable was not used in the subsequent analysis of the data, picking the sample from programs located in four geographic regions (New England, the north central states, Rocky Mountain and western prairies, and the Pacific Coast) helped but did not ensure a national dispersion of the sample. Because one-third of those interviewed were currently living and working in either the same state or a state nearby the one in which they pursued their undergraduate education, undersampled are those who reside in the southeastern, southern, and southwestern areas of the United States.

Table 6.1
Interviewed Sample, by Cohort, Gender, and Age

Cohort	Number	%Female	Age
TOTAL	76	59.2	25-44
I 1962-65	15	73.3	40-44
II 1966-70	22	50.0	35-39
III 1971-75	27	59.3	30-34
IV 1976-80	12	58.3	25-29

The cluster sample was grouped by five-year intervals in which the study abroad in Europe occurred (study abroad cohort) by gender and by age. This is depicted in Table 6.1.

The overall proportion of females in the sample (59.2 percent) is somewhat less than the proportion of women among the some 23,000 study abroad alumni/ae of the four institutions (62.6 percent). At the time of their interview, fifteen persons were between 40 and 44 (eleven of whom were women), twenty-two were between 35 and 39, twenty-seven between 30 and 34, and twelve between 25 and 29.

All individuals interviewed completed their bachelor's degree, and around 70 percent pursued graduate study, with close to 30 percent receiving a doctorate.

At the time of the interview, the vast majority (92 percent) were fully employed, almost two-thirds in professional/technical occupations and less than one-third in managerial/administrative work roles. More men were at work in professional/technical positions, whereas more women were employed as managers/administrators.

Two-thirds of the study abroad alumni/ae are married, and one-third are single or divorced. Three-fourths of the married have a family income of more than $35,000 a year; only two-fifths of the single/divorced earn over $35,000. Both marriage and childbearing tend to be delayed. And 10 percent of the sample have foreign-born spouses.

These overall characteristics of the study abroad alumni/ae sample are not greatly different from the characteristics of those segments of the American population from which they are drawn and to which they return and pursue further education, employment, family formation, and community involvement. Hence, we shall draw on the increasing number of data sets and the burgeoning literature on trends and changes in the American setting in order to contextualize the longer-term aftermaths of a study abroad experience.

To undertake a combined study of the lives and times of any segment of America's internationally mobile, highly educated implies critical choices that affect both the findings and the generalizations that can be drawn. (For a critical evaluation of the research tradition in this field, see Bowen et al. [1977] and the German Academic Exchange Service [DAAD, 1980].) Inasmuch as the sample is small and representativeness problematic, the findings developed in the analysis should be viewed as suggestive rather than conclusive.

To explore the longer-term meaning of study abroad in their lives, we shall examine their educational attainments, their work life, and more briefly noted, their family and community participation.

A. HIGHER EDUCATIONAL ASPIRATIONS, EXPECTATIONS, AND ATTAINMENTS

To provide a context for the results related to the educational aspirations and achievements of the study abroad alumni/ae, we looked at data collected by Astin and his associates of UCLA's Higher Education Research Institute. They surveyed each year—beginning in 1965—200,000 freshmen in all types of undergraduate postsecondary schools across the country. They found that even in their first year of college about half of the students queried felt that attaining graduate degrees was essential for fulfilling their ideal self and preferred occupational employment. Also noted by Astin and his colleagues was the steady increase in women's plans to pursue advanced degrees. For example, in 1966, 7 percent of the freshmen women planned on obtaining a doctorate; whereas in 1985 almost 15 percent were anticipating earning such a degree. The comparable percentages of freshmen men fell over this period from 21 percent to somewhat less than 16 percent (Astin, Green, and Korn, 1987). Commenting on these trends, the authors suggested:

These sex differences in degree aspirations no doubt reflect the effects of the women's movement. . . . The increase in women's degree aspirations began in 1969, just at the time when the women's movement was beginning to capture the attention of the media. And although the trends for women have more or less stabilized since 1977, men's aspirations for high level degrees have declined since that time. [P. 13]

The educational attainments of the study abroad alumni/ae far exceed the norms reported by Astin, Green, and Korn as well as the norms indicated in other studies we reviewed on aspirations for and attainment of educational experiences and degrees (Davis, 1964; Spaeth and Greeley, 1970; U.S. Department of Education, 1980, 1988).

All the alumni/ae interviewed did complete the bachelor's degree. A few did not complete it within four academic years because they either prolonged their

European stay or, while overseas, had missed a requirement for graduation that had to be made up.

Having earned a bachelor's degree puts the sampled alumni/ae in that 21 percent of the employed population (23 percent of the men and 20 percent of the women) who, in 1986, had minimally completed four years of undergraduate college (U.S. Department of Education, 1987, table 234). Not only did 100 percent complete their bachelor's, but also 80 percent of the men and 64 percent of the women had continued into post–bachelor's degree work.

As can be seen in Table 6.2, only 19.4 percent of the men and 35.6 percent of the women in the sample had no further formal education past the bachelor's degree. Also reported in Table 6.2 is the percentage distribution of higher education by study abroad cohorts (five-year intervals) and by sex.

Because of the small numbers involved, definitive statistical analyses could not be performed. However, research hypotheses can be generated by using χ^2 contingency tables. Accordingly, we collapsed contiguous categories to obtain cells with $N > 5$. For some of these analyses, the two older generations who entered college in the 1960s (Cohorts I and II) were put together, and the two younger generations who entered college in the 1970s (Cohorts III and IV) were collapsed. Table 6.3 reports the percentage distribution of educational attainment by sex and by the two ten-year-span generations.

Gender differences in the timing and level of education beyond the baccalaureate degree fit the gender trends in American higher education. A higher proportion of males than females go beyond the bachelor's degree (79 percent of the men and 64 percent of the women). Looking at only those men and women who pursue education past the baccalaureate degree, 72 percent of the men and 66 percent of the women earned a master's degree (not shown in the table). For women, the time elapsed between the bachelor's and master's was about a year longer than for the men. Forty-eight percent of the men pursued and were granted a doctoral degree (whether or not they took a master's), whereas only 34 percent of the women who went past the bachelor's have earned a doctorate. The older-age-grade males received their doctorates at an earlier age (twenty-eight) than the older females (thirty-one). However, there is no discrepancy in the age at which the younger-age-grade women and men received their doctorates.

Not shown in the table is the fact that one out of eight of those who hold a master's or doctorate has continued his or her education past that level by securing a second master's, special certification, or postdoctorate research training. For some, this participation in lifelong education is due to the need for additional education to move up into more complex work assignments; for others, it is to change directions in their employment areas; for still others, it reflects a need to update their knowledge base.

We anticipate that the complex factors affecting the life trajectories of American men and women who are involved in overseas study as undergraduates will result in lessening, rather than increasing, the differences between

Table 6.2
Percentage Distribution of SAP Alumni/ae Sample with Education Beyond Bachelor's Degree, by Study Abroad Cohort and Sex

SAP Cohort - Age	Education Beyond Bachelor's Degree			
	None	Some[1]	Master's	Doctorate
TOTAL 25-44	28.9	6.7	35.5	28.9
Males	19.4	3.2	38.7	38.7
Females	35.6	8.9	33.3	22.2
I 40-44	26.7	6.4	20.0	46.7
Males	--	--	50.0	50.0
Females	26.4	8.1	9.1	45.5
II 35-39	13.7	--	54.5	31.8
Males	9.1	--	45.5	45.5
Females	18.2	--	63.6	18.2
III 30-34	29.6	14.9	33.3	22.2
Males	36.4	9.1	18.2	36.4
Females	25.0	18.7	43.8	12.5
IV 25-29	58.3	--	25.0	16.7
Males	20.0	--	60.0	20.0
Females	76.8	8.9	--	14.3

[1] Formally enrolled in some post-bachelor's program but no degree

Table 6.3
Percentage Distribution of Educational Attainment of Study Abroad Alumni/ae, by Gender and Generation

Degrees	Sample	Gender		Cohort	
		Male	Female	I & II	III & IV
TOTAL	(76)	(31)	(45)	(37)	(39)
Bachelors	35.6	22.6	44.5	21.6	48.7
Masters	35.6	38.7	33.3	40.5	30.8
Doctorates	28.9	38.7	22.2	37.9	20.5

them—the so-called gender gap—as far as educational attainments are concerned. It is not so much that women will approach the "traditional" men's patterns or that men will become feminized but rather that the convergence will be over the centrality of a higher education, which includes cross-cultural experience for developing a style of work and life.

B. EMPLOYMENT HISTORY AND WORK LIFE

Major structural changes in America's political economy and social stratification system since World War II have engendered in its work force what has been termed the occupations of the "new middle class." By consensus of writers on this topic, these occupations are included in the U.S. Census categories: "Professional, technical and kindred workers" and "Managers, officials and proprietors, except farm." The highly educated men and, increasingly, women who occupy and often create these relatively high-status work roles in the central institutions of the society have respected authoritative knowledge and decision-making responsibilities. (For prescient interpretations of these changes, see Bell, 1973; Bledstein, 1976; Haber, 1974; Jencks and Riesman, 1968; Mills, 1956; Vanneman and Cannon, 1987.)

Ninety-two percent of the study abroad alumni/ae were, at the time of the interview, in work roles that are classified as "new middle class occupations"; that is, they were either in professional/technical or managerial/administrative positions. This puts the sample in that 16.8 percent of the total working force in the United States that in 1980 were classified as "new middle class." Approximately two-thirds of this category are men and one-third are women (U.S. Department of Education, 1980).

Table 6.4
Percentage Distribution of Employment Category, by Gender and Study Abroad Cohort

Employment Category	Total	Gender		Cohort	
		Male	Female	I & II	III & IV
	(76)	(31)	(45)	(37)	(39)
NMC Occup.[1]	92.1	93.6	91.1	94.6	89.8
Prof/Tech.[2]	61.8	71.0	55.5	64.9	59.0
Manag/Admin.[3]	30.3	22.6	35.6	29.7	30.8
Other	7.9	6.4	8.9	5.4	10.2

[1]New Middle Class Occupations

[2]Professional, technical and kindred workers

[3]Managers, officials, and proprietors except farm

The percentage distribution of job type by gender and study abroad cohort is reported in Table 6.4.

Maximizers and Minimalists

The question can be raised, In what ways were the European experiences of the study abroad alumni/ae incorporated into their new–middle-class work roles that ordinarily require higher education, and often continuing learning, for their performance? To explore this, we adapted the concepts of "maximizers" and "minimalists."

Maximizer refers to the forty-five individuals in the sample of seventy-six (59.2 percent) who incorporate their European study abroad and other significant transnational experiences into their career values and employment practices. *Minimalist* applies to the other thirty-one of the seventy-six (41.8 percent) who report that their student and subsequent foreign country experiences, if any, are valued in retrospect but feel that they are not appreciably relevant to their own work life. The meaning of the foreign study experience in other aspects of their lives, such as family and community life, will be looked at subsequently.

The sample, classified as "maximizers" or "minimalists," was further divided by gender, study abroad cohort, educational attainment, and occupational classification.

Of the men, 58.1 percent (eighteen out of thirty-one) were classified as maximizers; of the women, 60.0 percent (twenty-seven out of forty-five) were maximizers. The difference was nonsignificant.

Cross-classifying the maximizers and minimalists by cohort (Cohorts I and II, 35–44 years of age; Cohorts III and IV, 25–34 years of age) resulted in 56.8 percent of the older cohort and 61.5 percent of the younger cohort being maximizers. Again, the difference was nonsignificant.

When the maximizers and minimalists were subdivided by highest educational degree earned (two categories: bachelor's only and advanced degree earned beyond the bachelor's), twelve out of twenty-seven (44.4 percent) of those with only a bachelor's degree were utilizing their foreign experience in their work role, whereas 59.2 percent of those with advanced degrees are maximizers. The difference is significant ($\chi^2 = 10.8$, $p < .001$). Hence, those who have advanced degrees are more likely to incorporate their foreign experience into their work-related values and life.

Subclassifying the maximizers and minimalists by which type of new–middle-class work roles they held (professional/technical or managerial/administrative), it was found that 69.6 percent (thirty-two out of forty-six) of those in the professional/technical occupations are maximizers, and 43.3 percent (thirteen out of thirty) of those in the managerial/administrative are maximizers. The difference is significant ($\chi^2 = 5.17$, $p < .05$). Those in professional/technical roles tend to incorporate their foreign experiences more into the workplace than do those who are in managerial/administrative types of work.

Thus, neither gender nor age cohort alone seems to be related to whether or not the study abroad alumni/ae utilize their foreign experience in their work role, whereas advanced degrees and type of new–middle-class employment are.

In order to examine the question whether males and females from different study abroad cohorts, educational attainment categories, and type of employment category differ in their use of foreign experiences in their workplace, independent 2×2 contingency tables were constructed for maximizers and minimalists separately, using gender and each of the other three categories as independent variables. The results of this exercise suggest that the utilization of foreign experiences in the work role is a complex process that has largely been unstudied.

For example, maximizers tend to be twenty-five- to thirty-four-year-old males and thirty-five- to forty-four-year-old females ($\chi^2 = 3.01$, $.05 < p < .10$). Minimalists tend to be older males and younger females ($\chi^2 = 5.7$, $p < .05$). No significant difference was detected between men and women maximizers with respect to their educational achievement, but minimalists tend to be women with bachelor's degrees only and men with advanced degrees ($\chi^2 = 5.1$, $.05 < p < .10$). Maximizers are overwhelmingly professional/technical men

($p < .001$); but no significant difference was found among the minimalists for this cross-classification.

Dichotomizing, disembodying, and cross-classifying the variables give clues as to where to look for some of the constraints and opportunities for utilizing the study abroad and other foreign experiences in the workplace by the alumni/ae. However, such an exercise oversimplifies the great variety and extraordinary complexity of individuals and underestimates the untidy intricacies of day-to-day living.

To explore the relationship between the larger trends in American life in a global age and the individuals whose behavior is abtracted and summarized in those trends, we shall extend and refine the seminal formulation of "repertoire" developed by the comparative sociologist and cultural historian Charles Tilly. In his study of four centuries of French history, Tilly (1986) found:

Any population has a limited repertoire of collective action: alternative means of acting together on shared interests. . . . People know the general rules of performance more or less well and vary the performance to meet the purpose at hand. . . . The existing repertoire constrains collective action; far from the image we sometimes hold of mindless crowds, people tend to act within known limits, to innovate at the margins of existing forms. [P. 390]

Cross-Cultural Repertoires of Maximizers: Vignettes

Looking only at the forty-five of the seventy-six SAP alumni/ae who are classified as maximizers of their foreign experiences in the work role, we found that they could be sorted into five broad groupings: (1) those who had roles in educational institutions, (2) those with third cultural positions in transnational structures, (3) independent professionals, (4) maximizers of small chances in complex organizations, and (5) the deeply committed but situationally constrained. We shall illustrate these with vignettes drawn from the interviews and from the personal data sheets.

Roles in Educational Institutions. Beginning with the early 1960s, America's educational leadership responded to the new position of the United States as a world power by vigorously arguing for revamping the curricula both to produce an internationally aware public and to provide the basic skills for persons who could fulfill envisioned manpower needs in America's new commitments worldwide. The terms of reference were often stated as "introducing an international dimension," "infusing the curriculum with global knowledge," and "establishing foreign language and area study programs." Such recommended changes were unevenly built into the nation's educational systems. They were not without countermovements, as entrenched interests were threatened and were sometimes allowed to lapse as other social movements with urgent agendas made demands on educational institutions' time and resources. (For representative substantial accounts of the numerous conferences and occasional surveys, envisioned trends, and public policy interest, see Ad Hoc Committee on Global Education, 1987; Barber and Ilchman, 1980; Becker, 1979; President's Commission on Foreign Language and International Studies, 1980a, 1980b; Sanders and Ward, 1970.)

Personifying the cross-cultural repertoire used in the workplace by this grouping of maximizers, are a secondary school educator and a college professor.

SECONDARY SCHOOL EDUCATOR

In answer to the question, Did your study abroad experience prompt you to include an international dimension in your work? this person replied: "Yes, in almost every way. I'm chairman of a social studies department of a high school, and I teach international relations and world history. And so I use it all the time." Later in the interview he adds, "I'm very aware of some of the problems we're having in social studies, and one of the things right now are the fundamentalist rightists' attacks on global education. (See Report to the National Council of Social Studies [NCSS], 1987.) As a matter of fact, I have been very active in the Center for International Education. Phyllis Schlafly's legal forum is out to get them. I don't know what they will ever do if they get hold of my transcript because I have thirteen to twenty classes that have 'global' in the title. I'm going to be in trouble." While aware of his political vulnerability, he is untroubled about the validity of his active involvement in furthering "international awareness" within his professional work life.

As an undergraduate major in international relations, he went on a study abroad program to Bordeaux, France. A precipitating factor was an earlier European experience. "I, like everyone else in the early 1970s, had temporarily dropped out of college to hitchhike and backpack through Europe for about six months. That's when I made up my mind that when I re-enrolled I would go over there to study. I felt real inadequate with my weak language ability."

At Bordeaux, he met his future wife (at the time, a study abroad student from another university), who is now a teacher of Spanish and French. After finishing his bachelor's degree in 1977 and a secondary education master's degree the following year, they took teaching positions in a small city in a western prairie state. "Because both of us are teachers, we can take the summers to go to Western Europe about every three years to keep us up to date and for renewal. Although we always sort of concentrate on Western Europe, [our European experiences] sort of broadened our horizons for everything on an international level. I have a desire to go everywhere now. We did spend nine months living in France and took trips to the Soviet Union and East European bloc countries."

The primacy of his self-concept as a teacher is permeated by a worldview that he daily weaves into his work life. "[Having interacted personally with people from another society] dramatically forces you to look for the other side of the issue, and you find out real quickly how ethnocentric the American press and news coverage of events are. So it kind of forces you to be a little more open-minded about the situation. That's one of the major themes in my teaching.''

At the end of the interview, when queried if there was anything he would like to add, he went on at some length, illustrating the centrality of his international perspective in his role. ''Well, last Friday I invited people into two of my classes from Youth for Understanding. I am one of the big pushers for study abroad programs, and one of my students was selected for a big scholarship to study in Germany last year.

''In the school in which I teach we're real close to a SAC air force base. So 40 to 45 percent of my students are military dependents. So I can tell you absolutely without a doubt that these kids who have lived overseas are much more culturally aware. They're much less provincial than some of the local students who have never been any place else.''

The language of this global-minded high school educator contains a vision of interesting oncoming generations in his locality learning not only how to remember hard facts about the world but also how to think and feel about them so they can take the next steps with greater self-confidence.

COLLEGE TEACHER/SCHOLAR IN THE HUMANITIES

Two years before being interviewed, and after spending seven of the preceding nine years studying and teaching in foreign countries, this individual returned to his old undergraduate college to become an assistant professor of English. This career opportunity appealed to him because he felt that the international ambience of this church-related private college in the Great Lakes region assured his continuing renewal of his life's work values. These were succinctly stated at one point: ''I want to have experiences which challenge me intellectually.

''I see myself as molded in the American context—sort of the last waves of the 1960s. I only dimly understood what was really going on around me and only later came to understand it a bit better.'' While a study abroad student at Strasbourg, France, he felt frustrated with the intellectual challenge of the program and arranged through the study abroad director a number of alternatives, most notably studying with a French professor ''who seemed to have almost virtually unlimited time for this young, long-haired student who had these bizarre interests in provincial poetry.

''I traveled extensively in Europe; I had a Eurorail Pass but very little money, so often slept on the train at night. Although Europe was exciting, I decided that I wanted something more foreign than Western Europe, something that would cut me adrift from Western civilization.

''I had taken an overload of courses in earlier years and had completed all of my requirements, so my senior year I arranged for individualized study in French translation with a visiting professor from Paris. And I started studying

Mandarin (a self-study course with tapes and tests provided by a nearby university). Why? Quite simply because I had been interested in Chinese philosophy, paintings, and calligraphy.'' In the meantime, he was applying to a number of graduate schools, all of which accepted him, but he decided on Ann Arbor.

"And then I asked myself what it is that I really wanted to do. I knew I wanted to do graduate work, but I decided that I needed a different experience before going.'' He successfully applied for a temporary position of teaching English conversation and composition at the Taichung YMCA higher educational center in Taiwan. This Asian academic and societal experience "was undoubtedly the most remarkable and most influential year in my life to date. I flirted with the idea of staying many times. I had invitations to teach at universities even though I only had a B.A. at the time. However, I knew I wanted a graduate degree, and Ann Arbor would not grant a further extension.

"I finished the master's degree in eighteen months but decided that a doctorate in American literature there would prematurely specialize me, so I accepted a very generous offer of a teaching position in Montreal and enrolled in graduate work at McGill University.'' After being there for five years, he took an assistant professorship in Ontario, "which was not as exciting as bilingual Quebec; but still it is different. Then this opportunity opened up at my present college. An international commitment permeates the place, and the students are interested. This coming summer, on a grant from the college, I will study in Paris plus a short lecture tour in Jerusalem. I have never been to the Middle East. It's something I am quite looking forward to.

"I am a specialist in the late nineteenth- and twentieth-century American literature. But my passion and my other area of expertise is literary theory, which I see as applicable to any human society with a strong intellectual tradition. How does any people use literature to communicate their positions on the vital issues, including political issues, in their time and place in history? Literature is always written in response to what is happening to the individual writer in the present but draws upon the philosophy, the culture, the language, of the past. Critics of literary works also are trying to communicate their positions on current issues. In my pedagogy, I try to go beyond the inherent textual reading and introduce different methods for approaching the works.''

To summarize in our terms, this professor has introduced a "cross-cultural repertoire'' gained through diligent study and observations in both his study abroad program and his subsequent formal education, teaching, and experiences in foreign countries into his work role of college professor.

Third Cultural Positions in Transnational Structures. This grouping of the study abroad alumni/ae has positions in both the public and private sectors and in both national and international organizations, which carry out the actual work of interrelating the countries of the world system.

The defining commonalities of their positions are: (1) Location in the intermediate professional/managerial ranks of organizational hierarchies rather than in the senior-most political or policy-making positions and (2) their career lines call for combining aspects of both the professional and the managerial in a single role. They are highly educated in a specialized field of knowledge; they have pragmatic expertise in the language, behavior norms, and power structure of their foreign counterparts; and they have some sophisticated understanding of the enduring traditions and critical problems of a major world region.

This grouping of maximizers is exemplified by two midcareer persons, one employed with an international public sector organization and the other with an American firm involved in international business.

AN AFRICAN REGIONAL STAFF MEMBER OF
THE WORLD BANK

The World Bank is the world's primary venture in mobilizing financial support and policy-planning advice for strengthening the economic infrastructure and development of Third World countries.

In tracing the intricate pathways by which he arrived at his present position of coordinator for a World Bank program to control "river blindness" disease in eleven West African countries, this alumnus of an early (1962–63) study abroad program in France is illustrative of the type of complex self characteristic of "men in the middle of the third culture." (For the original formulation of this conceptualization, see Useem, Donoghue, and Useem, 1963.)

"I had come from a rather provincial background in the Midwest, and the study abroad period in France was my first meaningful experience with people who were different from myself. I found that you have to have the language to relate to people, but you also have to know something about their current concerns in order to have a conversation. This piqued my interest in political and economic issues, as well as international relations. Having been forced to look at those concerns in the foreign situation and to try to understand them carried over to domestic political interests. Right then the civil rights movement was getting started, and I became very interested in it because it involved people who were different from me—different backgrounds, different concerns, and also who were disadvantaged.

"By the time I graduated I was on the international relations track. . . . I'm quite happy with the way it all worked out. It was played by ear much of the way." Immediately after graduation, he became a Peace Corps volunteer teacher of English and physical education in French-speaking Africa. Upon returning to the United States, he earned two master's degrees, one in economics at the University of Michigan and one in international relations at Johns Hopkins University in 1971.

Over the next ten years, he held a succession of positions all based in Washington, D.C., but requiring frequent travel. These included international economist with the Departments of Agriculture and Treasury, deputy director of two offices concerned with international work in the Office of the Secretary of the Department of Treasury, senior policy adviser first to a congressman and then to a senator. He moved to the World Bank in 1982 as an evaluation officer in the Office of Policy Review and subsequently took his present position as program coordinator in the West Africa Department of the same institution.

From his Washington, D.C., organizational base he makes four to five trips yearly to French-speaking African countries, plus occasional trips to Europe and Asia for conferring with counterparts who represent their national governments. These interpersonal networks are small but influential segments in the world system.

"The people I interact with almost always have had some international experience." To move deftly in these international networks, "I find that I routinely spend a lot of time just keeping up with what's going on in other parts of the world—European countries, the developing countries, and right now, Africa."

In reflecting on the meaning of his study abroad experience for his subsequent career, he said, "The language has been lasting. It took me to a threshold that was very important to arrive at because of my work subsequently. And then an understanding of the people, how they think, that I couldn't have picked up without that in-depth experience at that time. That and an understanding of the French politically, which has helped me in understanding the African institutions, which are variants of the French system. I am interested in American international relations, and I feel this specialization requires both academic background in a functional area—mine is economics—and hands-on experience, which opens up opportunities. One of them by itself is not enough. More generally, it gave me an awareness of other cultures and a sensitivity to different ways of thinking and communicating, all of which is currently important to me professionally."

AN ATTORNEY IN AN INTERNATIONAL LAW FIRM

The intersections of the world system are filled with old and new nongovernmental organizations whose professional staffs mediate between the nominally private sector segments of interdependent nation-states. Such American-sponsored joint ventures have become commonplace in Third World countries. Among them is a New York City–based international law firm in which one of our alumni has been at work since 1986 in the sovereign debt restructuring of Chilean clients. (For an analysis of the critical issue of international public/private debt, see OECD, 1988.)

Of small-town origin in America's Midwest, this study abroad alumnus recalls his developing "interests in things international" during his young adult formative years. The first brief yet influential experience was in the summer between high school and college when his hometown Lion's Club sponsored his six-week visit to Finland. The Lion's Clubs of this region have an international exchange for youths with the old world homelands of Western Europe from which the members' parents and grandparents emigrated to America.

Entering college in 1975, he decided his discovered interests were in international economics, which he pursued further as a major field of study. He continued his study in his junior year abroad at Clérmont-Ferrand in Vichy, France. "I made it a real experience to know French people and French culture and to travel throughout Europe."

Upon graduation, he spent the next three years as an economic consultant to a firm in New York City. "I spent as much time as possible working on international economic issues even though that was not formally within my job. I tried to fit it into my job."

Anticipating further postgraduate training in a professional law school, "I ventured to learn before going something about a Third World region." He successfully applied for a Rotary Graduate Fellowship, studying French West African history for nine months at the University of Dakar in Senegal, took brief study tours of three of the region's countries, and got a good start on learning one of the main local languages.

Then came three years of professionalization at Columbia University's law school, specializing in, "I guess you could say, international law, and became editor-in-chief of *Columbia's Journal of International Law.*

"Meanwhile, I married. Both of us, in a sense, are internationalists. Her parents lived for ten years in Europe where her father, who is German, headed up the European corporate operation of an American company. She commuted once or twice a year to Germany the entire time she was in college and graduate school here." She is in theatrical history and doing her dissertation on German dance. "Together we have formed ties with a number of German scholars through exchange of visits and correspondence."

For adding to his language capabilities, on his own he spent an intensive period in Mexico to become adept at the language. In his role in the international law firm, he says, "I routinely use Spanish. It is a firm where everyone has command of foreign languages in the ordinary conduct of their work."

In summing up his foreign experiences, he commented: "I guess I want a career and lifestyle that have international influences throughout my life. I think I always want my job to have some sort of international dimension, and I always want to have friends from foreign countries. Which means that I will probably always live in a fairly large city and probably on the East Coast because those are the places more likely to have ready access to people from foreign countries. Not to mention the fact that that's where you're going to find the most ethnic restaurants and foreign films and Italian suits, and I can startle the Senegalese vendor by speaking to him in his native tongue. . . .

"And all of this is overlaid with my feeling about American politics and American foreign policy, especially with respect to developing countries. I don't want to put it into an oversimplified way of thinking that it is US versus THEM, democracy versus communism. You have to understand how local oligarchies and common people in regional areas view our policies. American policy is perceived differently abroad than it is perceived here. And you always have to look at it through a lens—a European lens or a regional lens or the lens of whatever country is being affected."

Independent Professionals. Our most heterogeneous grouping of maximizers are the "free" professionals, those who are not positioned in line organizations within bureaucratic structures. They are professionals in that they belong to "exclusive occupational groups applying somewhat abstract knowledge to particular cases" (Abbott, 1988, p. 8). At times they may be employed temporarily by, or perform special services for, bureaucratically organized structures, for example, as consultants. They are writers, lawyers, physicians, computer experts, journalists, freelancers in occupations that are as yet without any widely known designation.

For illustrating the category of autonomous professionals, we present two outstanding women—a musical composer in New England and a psychiatrist in California. Both include cross-cultural aspects in their life work.

MUSICAL COMPOSER AND PERFORMING ARTIST

This creative musical composer has been a lifelong resident of New England but has traveled extensively in both the United States and in foreign lands in pursuing her career.

Although she went to Freiburg, West Germany, with a group of undergraduate students, she explains, "I did it after my bachelor's but before my master's. I wasn't there as part of a special program where my whole degree hinged on getting the work done, but I certainly took courses and got a lot of my own work done." Her "own work," composing music, was primarily accomplished by studying composition and piano at the Freiburg Conservatory, "which I found very cosmopolitan. There were people from all over the world—South America, Africa, even North Vietnam. It was truly astounding."

She moved into private lodgings so she would not be speaking English with her American compatriots and avoided living with a family, "so I wouldn't have to help Germans practice their English. I was there really to have to sink or swim in German, so I made it uncomfortable for myself on purpose so I would have to learn German."

After her return she earned her master's degree in composition and theory in two years and had published her first "Performance Work." The many taped performances of original compositions since then have won prizes and led to her being recognized by inclusion in *Who's Who in American Music: Classical, International, Encyclopaedia of Women Composers,* among others, as well as being awarded a graduate teaching fellowship at Boston University, from which she eventually was awarded the doctorate.

In response to the query, Did your foreign experience make you more internationally aware? she pointed out: "I'm writing music, and I have to know what's happening [in my specialized field of work] all over the globe, or at least as much as I have access to, so my interest has always been international in scope.''

As for the language, "I use it all of the time. If I do research, often the only resource is in German. If I'm singing, I have to translate parts of the score for myself. Because I work with a semiprofessional choral group, we frequently do German works that need pronunciation, and I'm usually one of the people who knows German best. . . . I went as a chaperone with a children's ballet group [she had written the musical composition for it] to Austria, Yugoslavia, and Hungary, and it was my language abilities that got us through some rough spots.''

On the social side, "I'm much more open to meeting people from all over the world, and because I live in a college community, that's more possible. If the person is German speaking, I dust off my German and crank it into use whenever I can. But it is broader than that. I'm more likely to respond to something that has an international flavor, or at least a foreign flavor. This may seem weird, but even if it's a somewhat less familiar area of the United States, that also appeals to me—being different, simply different from the area in which I live.

"I urge my students [she teaches both private students and on the college level at various institutions] to go abroad and get a window on the world that they might not have if they only stay in America and not have any awareness of the other ways that the people work and think.''

Sometimes her husband travels with her or participates with her in her contacts with foreigners in the local community. He has a college degree in musicology and is music director of the local public television station. "Music ties us together, and it's because music is so international.''

PRIVATE PRACTICE PSYCHIATRIST AND ADJUNCT ACADEMIC LECTURER

Modern psychiatry as a medical practice and as a research field conceptually builds on and, in turn, contributes to an intricate set of paradigms drawn from the theories and knowledge base of the life, psychological, and social sciences. For understanding the individual requires considerable skills on the part of the psychiatrist as the sociocultural settings in which patients are embedded are becoming more complex and as the individual responds to the unexpected expectations of others due to high social and geographical mobility. (For one dimension of this, changing gender expectations, see Westkott, 1986.)

The second study abroad alumna illustrating the grouping of independent professionals is comparable in age grade, career status, and gender to the music composer but is a contrasting study of a transnational perspective and cognitive work life. Her education (B.A. in biochemistry in 1971; M.D. in 1975) and subsequent career as a psychiatrist with a private practice and as an adjunct professor with a prominent medical school are situated in the Los Angeles area. Her exchange student experience was in Scotland.

The ferment of the 1960s was at its peak when this alumna went on her study abroad program (1968–69) and was continuing on her return. In reflecting on this period in her life, this bright, high-achieving, upwardly mobile woman characterizes going abroad and returning as a "growth experience"—both exciting and painful. (For an insightful analysis of the growth experiences of others during this period, see Gitlin, 1987.)

Put in her words, "I think for a lot of reasons I found it a very growth-promoting experience. There's nothing like being there and experiencing it and seeing what comes up and seeing what happens when you're in an unfamiliar environment. Learning how to succeed in communicating when you both speak English but have different customs and values, or when you speak English and they don't [she meets often with a number of foreign students for whom English is not their native tongue] and you have to figure out what it is that they're expecting. I think you end up re-evaluating some of the social and political assumptions that you may have taken for granted. It's the personal contact. It's very thought-provoking and stimulating.

"Whenever I was over there it was when we were involved in the Vietnam War, and I think it was an eye-opener to see and to talk to other people who didn't have the same political view that I did. I thought I was pretty sophisticated when I went over there. It made me realize that maybe a lot of my attitudes were really very provincial."

Because she had taken advanced honors courses in biochemistry at her undergraduate college, "the academic experiences were real disappointing. I was way beyond the biochemistry being taught there. But I was fortunate in that I was free to focus on all the other social and personal issues that living there gave me." This included a "low point" in the spring "when I was homesick. The novelty of living in a foreign country had worn off, and some people were a little leery of becoming close friends because they knew you were leaving." She feels this experience has made her more sensitive to the foreign women medical students for whom she is a preceptor in an honors course she now teaches.

"I dropped out of school the first quarter I was back. I just had culture shock. Everything was going about three to four times faster than I had become accustomed to. And going back to living at home and commuting in the big city again. . . . And I found that people were more narrow-minded than I remembered.

"I think that politically before I went over there and to some extent when I came back, I was going to solve the problems of the world. But I think it [the whole experience of going to Scotland and returning to Los Angeles] brought home to me that maybe I really couldn't do that very effectively and maybe I'd be better off looking at my own backyard, so to speak. I think that that's certainly reflected in the kind of work that I do, which is very people intensive.

It's really one-on-one kind of work. I help people make internal changes so that the ripple effect is going to go from that focus outwards rather than trying to globally change things without paying attention to how individuals feel about it.''

She summed up by saying, ''I don't think that there's a strong international thread to my life except as it involves individuals that I have come in contact with.'' She has spent six months in Mexico where she learned Spanish, which she uses occasionally with patients or household help. She visited a family in Southeast Asia and has made trips to visit friends in Western Europe and the Middle East. ''I think that all of these contacts enhance my ability to see things from other people's point of view, to communicate with people of different backgrounds, people whose backgrounds are 'foreign' to me whether they are foreigners or not. This is something I use every day in the kinds of work which I do. It is very people oriented, really one-on-one kind of work.''

Maximizers of Small Chances in Complex Organizations. Our prior groups of alumni/ae who work in formal organizations have positions whose primary reason for being and main purpose is the performing of cross-culturally related roles. Our fourth-group members are also positioned in similar organizations, but their cross-cultural work is both valued and yet marginal, tangential or incidental to their work life.

We found two differing modes among the maximizers of these small chances for personally participating, often part-time or occasionally, in cross-cultural roles. One mode is composed of persons who select out for maximizing a facet of the cross-cultural that is accessible and appeals to them; the second is composed of persons who are called on to mediate inside the organization in cross-cultural situations.

SENIOR CUSTOMS INSPECTOR

A striking instance of self-selected, cross-cultural role maximizing is a woman of considerable status in an old-line federal bureaucratic structure. From 1968 to 1975, she was associated with the University of California at Santa Barbara. As an undergraduate she majored in French literature and European history, studied in her junior year at the University of Bordeaux, received her bachelor's degree, continued on for a master's degree in French literature and historiography, and was then picked by her French department to be a lecturer in English at Bordeaux for one year.

Since 1976, she has been employed by the U.S. Customs Service and has advanced to the senior ranks of that large-scale organization in which the professional staff impersonally encounters, one by one, strangers from all foreign lands at entry checkpoints. For her, these routine encounters are continuing ''small chances'' for personally and professionally renewing an interest in the world of human cultures.

Responding to the opening question of the telephone interview—Did your study abroad experience prompt you to include an international or intercultural dimension in your work activities?—she reviewed the twelve crowded years of her work life. "The answer is yes. Not that I got the job because of that particular interest at all, but I kept it because that was a dimension of the work experience that I love. I would not still be in the job that I'm in if it did not include that dimension. Just contact with people from other cultures is really critical to me to keep a balance and a perspective on my own self as an American and in the work I do. Although the contacts I have with people from other cultures are usually very brief, they're extremely satisfying and they're necessary to my life. I have an opportunity to have them every day."

Appraising her brief contacts with strangers, she also conveyed her own preference for using her knowledge of French culture and language. "Most of the people who come into the United States through the port of San Francisco are not from European areas; they are from Asian areas. And I don't speak their languages, but we do have a few European flights. And of course whenever the French-speaking people arrive from the Paris flights that connect through London, I jump on the opportunity to be their customs inspector. During the daytime I work at the pier area, and sometimes French-speaking people do come in and clear their personal effects, and I sure try to take the opportunity to be the one who does it.

"My employer has sent me abroad on an experience I never ever would have had a chance to take part in, had I not known the French language and culture so well. I was sent by Customs to the Ivory Coast for a drug conference, partly because of my customs experience but specifically because of my French-speaking abilities. I was the only one in the country selected to do this. Once again, it gave me that special feeling that only going abroad and getting to meet people from other kinds of cultures can give you. There's nothing else that gives me that feeling. It was short-lived, but an opportunity like that is very valuable to me, no matter how long it endures.

"In customs services, we have many different nationalities of people represented among the inspectors. A lot of people call upon me to explain the bothersome behavior of the French—their impoliteness, brusqueness, et cetera. It reminds me of when I was in France and I was constantly being called upon to justify the American point of view. I laugh and explain. It's the same thing in reverse, and I love it. And then I am also called upon to translate French documents at work."

IMPROVISED MEDIATORS

The second genre of maximizers of small chances might be called "improvised mediators." While not being illustrated by a vignette, the mode can be described as follows.

As the world penetrates ever more deeply into America's middle-sized urban communities, often the managerial leadership of local manufacturing and commercial companies, state government agencies, voluntary civic groups, and educational systems consists of relative newcomers to international transactions and interpersonal contacts with foreign counterparts. As a result, within these structures, there is a growth of untitled, recurrently improvised roles as translators, interpreters, ad hoc consultants, temporary special assistants to senior administrators, and so on.

To illustrate specifically from our sample, some of the alumni/ae have been brought in to check on the accuracy of translations of negotiated contracts, to make the arrangements for visiting foreign delegations, to travel abroad as an interpreter for a senior official, and others. All welcomed these opportunities to adapt their cross-cultural repertoires to fit their organization's new necessities in the global political economy.

The Deeply Committed But Situationally Constrained. There are a group of maximizers who utilize their cross-cultural skills in their present employment or underemployment but who, at the time of the interview (late 1980s), felt dissatisfied, restless, uneasy, bored, or trapped in their work role because it did not give them adequate scope for their continued growth in the utilization of their cross-cultural repertoire. All are actively seeking or planning on a change in employment that would afford them greater opportunities for making contributions to their central values that have evolved from their transnational educational opportunities and ongoing cross-cultural experiences.

The literature on the new–middle-class occupations suggests that such periods of stress are not uncommon among professional/technical and managerial/administrative workers. They are changing positions, organizations, and places of residence with greater frequency over a lifetime than was true in the pre–World War II period. These disjunctions in work life are experienced somewhat differently by men and women (see Bianchi and Spain, 1986).

All of our study abroad alumni/ae, both maximizers and minimalists, have experienced at least one of these periods in their work life. What distinguishes the maximizers from the minimalists is the source of the dissatisfaction, namely, not being able to utilize their cross-cultural repertoire as much as they would like. The minimalists may want better income or more responsibility or a different lifestyle but are not stressed by insufficient opportunity to express aspects related to their foreign education or experiences. Usually the process is a rather lengthy one to work out. Sometimes it is precipitated by a particular event, such as personal illness, but more often it is an accumulation of small stresses.

Illustrative of this category is a man who, as an undergraduate in history at the University of California, went to Göttingen in 1971–72 during his senior year. He then entered law school and received his J.D. in 1975. Even when filling out his résumé, he became aware that practicing law would not permit him to incorporate his interests in the larger world. "My uncle who was helping me fill out my résumé for a law position told me to take out any references to my interests in foreign travel and seeing foreign countries. . . . They'll think you want to take more than one or two weeks vacation and won't want to work sixty-five to seventy hours a week, day in and day out."

After a stint as a legal assistance officer in the U.S. Navy and as a staff attorney to the National Labor Relations Board, "I decided to become poor and teach school. I decided I could not continue the profession of lawyer, and I have never regretted it." He earned his teaching credentials in 1981, taught German in a high school, had a Fulbright teaching position in a German secondary school, married a woman with two children, and has had two children with her (one born in Germany). A few months before the interview, he took a new teaching job in another school system. "Currently I'm not teaching German, and I regret that. I would very much like to resume teaching German, and the possibilities are there if I move to another school. I'm considering that right now."

The second illustrative case is a 1970 alumna of a UC campus whose undergraduate majors were French and Spanish. Her junior year abroad was spent at Bordeaux, France. In the ensuing ten years, she earned a secondary teaching certificate and a master's degree in French, lived abroad for a year, and was for six years involved in the school system of southern California as a teacher of French, English as a second language, and bilingual science and mathematics.

"But I wanted to be internationally involved careerwise, and not being able to be was a source of frustration. I returned to school to get a master's degree in international management at the American Graduate School of International Management in Arizona. As it turned out, I just wasn't able to find a job in that field, which was, of course, a frustration. You see literature that says United States business needs people who understand international cultures, who can move from one to another culture without adversely affecting either the business or the family. But when it comes time to actually find that job, it's very, very difficult."

She took a job in a packing company for fresh artichokes in Arizona and has moved from assistant office manager to comptroller. At the time of the interview, she was a single parent with a 13-year-old daughter. She summed up her present situation in these words: "I make a good salary, and I'm involved in the community [among other cross-cultural activities, she sits on the school board and is supportive of bilingual education, etc.], but my job is not the one that I would like to have for the rest of my life. My daughter will be going to college in four or five years, and I will be able to move. For now, I'm in a holding pattern. I think generally I could say that in my personal life, education abroad has remained strong, but in my professional life it's been a source of frustration in not being able to do what I would like to do and feel capable of doing on the international scene." She is exploring job placement agencies, looking into possibilities in the Pacific Rim, assessing what additional skills she should develop "so that I will be ready when the time comes."

C. CONCLUDING COMMENTS

We have tried to show in some detail that a meaningful understanding of the longer-term effects of a study abroad experience in the subsequent life course of American undergraduates implies analysis not only of their biographies but also of the changing and complex contexts within which they respond and create their lives. More specifically we have described and analyzed only some aspects of their total biographies in relation to selected segments of American society within the present interdepedent world.

These particular generations of America's highly educated who have a Western European study abroad experience will continue to be part of the nation's new middle class until the end of this century, and the younger ones will go on into the early decades of the next century. There can be no methodological procedures for summarizing that which has not yet occurred in order to answer the question neatly and simply. Instead, we can, and have, constructed typologies of the combined personal and social meaning for their developing selves. Even then we have reported on only selective aspects, more particularly educational experiences and employment history. Thus, we have put aside other crucial dimensions of the self and society such as family and community life and the interactions between the United States and the rest of the world.

If there is one theme that is interwoven into nearly every aspect of their lives, it is the creative integration of their cosmopolitan and localite identities, the selective combining of socially derived cross-cultural and local-cultural repertoires. An interconnected theme, then, is that the majority of these persons are uniquely individuated men and women who not only have things happen to them but also make things happen. Most are persistent persons who, upon meeting obstacles, draw on their knowledge and experience to figure out alternative pathways that might enable them to fulfill their inner values.

Because of the contrasting contexts of their total experiences in both domestic and foreign settings, they are consciously aware of what they value and continuously re-evaluate. And because of their having more or less successfully confronted and made difficult choices in their own life histories, they feel confident, but not overly confident, that they can take some risks in pursuing their envisioned aims in life.

There have been over 300,000 American undergraduates who have studied abroad in Western Europe between the 1960s and 1980s and who now constitute a very small segment of the highly educated new middle classes within American society. If what we noted in our tiny sample can be generalized, then we can say that these widely and thinly distributed alumni/ae of European study abroad programs are making contributions in their microspaces to the larger society's reconstituting and reconceptualizing its interdependencies around the world.

7

THE SIGNIFICANCE OF THE STUDY'S FINDINGS: POLICY AND RESEARCH IMPLICATIONS

PRELIMINARY COMMENT

The preceding chapters have presented in some detail the design, methodology, and findings of the Study Abroad Evaluation Project with respect to U.S. participation. They have analyzed the extensive data collected in order to identify the outcomes of the study abroad experience for students and the relationship of certain characteristics of the students and of the sojourn abroad to these outcomes. Findings are presented on the long-term effects of study abroad on persons abroad five to twenty years ago, with special attention to whether and how they continued their international interests in their professional and personal lives.

The objectives of the SAEP when it was initially conceived in 1982 by the European project chair and the coordinator of the U.S. side have in large measure been achieved. Both the U.S. and European participants in the project wanted to know if the investments of staff, funds, and other resources to conduct study abroad and exchange programs are justified by their contribution to students' international education. However, whereas the Europeans tended to be more interested in the contribution of the experience abroad to students' ability to function professionally in another country and culture, the U.S. interest was more on students' gaining a greater knowledge of and concern for other countries and international issues as well as enhanced foreign language proficiency.

The findings for the full five-country project are reported in a two-volume publication of the European Institute of Education and Social Policy. As with the United States, separate publications report the project's findings on the Federal Republic of Germany and Sweden. Staffing and other constraints precluded reporting in this volume on the experience in the United States of students from higher education institutions in the four European countries.

A. THE FINDINGS IN THE CONTEXT OF OUR TIMES AND SOCIETY

This report on the U.S. experience in the SAEP comes at a timely moment for several reasons. First, study abroad is currently one of the most rapidly expanding fields in American higher education, and yet the little we know about its outcomes is mostly based on anecdotal information rather than on substantial and systematic research. In their examination of study abroad in *Abroad and Beyond,* Goodwin and Nacht (1988) refer to it as an "explosion" and warn that "leaders of American academe should recognize that this is a fast-moving field that they ignore at their peril." Thus, even though study abroad still involves only a small fraction of American undergraduates, its expanding role makes it imperative that we have more knowledge of it and what it can contribute to students' education.

The study is also timely because of the widening realization that the United States is irreversibly and increasingly interdependent with the rest of the world. In the United States, as in Europe, more and more professions require international knowledge and skills. These include the ability to work in cross-cultural situations, to relate to people of various backgrounds, to think comparatively, to possess certain interpersonal resources and flexibility, and to work and live in unstructured and ambiguous situations. Responsible informed citizenship increasingly requires a knowledge and understanding of other cultures and international issues. The Study Abroad Evaluation Project overwhelmingly documents the effectiveness of study abroad in significantly strengthening students' knowledge of other countries and their foreign language proficiency and in deepening their understanding of, concern for, and ways of thinking about international issues. In short, study abroad can play a crucial role in preparing future citizens and professionals to live and function in the global village that our world has become.

The timeliness of this study relates also to its findings that point up how study abroad contributes importantly to some of the goals of a liberal education in a period of redefinition and reaffirmation of these goals. For example, study abroad returnees are more independent-minded, intellectually inclined, and able to cope with ambiguity than they were before going abroad. More important to them after their study abroad experience are interdisciplinary approaches to learning and independent work. It is striking that in their period abroad (an academic year for most of the SAEP students), these students in large measure achieved a number of the goals of a liberal education in terms of personal and intellectual development.

While the focus of the project has been on international experience and international education, it is also relevant and timely for the domestic scene in the United States and the accelerating cultural diversity of the American people. Our college students do not come from, nor will they after college work and live in, a single homogeneous culture. To take only one aspect of the diversity, the high rate of increase of the Hispanic population (five times that of the rest of the population as a result of a high birthrate and the continuing stream of immigrants from Mexico and Central America) promises to make the American nation more and more diverse. To function successfully within it, most Americans must have the kinds of cross-cultural skills and sensitivity identified earlier. The study abroad experience by developing these skills is important in preparing students to function effectively not only in the global village but also as members of the increasingly diverse American culture and people.

Finally, this report should also be relevant to trends and developments in international education not only in the United States but also abroad. More and more higher education institutions—and in some cases, systems, for example, Japan—identify international education and the internationalization of these institutions as important strategies in preparing students for the growing number of careers with international dimensions and for living in an interdependent world. As part of becoming more international, these institutions may send more students abroad or enroll more students from other countries. To the extent that the U.S. experience in the SAEP suggests aspects of the experience abroad that appear to maximize students' international learning, the SAEP findings offer useful guidance to these internationalizing efforts and activities of higher education institutions at home and abroad, within, of course, the limitations of the Study Abroad Evaluation Project.

B. POLICY IMPLICATIONS

Introduction

What are the implications of the findings of the Study Abroad Evaluation Project for policy in the field? Should more students go abroad for study? What goals and criteria should govern their selection? Can any particular approaches to predeparture orientation, program activities, and management while abroad and post–study abroad programming strengthen students' international experience and learning? Should study abroad play a larger role in internationalizing colleges and universities, and how might this be achieved? What, if anything, does the SAEP suggest regarding the responsibilities of colleges and universities for study abroad? Does study abroad advance the national interest and hence merit public support?

While the findings of the SAEP provide insights on many of the foregoing questions, it should be emphasized that these findings may not apply to study abroad programs not sharing the characteristics of those examined in this project—for example, summer- or semester-only programs, study abroad elsewhere than in Western Europe, programs that do not integrate American students into host institutions abroad, or primarily graduate-level study abroad. In addition, U.S. higher education and other institutions interested in examining their own study abroad activities should not mechanically apply the instruments developed for the SAEP. Because they were shaped collaboratively by the European and American team members, a number of the questions are much more relevant to Europe than to the United States. Moreover, as the project to a large extent mapped new terrain in developing the instruments, it should be no surprise that some questionnaire items were found to be less useful than others. The original questionnaires are included in Appendix III in this volume. Interested users should pick and choose among items and select those that best fit their own circumstances and concerns.

Some Findings and Issues

The SAEP showed that students who study abroad are much more interested in international affairs after this experience than before and that their knowledge of their host country increases dramatically. This is especially the case with respect to what they experience directly, such as the cultural life, social structure, and higher education system. These findings might be viewed as mandating a major quantitative expansion in study abroad participation in order to achieve a more internationally informed and concerned citizenry. Such a conclusion is, however, far too simplistic and optimistic and, if carried out, would probably produce disappointing results.

Students who choose to study abroad—or those electing an academic year immersion study experience—are not typical of undergraduates in U.S. higher education. Our results suggest that efforts to expand student numbers without taking account of the factors conducive to their having a successful experience abroad may not be effective. It should also be recognized that not all undergraduates can study abroad or should be encouraged to do so. Some may find it impossible for personal, financial, or other reasons.

The following subsections attempt to deal with the implications of the SAEP findings for determining who should study abroad, recruitment and selection, program design, and how students' international learning through study abroad can be maximized. Finally, certain follow-up activities being conducted in Europe and in the United States whose initiation was significantly aided by SAEP findings will be described.

Who Should Study Abroad?

The SAEP findings show that study abroad by American students typically enrolls students from professional-level parents, students who are academic achievers, and a high proportion of students who have already been abroad.

The findings also show, however, that students from other backgrounds can successfully study abroad and have very worthwhile experiences. Thus, while 75 percent of the study abroad students' fathers had manager or other professional status and nearly half had a master's degree or higher, 25 percent were of middle or lower occupational status and 18 percent had only a high school diploma.

Similarly, the finding that close to three-fourths of the American SAEP students were majors in the humanities, social sciences, or business and two-thirds were female should be regarded as descriptive, not prescriptive. The one-third of the Kalamazoo study abroad students who were science or engineering majors and the 45 percent who were male found the experience no less important to their professional futures and personal development than did their humanities/social sciences and female colleagues. Efforts to expand participation in study abroad clearly can and should reach out beyond the traditional disciplines associated with study abroad to include students in the sciences and various professional fields.

An important question relating to expanding study abroad participation is whether, like an honors program, it should be limited to the most talented and high-achieving students, or whether study abroad students should be more representative of all American undergraduates? Regrettably, we cannot provide an answer to this question, as the United States students were overwhelmingly strong rather than uneven academically. However, the finding that the students who felt they performed well academically also learned most about their host country and were most satisfied with their experience abroad suggests that study abroad, at least of the kind that integrates students into host institutions, should probably not include students who are less able academically—at least not without special orientation and other programming.

Our findings on the personal characteristics of study abroad students also have implications for who should study abroad. It is striking that the study abroad students tended to be risk-takers, more critical of aspects of the United States, and less typically mainstream than the comparison group students (and on their return home, they rated the experience abroad particularly highly with regard to such values as self-discovery, critical thinking, independence, and intellectuality, coincidentally, as mentioned earlier, the values commonly associated with a liberal education). These students are much less committed to the immediate goals of their own financial survival than the students who chose not to study abroad, the latter being more task oriented, more concerned to get their degree and on to a job.

One faces the dilemma that it is probably the students who are already most international in their interests, most independent and analytical in their thinking, and relatively well equipped with coping and cross-cultural skills who elect to study abroad and, by the same token, may have less to gain from it than students choosing to stay home. Many of the latter, for whom the "value added" is likely to be greatest, may not conceive of themselves in study abroad, especially in programs that maximize interaction with the foreign culture and people.

Significant to study abroad participation are the SAEP findings that suggest that many of the students who choose not to study abroad make this decision because they doubt it will be relevant to their major or to their future career or because they fear it may prolong their studies. If the foregoing concerns can be addressed, more of these students, many of whom are presumably "mainstream," might opt to study abroad. Also, as is discussed later, more such students might make this choice if faculty members were more encouraging, rather than, especially in the sciences and professional fields, often being openly discouraging. The next subsection addresses strategies for recruiting more students to study abroad from those now not likely to do it.

Study Abroad Recruitment and Selection

For study abroad to enroll more students, selection can no longer be mainly through self-selection. Rather, it should adopt proactive strategies designed to expand the number of interested students. These, discussed in turn, relate to sexual stereotyping and career counseling, information dissemination, faculty support, reducing perceived deterrents, expanding the pool of internationally concerned students, and offering more programs that attract the more mainstream undergraduates.

To reduce the sex and discipline imbalances in student participation, male students and students in the sciences, engineering, and other professional fields should be given much more encouragement to study abroad. Staff in college career counseling offices should inform students about the relevance and value of a significant experience abroad to an increasing number of careers. U.S. colleges and universities should incorporate a study or internship abroad experience in the degree programs of students majoring in the sciences and professional fields as an integral part of the degree, as is becoming increasingly common in Western European postsecondary education. The very different distribution by sex and discipline of the European students in the intra-Europe study abroad programs reviewed by the SAEP can be regarded as something of a model and suggests that the American patterns should not be immutable. Males constituted close to 50 percent of the French and British students and about two-thirds of the Germans and Swedes. Some 60 percent of the European students were majors in the sciences, engineering, and other professional fields.

The need for more effective ways to inform qualified students about study abroad opportunities, underscored by SAEP findings, makes it important for colleges and universities to inform such students while still in high school about opportunities available through their study abroad programs. These students could then take this information into account in deciding where to apply for college, as do four-fifths of the Kalamazoo students. Also, because some undergraduates have difficulty in fitting an academic year or even a semester of study abroad into their degree programs, especially in disciplines with heavy requirements of sequenced courses such as engineering, the earlier possible student candidates know about and can start planning for study abroad, the likelier they can do it as an integral part of their degree studies.

Proactive recruitment should also involve much more effort by faculty members, as is documented by project findings on factors influencing the comparison group students' lack of interest in study abroad. These findings showed that 50 percent of these students saw study abroad as unnecessary for their academic program, whereas 40 percent viewed it as inappropriate. Faculty members who are well informed and enthusiastic about study abroad can and should counter such views if more students are to be motivated to seek this experience. In addition, faculty members should help students plan for study abroad so that it moves them toward, rather than delaying, their graduation, a concern of 46 percent of the respondents. In short, faculty advocates of study abroad should both disabuse students about misperceived obstacles and help students to overcome them.

Proactive recruitment to expand study abroad numbers clearly should address what 69 percent of the comparison group respondents identified as influencing their lack of interest in study abroad: its cost. An important need here is to communicate accurate information to students. Too often, as with the SAEP comparison group, study abroad is perceived as being much more expensive than the same period at the home campus, when this is not necessarily the case. This is not to deny the importance of financial assistance, and indeed a higher proportion of the study abroad group than the comparison group students received such support.

Because students who choose to study abroad tend to be internationally concerned, the expansion of study abroad participation can be furthered if more such students are identified and if the American education system and culture produce more of them. To be more specific, the study abroad students in the SAEP shared the following internationally oriented characteristics:

- Strong interest in current events, other countries, and European and international affairs;
- Prior experience abroad, typically one or two months in a tourist or living situation in Western Europe at age sixteen (62 percent of SAEP students);
- Prior foreign language study (for students going to foreign language countries); and
- A high level of motivation to experience another culture, live in and gain more understanding of another country, travel abroad, and use or improve knowledge of a foreign language.

The policy implications of the above include the following:

1. Study abroad and exchange programs at the high school level should be expanded to include many more young people because it is from an experience abroad at this

stage that many college students are motivated to study abroad, the "repeater" phenomenon;

2. Precollegiate and college-level foreign language instruction should aim at giving more students a working proficiency, knowledge of the foreign language country, and motivation to study abroad;

3. Colleges and universities should give all undergraduates a basic knowledge of at least one other country or world region and of significant world issues;

4. High schools and colleges, the latter especially at the lower division level, should strive to give students the kind of interest in and curiosity about other countries and cross-cultural skills in dealing with foreign people and cultures that students tend to gain from a high school–level experience abroad so that as college juniors or seniors they will be motivated to study abroad;

5. Participation in international clubs and contacts with foreign students should be deliberately fostered for undergraduates, especially those contemplating study abroad, not because the SAEP showed these activities to be important in stimulating student interest in it but because, on the contrary, it documented the woeful neglect of their international education potential.

The last approach for recruiting more study abroad students implicit in the SAEP findings is to develop more programs that attract "mainstream" Americans. Such programs should not offer a full cultural immersion experience, as this might turn off these students—and presumably not many would have the necessary foreign language proficiency—but should provide a more protected, even somewhat American-style setting and program, even though this may mean less international education. The SAEP showed that the more contact American students have with the host country, the more they learn about it and the greater their satisfaction. While this underscores the importance of maximizing this contact, it should not be at the cost of not recruiting the more mainstream students if they are to be attracted to study abroad. The immersion experience can be limited in a variety of ways—for example, by offering programs of a semester only rather than an academic year, by sending an accompanying faculty member to advise and assist the students as necessary, by having the American students in classes mainly with each other instead of with students of the host country, and so on. While, as pointed out earlier, the extent to which programs offering less-than-full immersion in the host culture contribute to students' international education—because it was not a focus of the SAEP—is an unknown, presumably it is much more worthwhile than no immersion at all.

Other kinds of study abroad programs that might attract more of the kinds of students who generally do not think of or seek to study abroad are those programs deliberately directed at enabling such students to meet some of their academic requirements while abroad. For example, this might include general education or distribution requirements, depending on the institutions involved. This approach might also involve programs to enable students to complete some major requirements abroad, thus making study abroad more attractive to the students who are less inclined to be risk-takers. Such programs might also be useful to the risk-takers in enabling them to avoid some of the letdown many now feel when they return from abroad.

Program Design and Maximizing Student Learning

Although how much students gain from study abroad depends on many variables, lessons learned from the Study Abroad Evaluation Project point up the importance of the following program characteristics, activities, and policies:

• Early planning for study abroad, preferably during freshman year, so that students have as wide a choice as possible of program location and content, when and for how long they study abroad, and how to mesh this with major and other requirements;

• Careful preparation and orientation of students for study abroad so that cross-cultural differences, dissimilar approaches to teaching and to students at the host institutions, and inadequate foreign language skills do not impede the Americans' international learning;

• The participation of faculty members in advising students and helping them to plan their study program abroad in order to ensure that it will be granted appropriate academic credit;

• Requiring high standards for students' academic performance while on study abroad in light of the SAEP finding that it is the high academic achievers who gain most in international knowledge and commitment;

• Provision in students' program abroad for continuous opportunities to increase their knowledge of the host country and its language and culture;

• Facilitating and encouraging periods of free travel while abroad, whether during or at the end of the program, because of its important contribution to students' international education;

• To the extent feasible, integrating American undergraduates abroad into the host culture through their living arrangements and in attending classes with host country students; and

• Offering to returned study abroad students courses and programs that enable them to capitalize and build on their learning acquired abroad, including foreign language skills, and thereby also helping to reduce their sense of alienation so common on re-entry.

Some National Policy Needs

The preceding recommendations have mostly addressed institutions of post-secondary education, especially the faculty members and administrators who are involved with, and can affect, study abroad programs and policies. Some aims were set forth, however, whose implementation requires broader public support and national action. These are addressed in the following recommendations:

1. The national leadership concerned about the urgent need for internationally educated Americans should be made aware of the key findings of the Study Abroad Evaluation Project, namely, that for American undergraduates a significant study abroad experience dramatically strengthens their international knowledge and concern. This applies especially to their knowledge of the host country and its language and their ways of thinking about the world and far exceeds the international learning achieved by comparison group students electing to stay home.

2. In keeping with this finding, college and university presidents, professional associations, and foundations and other opportunities involved with education and international studies should give major recognition and priority to serious undergraduate study abroad in enunciating educational goals and in allocating resources.

3. Because cost can be an important deterrent to study abroad for many undergraduates, federal financial aid to students should provide incentive grants toward study abroad costs, with matching requirements for the home campuses, in order to encourage and accord recognition to their commitment.

4. For students at the high school and lower division college level, cross-cultural and international studies programs should be encouraged and strengthened, which, like high school study abroad, fire students' interest in other countries and give them the language and intercultural skills that motivate them to study abroad as college juniors and seniors.

5. Given the need for Americans to have much more knowledge of the non-Western and developing worlds and the paucity of study abroad programs targeted to the countries and regions concerned, federal and other funding should encourage a major expansion of such programs because of the effectiveness of study abroad documented in the SAEP in strengthening international education.

Follow-Up to the SAEP

In both Western Europe and the United States the Study Abroad Evaluation Project has been important in stimulating and contributing to the development of further activity, although quite different in the two geographic areas.

In Western Europe the very positive findings of the SAEP's evaluation of intra-European exchanges of students, a large number of which comprised Joint Study Programs (JSPs) funded under the European Community (EC), helped in making the case for ERASMUS. Approved by the EC in May 1987, ERASMUS (the European Action Scheme for Mobility of University Students) funds costs involved in developing an EC network of cooperation between higher education institutions in EC countries. Much of the funding goes to support the costs of students studying in another EC country for several months or longer as an integral part of their degree program for their home institution, the same model as for the JSP. The goal of ERASMUS is to make it possible by 1992 for 10 percent of higher education students in the European Community to study in another EC country, up from less than 1 percent in the 1980s, thereby "Europeanizing" professional education in the European Community.

The follow-up to the SAEP in the United States also promises to be critical to the future of study abroad. Funded by the Ford Foundation, the so-called Articulation Project encourages policies and programs that enable study abroad to have a more central part in internationalizing undergraduate students' total degree programs. The project's name is derived from its emphasis on articulating students' study abroad experience with their home campus studies so that, rather than being apart or "time out" from their degree studies, study abroad is an integral part of these studies.

The eight U.S. colleges and universities participating in the "Articulation Project" have addressed various issues identified in the SAEP: the best timing of and time period for study abroad, the articulation of study abroad with home campus study so that major and other requirements can be met in part through study abroad, pre–study abroad orientation to help prepare students for the teaching approaches and learning expectations of host countries, post–study abroad programs that sustain language proficiency gained abroad and capitalize on students' increased international knowledge, and strategies for enlisting more faculty support for study abroad.

As a final note, it is interesting that in Western Europe, ERASMUS includes as a related project the development of an academic credit system in European higher education, thus bringing it closer to the U.S. model, whereas the follow-up in the United States, the Articulation Project, to a considerable extent has aimed at the JSP model, now under ERASMUS, whereby study abroad is an integral part of study in one's major field.

C. IMPLICATIONS FOR FUTURE RESEARCH

As noted earlier in this book, the Study Abroad Evaluation Project focused on selected aspects of study abroad and exchanges because they represented shared concerns of the five-country project team and of agencies funding the project. Many aspects of study abroad were therefore deliberately not part of the SAEP, including other kinds of study abroad program models. Project findings suggest, however, that these other models and aspects are important to the field and to students' international learning and hence merit serious research. Research is also called for on some of the aspects of study abroad that were the focus of the SAEP because its findings both underscore the need to know much more about them and also prompt additional related questions.

Moreover, the fact that the SAEP documents the importance of study abroad to students' international learning should provide important impetus to the pursuit of research that looks at the larger issues involved in the internationalization of higher education. Important in this is the American university's response to the increasing international interdependence of the United States. The remainder of this chapter discusses these three different categories of research needs.

Research Needs Related to the SAEP Findings

While the Study Abroad Evaluation Project provided valuable data and insights on a number of aspects and issues relating to study abroad, many of them call for further research if the outcomes of the study abroad experience are to be understood and assessed more fully. The following listing does not purport to be exhaustive.

- How should predeparture and orientation programs be designed in order to provide the most effective preparation for the study abroad experience, a widely perceived problem area pointed up by the SAEP?
- Because interaction with foreign students is an important but mostly neglected resource for the international education of American study abroad students, what strategies might catalyze more such interaction?
- The SAEP findings that American pre–study abroad students tend to be relatively uninformed about their prospective host country and return home much more but unevenly knowledgeable about it make it important to explore and evaluate the best means to ensure their having a maximum and continuing level of learning about the host country while abroad.
- Although the SAEP collected certain demographic and other data on study abroad and comparison group students, limitations in the data and other factors precluded examining important interrelationships between some student and/or program characteristics and the degree of international learning achieved. More research is needed on the interrelationship, if any, between international learning from study abroad, including increased proficiency in the host country's language, and (1) students' sex, major field, prior experience abroad, relevant language proficiency (if any), and parents' socioeconomic circumstances and employment status and (2) the geographic location of programs and their disciplinary focus or foci.
- An important SAEP finding that merits much more research involves the sense of alienation experienced by many study abroad returnees, including factors producing it and possible strategies for reducing or avoiding it, for example, by more effectively integrating their study abroad experiences into their subsequent home campus programs.
- The SAEP finding on the frequent lack of faculty support for study abroad calls for much closer examination and research because of the crucial role played by faculty in encouraging and facilitating or discouraging and impeding study abroad.

Other Research Issues Prompted by the SAEP

A whole range of study abroad characteristics and models fell outside the scope of the SAEP because they did not fit its chosen focus, namely, study abroad programs aimed at integrating U.S. students into host country institutions, typically for an academic year, in the UK, France, West Germany, and Sweden. Some of these other models become particularly important as U.S. colleges and universities expand their study abroad programs and services in keeping with burgeoning student interest. Research on non–SAEP program models and characteristics should target programs that involve shorter time periods than an academic year, that utilize geographic areas other than Western Europe, that provide at most only partial immersion in the host country and culture and do not integrate students into higher education institutions abroad, that are accessible to students with a wide range of academic ability, and that send students abroad other than for their junior year.

Other aspects of study abroad on which the importance of research was pointed up by the SAEP include: study abroad pursued by students individually rather than through group arrangements, study abroad for minorities and other under-represented student groups (blacks, science and engineering majors, males, etc.), and study abroad for students who, unlike the more typical study abroad students, tend not to be risk-takers.

Also neglected by the SAEP but extremely important in strengthening our understanding of the role of study abroad and exchanges in the international education of Americans is the difficult issue of what kind of educational cross-cultural experience might be a "domestic equivalent" to study abroad for those students who cannot or choose not to study abroad, that is, the kind of trans-forming international education gained through successful experience studying in another country. This calls for highly pragmatic and multidisciplinary re-search in cross-cultural learning and outcomes.

Finally, as implied by the last point, more knowledge and understanding are needed of unsuccessful study abroad programs and experiences, presumably resulting in little international learning. With which, if any, characteristics of study abroad programs or students or both does this correlate?

Some Wider Institutional and National Issues

Apart from the foregoing rather specific issues and topics on which research would expand knowledge of study abroad's contribution to international edu-cation, the increasing responsibilities imposed on colleges and universities by the expanding international interdependence of the world community challenge faculty and administrators to examine a number of issues and research ques-tions. Some of the questions that suggest themselves are:

1. What does an "internationalized" university or college mean? Why is it important?

2. What are the implications of internationalizing an institution's programs and curri-cula? What are the costs and what are the benefits?

3. How will internationalization affect the content of academic disciplines and disci-plinary research?

4. What types of programs or student exchanges best meet the goals and objectives of a specific institution or type of institution?

5. What are the most important criteria for the success of faculty and/or student exchange programs? Should they be reciprocal? Focused on a single discipline? Involve a short or long time period?

6. How and to what extent will the entire enterprise of international educational exchange be studied and evaluated? How and to what extent will scholarly inquiry and research be supported?

7. How will the results of systematic, scholarly inquiry into study abroad be used to inform policy and future developments?

The list of questions, although not exhaustive, is indicative of the breadth and complexity of the research agenda that needs to be developed. In order for knowledge to advance in the area of international educational exchange, the cooperation of scholars from a variety of fields will be necessary, including the sciences, social sciences, and humanities.

Since empirical research on international educational exchange tends to be driven more from pragmatic than theoretical considerations, it will be necessary to develop theory that will serve to guide the formulation and operationalization of research questions. This suggests that while the study of international educational exchange may in and of itself not constitute a bona fide area of disciplined inquiry, it can be the focus of disciplined inquiry employing a variety of intellectual and empirical traditions. For example, the exploration of the goals and purposes of education and how international exchange relates to these could involve participation of scholars from philosophy, history, economics, and sociology. The study of attitude change and development and/or change in linguistic awareness and ability may utilize the knowledge base and methods of social psychology, cognitive psychology, linguistics, and anthropology.

In summary, it is exceedingly important that a solid research tradition be developed in the area of international educational exchange. This will require the cooperation of individuals representing a variety of disciplinary and intellectual traditions as well as university and college administrators. Research in international education is necessary to inform policy and practice and at the same time can make significant contributions to traditional areas of disciplined inquiry. If the Study Abroad Evaluation Project, in addition to blazing new terrain and documenting the importance of study abroad to the international education of American (and European) undergraduates, has pointed up the need for much more knowledge of international educational exchange, it will have rendered an extremely important service to the field.

APPENDIX I

PARTICIPATION OF KALAMAZOO COLLEGE IN THE STUDY ABROAD EVALUATION PROJECT

Kalamazoo College was deliberately invited to participate in the Study Abroad Evaluation Project for two main reasons. First, its impressive record of activity in and commitment to international education and the fact that 85 to 95 percent of its students participate in study abroad are in contrast to most U.S. colleges and universities, including the three universities included in the study. Second, also in contrast to these universities, Kalamazoo is a small, private, midwestern, liberal arts undergraduate college; by typifying to a degree a different and important strand in American higher education, Kalamazoo's inclusion made the SAEP more representative of U.S. higher education. The willingness of David Breneman, President of the college, and of Dr. Joe Fugate, its Director of Foreign Study, to collaborate with the project and of Dr. Fugate's office to take on the time-consuming data-gathering and other work of institutional participation was indispensable to Kalamazoo's involvement. Obviously so, too, was its offering study abroad opportunities to the four SAEP target countries of Western Europe, even though with limited reciprocity, and its maintaining records of study abroad alumni/ae going back at least two decades ago and knowing how to contact them for the SAEP longitudinal survey.

SOME BACKGROUND ON KALAMAZOO COLLEGE

With over 1,100 students Kalamazoo is one of the nationally more prestigious among the 405 private colleges whose full-time undergraduate enrollment ranges between 1,000 and 2,500 students.[1] These 405 institutions, while separately small, altogether have over 620,000 enrollees. (The 1,349 four-year private colleges of all sizes, but none over 10,000, together educate over 1.7 million undergraduates annually [Grant and Snyder, 1984]). The relative independence of these colleges from control on the national and state levels stems from their often having originated in culturally autonomous and self-sustaining Protestant religious communities. Up to World War II, most college students studied in one of these church-related private colleges. In the north central states in which Kalamazoo is located, 468 such colleges continue to function, commonly retaining their original underlying values but opening educational opportunities to widening segments of students, irrespective of their socioeconomic backgrounds and religious preferences.

Kalamazoo has a long-time respected reputation for producing graduates whose careers are based on solid academic education. Thus, a survey made in the depths of the Depression of the 1930s of the 1,754 reachable alumni found over half were either pursuing graduate work or professional careers. One-fifth were corporate executives, owners/managers of business firms, or holders of elected or appointed upper-level government positions. Another fifth held positions as teachers or administrators in local schools. The rest mostly had work roles in nonprofit organizations in the region's civic agencies and in the colonial world of several continents as mission-related paraprofessionals and full professionals engaged in educational and welfare services (Goodsell and Dunbar, 1933).

Most influential in its earning of national respect in the circles of physical and life scientists and among knowledgeable scholars of undergraduate education has been its impressive fifty-year performance in the intellectual and personal development of proportionately numerous future research scientists of eminence (Davis-Van Atta, Carrier, and Frankfort, 1985; Goodrich, Knapp, and Boehm, 1951; Mulder, 1958).

Perhaps coincidentally, but we do not think so, among America's foremost small and independent undergraduate colleges that contribute, disproportionately to their size, considerable numbers of future highly productive natural scientists, nearly all have institutional ties into the larger world systems of modern science and higher education outside the United States.[2] Kalamazoo is one of them.

This rich heritage of Kalamazoo—with its subtle ambience of the older "Protestant work ethic," its commitment to service both at home and around the world, and its augmentation by the newer scholarly quality of its educational standards (which has diffused to all fields of study)—is one of three reasons the institution has developed a strong study abroad program. Having this collective identity, two additional factors enable the program to work: (1) an imaginative and wealthy chairman of the board of trustees endowed Kalamazoo with the funds to accomplish its goals, and (2) the willingness of the college administrators and professors to trust, at least most of the time, a few tough-minded and deeply committed faculty members to make the decisions about the conduct of the program.

Eighty-five percent of Kalamazoo's undergraduate participate in the program, and it is a major contributor to the patterns of everyday student life. Within the academic community, the program is a centerpiece of the curriculum.

With a preliminary grant of funds, a pilot program was self-consciously begun in 1958. A group of advanced undergraduate students were rigorously screened for strong performance records and foreign language aptitudes but without concern for their major field or personal finances. An improvised nine-week course of studies was tried out at the universities in Caen, Bonn, and Madrid. Complementing the academic-centered experience was an intimate cultural experience of living in the home of a local family. This beginning, which seemed to everyone an exciting success, quickly was extended into a "five-year experiment" for a large number. The recurring positive assessments of the educational value and personal enrichment of foreign study and experience encouraged further strengthening of the study abroad program. By the academic year 1962, it was regularized as an integral part of undergraduate education and a normal part of a student's four years at Kalamazoo College.

Thus far, among those studying abroad about nine out of ten are juniors; most attend courses at Bonn, Erlangen-Nürnberg, Hannover, or Münster, in West Germany, and Aix-en-Provence, Avignon, Caen, Clérmont-Ferrand, or Strasbourg, in France; lesser numbers have gone to the UK, Spain, Italy, Denmark, and Greece; even fewer have been to Third World countries except Africa.③ Organized as a year-round academic program, with one to three-quarters overseas, Kalamazoo College's study abroad program is manageable for most of its students.

Perhaps the concluding statements of two retrospective evaluations are a useful summary of the outcome of the last twenty-five years of having had study abroad at Kalamazoo College: "There can be little doubt that the entire character of the institution would change rapidly if it were not for the foreign study abroad program" and "In all planning at the institution, continuation of the Foreign Study Program continues to play a major role."

STUDENT PROFILE

It is hardly surprising that the Kalamazoo study abroad students, because they compose 85 percent or more of all students at the college, show a very different profile from that of the California, Colorado, and Massachusetts SAEP students. The latter constitute only 5 percent or less of undergraduate enrollments at their institutions.

Kalamazoo study abroad students were close to 45 percent male and 55 percent female, compared with a male/female ratio at the universities of about 1:2. While the greater majority of study abroad students' parents were U.S. citizens at birth and had not lived for a considerable period abroad, this proportion was highest for Kalamazoo students. A somewhat lower percentage of Kalamazoo students' parents had postgraduate degrees and were in occupations defined as manager/top administrator than the study abroad students at the three universities. A much higher percentage of Kalamazoo students were majoring in science, engineering, premedical studies, and related fields (over 30 percent compared with 12 to 15 percent) and a much lower percentage in humanities and fine arts (26 versus 42 to 46 percent for the universities' students). With respect to the above factors, Kalamazoo students resemble more the comparison group students at California and Massachusetts than the other study abroad students, no doubt because they represent more of a cross section of students at ranking higher education institutions in the United States than of the small fraction of U.S. students nationally who study abroad.

Consistent with the above, the Kalamazoo students showed a pattern of being less interested in things international than the other SAEP students. They read less, made fewer consultations before going on study abroad, and showed less desire to gain new perspectives on the United States or to have a break from routine. They were less likely to see study abroad as an opportunity for academic development—more likely, in fact, not to have thought about it at all (except many chose to go to Kalamazoo because of its study abroad opportunities). The Kalamazoo students were, however, more desirous of using a foreign language and had spent relatively more time learning it. Being with friends was much more a motivation for Kalamazoo students in their study abroad decisions than was true for the other study abroad students, but, of course, this is much more an option for Kalamazoo students where study abroad is the rule than for the university students for whom it is an exception.

The project data suggest that Kalamazoo students were less aware of world problems, less critical of U.S. foreign policy, less concerned about international peace or finding solutions to global hunger, and so on. They saw less need for closer cooperation among nations and participated less in activities aimed at international understanding. The Kalamazoo students showed more negative feelings about foreigners and less desire to meet them. They were less tolerant of non–U.S. values than the other study abroad students, were more patriotic, and were more opposed to foreign businesses and to foreign immigrants to the United States. Like the California, Colorado, and Massachusetts students, they became more pessimistic about the future while on study abroad and changed more in this regard than did the other students. While the Kalamazoo students along with the others reacted positively to their study abroad experience, they were less positive, for example, about its worthwhileness, exposure to new subject matter, and becoming acquainted with new people. Kalamazoo students were also somewhat less positive about the value of acquiring a new perspective on the United States and gave less value to study abroad as a break from their surroundings, an opportunity for personal growth and expanded self-confidence, and a chance to reflect on their own values. One can conjecture that Kalamazoo students had these reactions because study abroad was an expected part of their academic program, whereas for the study abroad students at the universities it was exceptional and hence made more of an impact.

As the foregoing statements point up, the Kalamazoo students differ in a number of respects from the study abroad students at California, Colorado, and Massachusetts; the former constitute the overwhelming majority at their college, whereas the latter compose a small highly selected and self-selected minority. The fact that study abroad is an assumed activity for nearly all Kalamazoo students and for most involves a precollege decision contrasts sharply with the experience of students from the three universities participating in the study. That some of the Kalamazoo students tend to be less integrated into their host institutions abroad than the latter students is yet another difference. Expectations and potential for impact are, if not less, at least different for Kalamazoo students.

If study abroad is to achieve more priority in American higher education and hence to involve more students than has so far been the case, much can be learned from the Kalamazoo students' experience. Even though they can hardly be regraded as representative of American undergraduates generally, they are probably more representative of the wider pool of students who would study abroad if the number expanded significantly. Efforts to increase the number by recruiting, for example, more male students, more in the sciences and professional fields, and more students whose parents are not among the highly educated would undoubtedly profit from examining study abroad at Kalamazoo College.

NOTES

1. The primary author of the section "Student Profile" was Dr. James L. Buschman, formerly Assistant Director of the Foreign Study Program at Kalamazoo College.
2. For instance, among forty-five out of forty-eight colleges for which there are re-

cent data, the median college had thirty foreign undergraduate students in 1979–80 and fifty in 1983–84.

3. Kalamazoo College has the oldest and most extensive university-integrated study abroad program in sub-Saharan Africa of any college or university in the United States.

APPENDIX II

EUROPEAN MEMBERS OF THE SAEP TEAM

Dr. Ladislav Cerych, Director, European Institute of Education and Social Policy, Paris

Mr. Alan Smith, Director ERASMUS Bureau, European Institute of Education and Social Policy, Brussels

Professor Ulrich Teichler, Center for Research on Higher Education and Work, Gesamthochschule-Kassel, Federal Republic of Germany

Ms. Britta Baron, Assistant to the President of the Board and to the Secretary General, German Academic Exchange Service, Bonn

Ms. Dényse Saab, Project Assistant, European Institute of Education and Social Policy, Paris

Dr. Susan Opper, Associate Director for Research, Education Abroad Program, University of California; formerly Research Associate for the SAEP at the European Institute of Education and Social Policy, Paris and Brussels

Mr. Wolfgang Steube, Project Assistant, Center for Research on Higher Education and Work, Gesamthochschule-Kassel, Federal Republic of Germany

APPENDIX III

Instruments Used in the Study

Six research instruments were used in the present study: two premeasure questionnaires (one for the study abroad group and one for the comparison group); two postmeasure questionnaires (one for the study abroad group and one for the comparison group); an alumna/us profile questionnaire; and a focused-interview questionnaire, which served as the basis for telephone interviews with study abroad alumni/ae.

These instruments are presented in Appendix III as follows:

A: Premeasure Comparison Group Questionnaire

Name: _____

UC Campus: _____

Permanent Address: _____

_____

(To be returned with completed questionnaire)

I.   BACKGROUND DATA

In order for us to interpret as accurately as possible the information you provide us in later sections of this questionnaire, it would be helpful for us to obtain some information about you and your background.

1.   Year of birth: _____

2.   Sex: Female _____   Male _____

3.   What is your present nationality?

U.S. _____   Other Nationality: _____

4.   What was your nationality at birth?

U.S. _____   Other Nationality: _____

5.   Were your parents born in a country other than that of your present nationality? (Circle)

Father   YES, Country of birth: _____   NO.

Mother   YES, Country of birth: _____   NO.

6.   Have your parents, brothers/sisters lived for a considerable period of time (minimum 3 consecutive months) in a country other than that in which they are currently residing? (Circle)

Father   YES, Country _____   NO.

Mother   YES, Country _____   NO.

Brother(s)/ YES, Country _____   NO.
Sister(s)

7.   What is the highest level of education your father and mother reached? (If you are not sure, please give your best guess.)

	father	mother
Eighth Grade	_____	_____
High School	_____	_____
Bachelors Degree	_____	_____
Masters Degree	_____	_____
Ph.D.	_____	_____
Other (please specify)	_____	_____

8. Please state the occupation of your father and mother. If your parents are retired, deceased or unemployed, please indicate their last occupation.

OCCUPATIONAL CATEGORIES	FATHER	MOTHER
1) Managers, top administrators and civil servants	_____	_____
2) Education professions (includes all educational levels; teachers as well as researchers)	_____	_____
3) Health professions (doctors, nurses; as distinct from category 9, below)	_____	_____
4) Writers, artists, athletes and kindred professions	_____	_____
5) Engineers, natural scientists	_____	_____
6) Other professions (please specify) _____	_____	_____
7) Technicians, foremen	_____	_____
8) Middle level managers (e.g. in sales, clerical, service areas)	_____	_____
9) Other middle level personnel (e.g. in medical, community and social services)	_____	_____
10) Agricultural*, forestry and fishing occupations (* as distinct from 11, below)	_____	_____
11) Production and transport operatives, farm laborers	_____	_____
12) Clerical, sales and service workers	_____	_____
13) Other (please specify) _____	_____	_____

9. Do you live

   Alone?____   With parents?____   With partner?____   With friends?____

10. Do you have any children?

   No.   YES. How many? _____

11. Do you live in

   _____University dormitory/residence hall?
   _____Room in private home (with another family)?
   _____Apartment/house?
   _____Other? Please specify:_____

12. What is the distance between your institution of higher education and your parents' residence?

_____Up to 50 miles
_____50 - 100 miles
_____100 - 200 miles
_____More than 200 miles

13. Did you spend any period of at least 6 consecutive months doing something which is not part of the general educational career pattern you are now following?

NO

YES If "YES", please indicate the type of activity in which you were engaged, and for how long.

ACTIVITY	TIME PERIOD
A different type of education, training	_____
Employment	_____
Military/conscientious objector service	_____
Volunteer Work	_____
Travel	_____
Unemployed	_____
Care of household/children	_____
Other	_____

14. How long have you studied at your home institution?
(Transfer students: How long have you been in higher education?)

_____Up to 2 semesters/3 quarters
_____2-4 semesters/3-6 quarters
_____5-6 semesters/7-9 quarters
_____More than 6 semesters/more than 9 quarters

15. How important were the following in your choice of home institution?
(Circle one number)

	very important			not at all important	
1) Institution strong in certain subject areas	1	2	3	4	5
2) Prestige of institution	1	2	3	4	5
3) Like the area in which institution is located	1	2	3	4	5

		very important				not at all important
4)	Proximity of institution (e.g. to work, family)	1	2	3	4	5
5)	Not admitted to institution you really wanted to attend	1	2	3	4	5
6)	Amount of tuition required	1	2	3	4	5
7)	Chance, no special reason	1	2	3	4	5
8)	Other, please specify: _____	1	2	3	4	5

16. What is your primary field/major field of study? (Check one only)

____ Humanities, fine arts

____ Education (including teacher training)

____ Social science

____ Economics, business studies

____ Law

____ Natural (pure) sciences, mathematics

____ Engineering, technical studies, architecture, agriculture, environmental science

____ Medicine, dentistry, other health sciences

____ Undeclared

____ Other, please specify: _____

17. Why did you choose your major field of study? (Circle one number)
(Skip to #18 if non-declared major)

	very important				not at all important
Interest in the subject area	1	2	3	4	5
Interest in occupation/career for which this field is preparation	1	2	3	4	5
Career prospects	1	2	3	4	5
You believe you are strong in the subject area	1	2	3	4	5
Institution is strong in the subject area	1	2	3	4	5

	very important			not at all important	
Major was recommended to you	1	2	3	4	5
Other, please specify: _____	1	2	3	4	5
No particular reason	1	2	3	4	5

18. What subjects or fields have you studied during the past year?

_____

19. What is your grade point average? _____ (Scale of _____)

20. How would you rate your academic achievement (i.e. grades, results on examinations, etc.) in higher education? In making this estimation, compare yourself with other students in your field of study and at the same institution. Circle one of the numbers below, on a scale of 1 (= far above average) to 5 (= far below average).

Far above   Far below
average   average

   1   2   3   4   5

21. How have you financed your studies in higher education? Please estimate percentages.

Cash or other contributions from parents (e.g. rent free while living with them*)	_____%
Income from your own work	_____%
Grants, scholarships, loans	_____%
Other (please specify below)	_____%
TOTAL	100 %

*If you live with your family rent-free, please consider this as a contribution of 30%

22. To what extent are you interested in current events, other countries, European and/or international affairs?

Extremely   Not at all
interested   interested

   1   2   3   4   5

23. What are your major sources of information about other countries? MULTIPLE REPLY POSSIBLE. Check <u>only</u> the 3 most frequently consulted sources.

_____ Books published in your own country

_____ Newspapers/magazines published in your own country

_____ Foreign newspapers/magazines

_____ Books published in foreign countries

_____ Television, radio news

_____ Family/relatives

_____ Friends, contacts from your own country

_____ Friends, contacts from other countries

24. Have you been abroad for any reason?

NO

YES   If "YES" indicate where: Country 1 _____

Country 2 _____

<u>TYPE OF EXPERIENCE</u> (use additional space at end of question if necessary)

	no. months	where	age
Living	_____	_____	____
Attending school/university	_____	_____	____
Working	_____	_____	____
Touristic	_____	_____	____

25. Please indicate the frequency with which you spend time in each category of activity.

	very frequently				never
Participating in sports	1	2	3	4	5
Performing in music, arts, etc.	1	2	3	4	5

	very frequently				never
Participating in clubs (e.g. social, political or religious organizations)	1	2	3	4	5
Working (i.e. employment <u>during</u> academic year such as giving private lessons, work study or off-campus job)	1	2	3	4	5
Visiting museums, attending concerts, theater, film, etc.	1	2	3	4	5
Attending sports events (i.e. spectator sports)	1	2	3	4	5
Traveling	1	2	3	4	5
Reading (i.e. literature other than coursework), watching TV	1	2	3	4	5
Other, please specify: _____	1	2	3	4	5

26. To what extent have you had contact with foreigners?

	Constant		Occasional		None
General contact with foreigners	1	2	3	4	5
Contact with people from a specific country: _____	1	2	3	4	5
Contact with foreign students	1	2	3	4	5
Contact with students from a specific country: _____	1	2	3	4	5

27. To what extent have you participated in any international clubs?

Constantly		Occasionally		Never
1	2	3	4	5

II. KNOWLEDGE AND VIEWS OF OTHER COUNTRIES AND INTERNATIONAL AFFAIRS

28. Omitted

29. Omitted

30. Please indicate your attitude toward each of the following in the
foreign country which you feel you know best. Indicate
country:_____

	Highly positive		Highly negative		No opinion

Post-secondary or higher education   1   2   3   4   5   x

Governmental foreign policies in general 1   2   3   4   5   x

Cultural life (e.g. art, music, theater,
cinema, literature)   1   2   3   4   5   x

Television, radio, newspapers, magazines 1   2   3   4   5   x

Customs, traditions   1   2   3   4   5   x

Treatment of recently arrived immigrant
groups   1   2   3   4   5   x

Social structure (e.g. family, class
system)   1   2   3   4   5   x

31. Please indicate how you assess the quality of each of the following in
the U.S.

	Highly positive		Highly negative		No opinion

Post-secondary or higher education   1   2   3   4   5   x

Governmental foreign policies in general 1   2   3   4   5   x

Cultural life (e.g. art, music, theater,
cinema, literature)   1   2   3   4   5   x

Television, radio, newspapers, magazines 1   2   3   4   5   x

Customs, traditions   1   2   3   4   5   x

Treatment of recently arrived immigrant
groups   1   2   3   4   5   x

Social structure (e.g. family, class
system)   1   2   3   4   5   x

32. How would you rate your level of knowledge concerning the attitudes and
values of persons living in the foreign country which you know best?

	Extensive			Moderate		Minimal	

Human rights   1   2   3   4   5   6   7

Significance of education   1   2   3   4   5   6   7

	Extensive			Moderate		Minimal	
Foreigners	1	2	3	4	5	6	7
International (regional) cooperation	1	2	3	4	5	6	7
Your home country	1	2	3	4	5	6	7
The Third World	1	2	3	4	5	6	7
International Affairs	1	2	3	4	5	6	7
East-West relations	1	2	3	4	5	6	7
Nationals of your home country	1	2	3	4	5	6	7
Recent immigrant groups	1	2	3	4	5	6	7
Social welfare	1	2	3	4	5	6	7
International peace	1	2	3	4	5	6	7
Business as a career	1	2	3	4	5	6	7
International cooperation in business and finance	1	2	3	4	5	6	7

33. How would you describe your position on the following?

	Ex-tensive	Con-siderate	Fair	Slight		Non-Existent
Awareness of problems common to many nations.	1	2	3	4	5	6	7
Concern with problems of Third World countries.	1	2	3	4	5	6	7
Desire for international peace.	1	2	3	4	5	6	7
Wish to help find solutions to global problems such as hunger, disease, etc.	1	2	3	4	5	6	7
Respect for historical, cultural, etc. traditions and achievement of nations other than your own.	1	2	3	4	5	6	7
Need for closer cooperation among nations.	1	2	3	4	5	6	7
Desire to meet and interact with persons not from your home country.	1	2	3	4	5	6	7

	Ex-tensive	Con-siderate	Fair	Slight	Non-Existent
Actual or desired travel to foreign nations.	1	2	3	4	5	6	7
Actual participation in activities aimed at affecting greater international understanding.	1	2	3	4	5	6	7
Negative feelings about foreigners.	1	2	3	4	5	6	7
Critical views of your own country.	1	2	3	4	5	6	7
View that values of your own society are not universal and that values of other societies are just as valid.	1	2	3	4	5	6	7
Respect for traditions, culture, way of life, etc. of other cultures.	1	2	3	4	5	6	7
Belief that problems of developing nations should be of no concern to the developed ones.	1	2	3	4	5	6	7
Belief that conflicts among particular nations do not affect the rest of the world.	1	2	3	4	5	6	7
Interest in learning more languages.	1	2	3	4	5	6	7
Membership in organizations concerned with international issues and problems.	1	2	3	4	5	6	7

34. For the following statements please decide whether or not you agree. After you have read each statement, please circle the number in the line below to indicate your response.

Strongly Disagree	Moderately Disagree	Slightly Disagree	Indifferent	Slightly Agree	Moderately Agree	Strongly Agree
1	2	3	4	5	6	7

Pacific demonstrations--picketing missile bases, peace walks, etc.--are harmful to the best interests of my home country.

1	2	3	4	5	6	7

Strongly Disagree	Moderately Disagree	Slightly Disagree	Indifferent	Slightly Agree	Moderately Agree	Strongly Agree
1	2	3	4	5	6	7

I believe that my country should send food and materials to any country that needs them.

| 1 | 2 | 3 | 4 | 5 | 6 | 7 |

The immigration of foreigners to my country should be kept down so that we can provide for our own people first.

| 1 | 2 | 3 | 4 | 5 | 6 | 7 |

Since the world's supplies of essential minerals are limited, the mining and distribution of mineral resources should be controlled by an international authority.

| 1 | 2 | 3 | 4 | 5 | 6 | 7 |

We should not allow foreign business enterprises to have substantial holdings in our country.

| 1 | 2 | 3 | 4 | 5 | 6 | 7 |

Patriotism and loyalty are the first and most important requirements of a good citizen.

| 1 | 2 | 3 | 4 | 5 | 6 | 7 |

Immigrants should not be permitted to come into our country if they compete with our own workers.

| 1 | 2 | 3 | 4 | 5 | 6 | 7 |

We should have a World Government with the power to make laws that would be binding to all its member nations.

| 1 | 2 | 3 | 4 | 5 | 6 | 7 |

An international authority should be established and given direct control over the production of nuclear energy in all countries.

| 1 | 2 | 3 | 4 | 5 | 6 | 7 |

It is our responsibility to do everything possible to prevent people from starving anywhere in the world.

| 1 | 2 | 3 | 4 | 5 | 6 | 7 |

It is none of our business if other governments restrict the personal freedom of their citizens.

| 1 | 2 | 3 | 4 | 5 | 6 | 7 |

Strongly Disagree	Moderately Disagree	Slightly Disagree	Indifferent	Slightly Agree	Moderately Agree	Strongly Agree
1	2	3	4	5	6	7

No duties are more important than duties towards one's country.

1	2	3	4	5	6	7

I prefer to be a citizen of the world rather than of any country.

1	2	3	4	5	6	7

III. ASSESSMENT OF LEARNING STYLES, ABILITIES AND ACCOMPLISHMENTS.

35. Please indicate whether you see yourself as being strong or weak with respect to each of the following:

	very strong				very weak
Working continuously (rather than leaving everything to the last minute).	1	2	3	4	5
Discipline in learning (e.g. not easily distracted from your studies)	1	2	3	4	5
Assuming a heavy workload	1	2	3	4	5
Working under time pressure	1	2	3	4	5
Figuring out what is most significant to learn	1	2	3	4	5
Accepting criticism as a stimulus for further learning	1	2	3	4	5
Developing your own points of view	1	2	3	4	5
Cooperating with others in academic work	1	2	3	4	5
Good memory	1	2	3	4	5
Applying theories, abstract knowledge to practical issues	1	2	3	4	5
Quick understanding	1	2	3	4	5
Tackling abstract problems, working with theories	1	2	3	4	5
Motivating other people	1	2	3	4	5
Articulate, being able to express your own thoughts, views	1	2	3	4	5
Planning and following through accordingly	1	2	3	4	5

	very strong				very weak
Ability to formulate hypotheses and use them in analysis	1	2	3	4	5
Fantasy	1	2	3	4	5
Knowledge of your field	1	2	3	4	5
Choosing tasks commensurate with your abilities	1	2	3	4	5
Coping with ambiguity	1	2	3	4	5
Developing comparative perspectives	1	2	3	4	5
Understanding approaches from several disciplines	1	2	3	4	5
Knowledge of research in your field conducted abroad	1	2	3	4	5
Knowledge of other cultures, countries, international/ European affairs	1	2	3	4	5

36. To what extent: a) does your institution emphasize b) should your institution emphasize the following learning characteristics?

	a. Does strongly emphasize				not at all emphasize	b. Should strongly emphasize				not at all emphasize
Learning facts	1	2	3	4	5	1	2.	3	4	5
Understanding theories	1	2	3	4	5	1	2	3	4	5
Applying knowledge to practical issues	1	2	3	4	5	1	2	3	4	5
Applying research methods, approaches	1	2	3	4	5	1	2	3	4	5
Systematic thinking	1	2	3	4	5	1	2	3	4	5
Familiarity with views from different schools of thought	1	2	3	4	5	1	2	3	4	5
Obtaining international/intercultural, comparative perspectives	1	2	3	4	5	1	2	3	4	5
Utilizing publications in foreign languages	1	2	3	4	5	1	2	3	4	5
Awareness of social, political implications of knowledge, research	1	2	3	4	5	1	2	3	4	5
Obtaining knowledge of different disciplines	1	2	3	4	5	1	2	3	4	5
Regular class attendance	1	2	3	4	5	1	2	3	4	5
Developing one's own point of view, means of analysis	1	2	3	4	5	1	2	3	4	5
Freedom to choose areas of study within courses and independent work	1	2	3	4	5	1	2	3	4	5
Active participation in class discussions	1	2	3	4	5	1	2	3	4	5
Communication between students and teaching staff	1	2	3	4	5	1	2	3	4	5

| | a. Does | | | | | b. Should | | | | |
	strongly emphasize			not at all emphasize		strongly emphasize			not at all emphasize	
Regarding teacher as major source of information	1	2	3	4	5	1	2	3	4	5
Studying to get good grades	1	2	3	4	5	1	2	3	4	5
Taking on a heavy workload	1	2	3	4	5	1	2	3	4	5
Selecting demanding courses	1	2	3	4	5	1	2	3	4	5

151

37. From your experience, rate the following statements:

	Very true for me			Not at all true for me
Some students find it hard to make friends	1	2	3	4
Some students feel there are a lot of things about themselves they would change if they could	1	2	3	4
Some students have a lot of friends	1	2	3	4
Some students are pretty sure of themselves	1	2	3	4
Some students don't think they are a very important member of their group	1	2	3	4
Some students feel good about the way they act	1	2	3	4
Some students are always doing things with a lot of kids	1	2	3	4
Some students think maybe they are not a very good person	1	2	3	4
Some students wish more people liked them				
Some people are very happy being the way they are	1	2	3	4
Some students are popular with their classmates	1	2	3	4
Some people aren't very happy with the way they do a lot of things	1	2	3	4
Some people are really easy to like	1	2	3	4
Some people are usually sure that what they are doing is the right thing	1	2	3	4

IV. CAREER PROSPECTS

38. Indicate briefly but as specifically as possible the professional career which you are most likely to pursue:

_____

_____

39. How set are these career goals?

         very   not at all
         determined   determined

              1   2   3   4   5

40. Do you presently anticipate that your career will involve
    (MULTIPLE REPLY POSSIBLE)

    ____Utilizing your particular expertise with regard to a specific
        foreign country? Specify: _____

    ____Utilizing the general international experience you will obtain
        as a consequence of overseas study?

    ____Considerable contact/cooperating with a specific foreign country
        (regardless of where you are living and working)? Specify: _____

    ____Considerable international contact/cooperation?

    ____Your living and working where you will study abroad?

    ____Your living and working in another foreign country?

V. LANGUAGE PROFICIENCY

Are you proficient in a foreign language? NO ____ YES ____ Please specify _____

Have you studied a foreign language? NO ____ YES ____ Please specify _____

How many semesters/quarters have you studied it? Semesters _____ Quarters _____

         Intensive _____   Non-intensive _____

41. Please check all the phrases below, which describe what you can do quite easily
    in a foreign language. MULTIPLE REPLY POSSIBLE!

              Specify language: _____

Count to 10 in the language   ____

Say the day of the week   ____

Give the current date (month, day, year)   ____

Order a simple meal in a restaurant   ____

Ask for directions on the street   ____

Buy clothes in a department store   ____

Introduce yourself in social situations and use appropriate
greetings and leave-taking expressions   _____

Give simple biographical information about yourself (place of birth,
composition of family, early schooling, etc.)   _____

Talk about your favorite hobby at some length, using appropriate
vocabulary   _____

Describe your present job, studies, or other major life activities
accurately and in detail   _____

Tell what you plan to be doing five years from now, using appropriate
vocabulary   _____

Describe your country's educational system in some detail   _____

State and support with examples and reasons a position on a
controversial topic (for example, birth control, nuclear safety,
environmental pollution)   _____

Describe the system of government of your country   _____

Listening Comprehension

Understand very simple statements or questions in the language ("Hello,
How are You", "What is your name?", "Where do you live?", etc.)   _____

In face-to-face conversation, understand a native speaker who is speaking
slowly and carefully (deliberately adapting his or her speech to suit you) _____

On the telephone, understand a native speaker who is speaking to you slowly
and carefully (deliberately adapting his or her speech to suit you)   _____

In face-to-face conversation with a native speaker who is speaking slowly
and carefully, tell whether the speaker is referring to past, present, or
future events   _____

In face-to-face conversation, understand a native speaker who is speaking
as quickly and is colloquially as he or she would to another native speaker _____

Understand movies without subtitles   _____

Understand news broadcasts on the radio   _____

From the radio, understand the words of a popular song you have
not heard before   _____

Understand play-by-play descriptions of sports events (for example,
a soccer match) on the radio   _____

Understand two native speakers when they are talking rapidly with one another _____

On the telephone, understand a native speaker who is talking as quickly
and as colloquially as he or she would to another native speaker _____

Reading Proficiency

Read handwritten personal letters or notes written to you in which the
writer has deliberately used simple words and constructions _____

Read on store fronts the type of store or the services provided (for
example, "dry cleaning," "book store," or "butcher") _____

Understand newspaper headlines _____

Read handwritten personal letters and notes written as they would be to a
native user of the language _____

Read and understand magazine articles at a level similar to those found
in a publication such as Time, Der Speigel or Express without using a
dictionary _____

Read technical material in a particular academic or professional field with
not use or only very infrequent use of a dictionary _____

Read popular novels without using a dictionary _____

Read newspaper "want ads" with comprehension, even when many abbreviations
are used _____

42. Please assess the level of your writing ability in your language of proficiency.
     Check only the one paragraph which best describes your writing ability.

I cannot really communicate any information in writing. _____

I can write a few sentences using very basic vocabulary and structures. _____

I can write relatively simple items (such as a short note to a friend)
that communicate basic messages but usually contain a considerable number
of misspellings and/or grammatical errors. _____

I can write fairly long personal letters as well as uncomplicated
business letters, which convey meaning accurately and which contain
relatively few errors, although they are not completely idiomatic
in expression. _____

I can write complex personal and business letters, as well a s many other
kinds of documents (for example a "letter to the editor" of the local
newspaper) using in each case that particular vocabulary and style of
expression appropriate to the particular writing situation. There is
only an occasional hint that I am not a native writer of the language. _____

My writing, in all situations, cannot be distinguished from that of an educated native speaker of the language.   _____

43. What is your present knowledge of other foreign languages?

FOREIGN LANGUAGE	Fluent			Minimal	
_____	1	2	3	4	5
_____	1	2	3	4	5
_____	1	2	3	4	5

VI. STUDY ABROAD

We very much appreciate your completing this survey. Your responses will enable us to judge more accurately those students who will be studying abroad. We would also like to know what you think about the opportunity to study overseas. Your university or college sponsors a large number of overseas study programs to many countries. It is possible for students in most major to study abroad during the junior or senior year for a semester or a year. Cost for these programs in some cases may be somewhat higher than the cost of study at home, but there are many programs for which costs are quite close to your home expenses. Most loans and scholarship aid can be applied to study abroad, but you should verify these details with your Study Abroad Office.

Given these facts, we would ask you to answer these final questions:

44. How interested are you in studying abroad?

Extremely		Moderately		Not at all
1	2	3	4	5

45. How willing would you be to commit your time and money by enrolling?

Extremely		Moderately		Not at all
1	2	3	4	5

46. If you have little or no interest in such a program, please check the factors which influenced your choice:

_____ Unnecessary for my curriculum

_____ Dislike foreign travel

_____ Family obligations

_____ Inappropriate for my major

_____ Might delay my graduation

_____ Cost

_____ Concern for credit transfer

_____ Uncomfortable with foreigners

47. If you do have interest, which country would appeal to you most?

_____

ADDITIONAL COMMENTS:

THANK YOU FOR YOUR ASSISTANCE!

B: PREMEASURE STUDY ABROAD GROUP QUESTIONNAIRE

I. BACKGROUND DATA

In order for us to interpret as accurately as possible the information you provide us in later sections of this questionnaire, it would be helpful for us to obtain some information about you and your background.

1. Year of birth: _____

2. Sex: Female _____   Male _____

3. What is your present nationality?

    U.S. _____   Other Nationality: _____

4. What was your nationality at birth?

    U.S. _____   Other Nationality: _____

5. Were your parents born in a country other than that of your present nationality? (Circle)

    Father   YES, Country of birth: _____   NO.

    Mother   YES, Country of birth: _____   NO.

6. Have your parents, brothers/sisters lived for a considerable period of time (minimum 3 consecutive months) in a country other than that in which they are currently residing? (Circle)

    Father   YES, Country _____   NO.

    Mother   YES, Country _____   NO.

    Brother(s)/ YES, Country _____   NO.
    Sister(s)

7. What is the highest level of education your father and mother reached? (If you are not sure, please give your best guess.)

	father	mother
Eighth Grade	_____	_____
High School	_____	_____
Bachelors Degree	_____	_____
Masters Degree	_____	_____
Ph.D.	_____	_____
Other (please specify)	_____	_____

8. Please state the occupation of your father and mother. If your parents are retired, deceased or unemployed, please indicate their last occupation.

OCCUPATIONAL CATEGORIES   FATHER   MOTHER

1) Managers, top administrators and civil servants   _____   _____

2) Education professions (includes all educational
    levels; teachers as well as researchers)   _____   _____

3) Health professions (doctors, nurses; as distinct
    from category 9, below)   _____   _____

4) Writers, artists, athletes and kindred professions   _____   _____

5) Engineers, natural scientists   _____   _____

6) Other professions (please specify) _____   _____   _____

7) Technicians, foremen   _____   _____

8) Middle level managers (e.g. in sales, clerical,
    service areas)   _____   _____

9) Other middle level personnel (e.g. in medical,
    community and social services)   _____   _____

10) Agricultural*, forestry and fishing occupations
    (* as distinct from 11, below)   _____   _____

11) Production and transport operatives, farm laborers   _____   _____

12) Clerical, sales and service workers   _____   _____

13) Other (please specify) _____   _____   _____

9. Do you live

    Alone?____   With parents?____   With partner?____   With friends?____

10. Do you have any children?

    No.   YES. How many? _____

11. Do you live in

    ____University dormitory/residence hall?
    ____Room in private home (with another family)?
    ____Apartment/house?
    ____Other? Please specify:_____

12. What is the distance between your institution of higher education and your parents' residence?

_____ Up to 50 miles
_____ 50 - 100 miles
_____ 100 - 200 miles
_____ More than 200 miles

13. Did you spend any period of at least 6 consecutive months doing something which is not part of the general educational career pattern you are now following?

NO

YES If "YES", please indicate the type of activity in which you were engaged, and for how long.

ACTIVITY	TIME PERIOD
A different type of education, training	_____
Employment	_____
Military/conscientious objector service	_____
Volunteer Work	_____
Travel	_____
Unemployed	_____
Care of household/children	_____
Other	_____

14. How long have you studied at your home institution?
(Transfer students: How long have you been in higher education?)

_____ Up to 2 semesters/3 quarters
_____ 2-4 semesters/3-6 quarters
_____ 5-6 semesters/7-9 quarters
_____ More than 6 semesters/more than 9 quarters

15. How important were the following in your choice of home institution?
(Circle one number)

	very important			not at all important
1) Institution strong in certain subject areas	1 2	3	4	5
2) Prestige of institution	1 2	3	4	5
3) Like the area in which institution is located	1 2	3	4	5

		very important			not at all important	

4) Proximity of institution (e.g. to work, family)   1   2   3   4   5

5) Not admitted to institution you really wanted   1   2   3   4   5
   to attend

6) Amount of tuition required   1   2   3   4   5

7) Chance, no special reason   1   2   3   4   5

8) Other, please specify: _____   1   2   3   4   5

16. What is your primary field/major field of study? (Check one only)

   ____ Humanities, fine arts

   ____ Education (including teacher training)

   ____ Social science

   ____ Economics, business studies

   ____ Law

   ____ Natural (pure) sciences, mathematics

   ____ Engineering, technical studies, architecture, agriculture,
        environmental science

   ____ Medicine, dentistry, other health sciences

   ____ Undeclared

   ____ Other, please specify: _____

17. Why did you choose your major field of study? (Circle one number)

	very important			not at all important	

Major not yet chosen   1   2   3   4   5

Interest in the subject area   1   2   3   4   5

Interest in occupation/career for which
this field is preparation   1   2   3   4   5

Career prospects   1   2   3   4   5

You believe you are strong in the subject area   1   2   3   4   5

	very important			not at all important	
Institution is strong in the subject area	1	2	3	4	5
Major was recommended to you	1	2	3	4	5
Other, please specify: _____	1	2	3	4	5
No particular reason	1	2	3	4	5

18. What subjects or fields have you studied during the past year?

   _____

19. What is your grade point average? _____ (Scale of _____)

20. How would you rate your academic achievement (i.e. grades, results on examinations, etc.) in higher education? In making this estimation, compare yourself with other students in your field of study and at the same institution. Circle one of the numbers below, on a scale of 1 (= far above average) to 5 (= far below average).

   Far above   Far below
   average   average

     1   2   3   4   5

21. How have you financed your studies in higher education?
    Please estimate percentages.

Cash or other contributions from parents (e.g. rent free while living with them*)	_____	%
Income from your own work	_____	%
Grants, scholarships, loans	_____	%
Other (please specify below)	_____	%
TOTAL	100	%

   *If you live with your family rent-free, please consider this as a contribution of 30%

22. To what extent are you interested in current events, other countries, European and/or international affairs?

        Extremely   Not at all
        interested   interested

          1   2   3   4   5

23. What are your major sources of information about other countries? MULTIPLE REPLY POSSIBLE. Check only the 3 most frequently consulted sources.

_____ Books published in your own country

_____ Newspapers/magazines published in your own country

_____ Foreign newspapers/magazines

_____ Books published in foreign countries

_____ Television, radio news

_____ Family/relatives

_____ Friends, contacts from your own country

_____ Friends, contacts from other countries

24. Have you been abroad for any reason?

NO

YES   If "YES" indicate where: Country 1 _____

                               Country 2 _____

TYPE OF EXPERIENCE (use additional space at end of question if necessary)

	no. months	where	age
Living	_____	_____	____
Attending school/university	_____	_____	____
Working	_____	_____	____
Touristic	_____	_____	____

25. Please indicate the frequency with which you spend time in each category of activity.

	very frequently				never
Participating in sports	1	2	3	4	5
Performing in music, arts, etc.	1	2	3	4	5
Participating in clubs (e.g. social, political or religious organizations)	1	2	3	4	5
Working (i.e. employment during academic year such as giving private lessons, work study or off-campus job)	1	2	3	4	5
Visiting museums, attending concerts, theater, film, etc.	1	2	3	4	5
Attending sports events (i.e. spectator sports)	1	2	3	4	5
Traveling	1	2	3	4	5
Reading (i.e. literature other than coursework), watching TV	1	2	3	4	5
Other, please specify: _____	1	2	3	4	5

26. To what extent have you had contact with foreigners?

	Constant		Occasional		None
General contact with foreigners	1	2	3	4	5
Contact with people from a specific country: _____	1	2	3	4	5
Contact with foreign students	1	2	3	4	5
Contact with students from a specific country: _____	1	2	3	4	5

27. To what extent have you participated in any international clubs?

Constantly		Occasionally		Never
1	2	3	4	5

II. KNOWLEDGE AND VIEWS OF OTHER COUNTRIES AND INTERNATIONAL AFFAIRS

28. How would you rate your level of knowledge of the Foreign country which you feel you know best? Indicate country: _____

	YOUR LEVEL OF KNOWLEDGE				
	extensive			minimal	
Political system and institutions	1	2	3	4	5
Governmental foreign policies in general	1	2	3	4	5
Governmental policy toward your own country	1	2	3	4	5
System of post-secondary or higher education	1	2	3	4	5
Cultural life (e.g. art, music, theater, cinema, literature)	1	2	3	4	5
Economic system	1	2	3	4	5
The country's geography	1	2	3	4	5
Social structure (e.g. family, class system)	1	2	3	4	5
Customs, traditions (including religious)	1	2	3	4	5
Attitude toward recently arrived immigant groups	1	2	3	4	5
Television, radio, newspapers, magazines	1	2	3	4	5
Sports, leisure/recreational activities	1	2	3	4	5

29. Please indicate in order of significance the main areas in which you especially hope to gain more knowledge about a foreign country in the coming year.

Indicate country: _____

_____

_____

_____

30. Please indicate your attitude toward each of the following in the
     foreign country which you feel you know best. Indicate
     country:_____

	Highly positive		Highly negative		No opinion
Post-secondary or higher education	1	2	3	4	5	x
Governmental foreign policies in general	1	2	3	4	5	x
Cultural life (e.g. art, music, theater, cinema, literature)	1	2	3	4	5	x
Television, radio, newspapers, magazines	1	2	3	4	5	x
Customs, traditions	1	2	3	4	5	x
Treatment of recently arrived immigrant groups	1	2	3	4	5	x
Social structure (e.g. family, class system)	1	2	3	4	5	x

31. Please indicate how you assess the quality of each of the following in
     the U.S.

	Highly positive		Highly negative		No opinion
Post-secondary or higher education	1	2	3	4	5	x
Governmental foreign policies in general	1	2	3	4	5	x
Cultural life (e.g. art, music, theater, cinema, literature)	1	2	3	4	5	x
Television, radio, newspapers, magazines	1	2	3	4	5	x
Customs, traditions	1	2	3	4	5	x
Treatment of recently arrived immigrant groups	1	2	3	4	5	x
Social structure (e.g. family, class system)	1	2	3	4	5	x

32. How would you rate your level of <u>knowledge</u> concerning the attitudes and
     values of persons living in the foreign country which you know best?

	Extensive		Moderate		Minimal	
Human rights	1	2	3	4	5	6	7
Significance of education	1	2	3	4	5	6	7

	Extensive		Moderate		Minimal	
Foreigners	1	2	3	4	5	6	7
International (regional) cooperation	1	2	3	4	5	6	7
Your home country	1	2	3	4	5	6	7
The Third World	1	2	3	4	5	6	7
International Affairs	1	2	3	4	5	6	7
East-West relations	1	2	3	4	5	6	7
Nationals of your home country	1	2	3	4	5	6	7
Recent immigrant groups	1	2	3	4	5	6	7
Social welfare	1	2	3	4	5	6	7
International peace	1	2	3	4	5	6	7
Business as a career	1	2	3	4	5	6	7
International cooperation in business and finance	1	2	3	4	5	6	7

33. How would you describe your position on the following?

	Ex-tensive	Con-siderate	Fair	Slight	Non-Existent
Awareness of problems common to many nations.	1	2 3	4	5 6	7
Concern with problems of Third World countries.	1	2 3	4	5 6	7
Desire for international peace.	1	2 3	4	5 6	7
Wish to help find solutions to global problems such as hunger, disease, etc.	1	2 3	4	5 6	7
Respect for historical, cultural, etc. traditions and achievement of nations other than your own.	1	2 3	4	5 6	7
Need for closer cooperation among nations.	1	2 3	4	5 6	7
Desire to meet and interact with persons not from your home country.	1	2 3	4	5 6	7

	Ex- tensive	Con- siderate	Fair	Slight	Non- Existent
Actual or desired travel to foreign nations.	1	2	3	4	5	6	7
Actual participation in activities aimed at affecting greater international understanding.	1	2	3	4	5	6	7
Negative feelings about foreigners.	1	2	3	4	5	6	7
Critical views of your own country.	1	2	3	4	5	6	7
View that values of your own society are not universal and that values of other societies are just as valid.	1	2	3	4	5	6	7
Respect for traditions, culture, way of life, etc. of other cultures.	1	2	3	4	5	6	7
Belief that problems of developing nations should be of no concern to the developed ones.	1	2	3	4	5	6	7
Belief that conflicts among particular nations do not affect the rest of the world.	1	2	3	4	5	6	7
Interest in learning more languages.	1	2	3	4	5	6	7
Membership in organizations concerned with international issues and problems.	1	2	3	4	5	6	7

34. For the following statements please decide whether or not you agree. After you have read each statement, please circle the number in the line below to indicate your response.

Strongly Disagree	Moderately Disagree	Slightly Disagree	Indifferent	Slightly Agree	Moderately Agree	Strongly Agree
1	2	3	4	5	6	7

Pacific demonstrations--picketing missile bases, peace walks, etc.--are harmful to the best interests of my home country.

1	2	3	4	5	6	7

Strongly Disagree	Moderately Disagree	Slightly Disagree	Indifferent	Slightly Agree	Moderately Agree	Strongly Agree
1	2	3	4	5	6	7

I believe that my country should send food and materials to any country that needs them.

| 1 | 2 | 3 | 4 | 5 | 6 | 7 |

The immigration of foreigners to my country should be kept down so that we can provide for our own people first.

| 1 | 2 | 3 | 4 | 5 | 6 | 7 |

Since the world's supplies of essential minerals are limited, the mining and distribution of mineral resources should be controlled by an international authority.

| 1 | 2 | 3 | 4 | 5 | 6 | 7 |

We should not allow foreign business enterprises to have substantial holdings in our country.

| 1 | 2 | 3 | 4 | 5 | 6 | 7 |

Patriotism and loyalty are the first and most important requirements of a good citizen.

| 1 | 2 | 3 | 4 | 5 | 6 | 7 |

Immigrants should not be permitted to come into our country if they compete with our own workers.

| 1 | 2 | 3 | 4 | 5 | 6 | 7 |

We should have a World Government with the power to make laws that would be binding to all its member nations.

| 1 | 2 | 3 | 4 | 5 | 6 | 7 |

An international authority should be established and given direct control over the production of nuclear energy in all countries.

| 1 | 2 | 3 | 4 | 5 | 6 | 7 |

It is our responsibility to do everything possible to prevent people from starving anywhere in the world.

| 1 | 2 | 3 | 4 | 5 | 6 | 7 |

It is none of our business if other governments restrict the personal freedom of their citizens.

| 1 | 2 | 3 | 4 | 5 | 6 | 7 |

Strongly Disagree	Moderately Disagree	Slightly Disagree	Indifferent	Slightly Agree	Moderately Agree	Strongly Agree
1	2	3	4	5	6	7

No duties are more important than duties towards one's country.

1	2	3	4	5	6	7

I prefer to be a citizen of the world rather than of any country.

1	2	3	4	5	6	7

III. ASSESSMENT OF LEARNING STYLES, ABILITIES AND ACCOMPLISHMENTS.

35. Please indicate whether you see yourself as being strong or weak with respect to each of the following:

	very strong				very weak
Working continuously (rather than leaving everything to the last minute).	1	2	3	4	5
Discipline in learning (e.g. not easily distracted from your studies)	1	2	3	4	5
Assuming a heavy workload	1	2	3	4	5
Working under time pressure	1	2	3	4	5
Figuring out what is most significant to learn	1	2	3	4	5
Accepting criticism as a stimulus for further learning	1	2	3	4	5
Developing your own points of view	1	2	3	4	5
Cooperating with others in academic work	1	2	3	4	5
Good memory	1	2	3	4	5
Applying theories, abstract knowledge to practical issues	1	2	3	4	5
Quick understanding	1	2	3	4	5
Tackling abstract problems, working with theories	1	2	3	4	5
Motivating other people	1	2	3	4	5
Articulate, being able to express your own thoughts, views	1	2	3	4	5
Planning and following through accordingly	1	2	3	4	5

	very strong				very weak
Ability to formulate hypotheses and use them in analysis	1	2	3	4	5
Fantasy	1	2	3	4	5
Knowledge of your field	1	2	3	4	5
Choosing tasks commensurate with your abilities	1	2	3	4	5
Coping with ambiguity	1	2	3	4	5
Developing comparative perspectives	1	2	3	4	5
Understanding approaches from several disciplines	1	2	3	4	5
Knowledge of research in your field conducted abroad	1	2	3	4	5
Knowledge of other cultures, countries, international/ European affairs	1	2	3	4	5

36. To what extent: a) does your institution emphasize b) should your institution emphasize the following learning characteristics?

	a. Does strongly emphasize				not at all emphasize	b. Should strongly emphasize				not at all emphasize
Learning facts	1	2	3	4	5	1	2	3	4	5
Understanding theories	1	2	3	4	5	1	2	3	4	5
Applying knowledge to practical issues	1	2	3	4	5	1	2	3	4	5
Applying research methods, approaches	1	2	3	4	5	1	2	3	4	5
Systematic thinking	1	2	3	4	5	1	2	3	4	5
Familiarity with views from different schools of thought	1	2	3	4	5	1	2	3	4	5
Obtaining international/intercultural, comparative perspectives	1	2	3	4	5	1	2	3	4	5
Utilizing publications in foreign languages	1	2	3	4	5	1	2	3	4	5
Awareness of social, political implications of knowledge, research	1	2	3	4	5	1	2	3	4	5
Obtaining knowledge of different disciplines	1	2	3	4	5	1	2	3	4	5
Regular class attendance	1	2	3	4	5	1	2	3	4	5
Developing one's own point of view, means of analysis	1	2	3	4	5	1	2	3	4	5
Freedom to choose areas of study within courses and independent work	1	2	3	4	5	1	2	3	4	5
Active participation in class discussions	1	2	3	4	5	1	2	3	4	5
Communication between students and teaching staff	1	2	3	4	5	1	2	3	4	5

172

| | a. Does | | | | | b. Should | | | | |
	strongly emphasize			not at all emphasize		strongly emphasize			not at all emphasize	
Regarding teacher as major source of information	1	2	3	4	5	1	2	3	4	5
Studying to get good grades	1	2	3	4	5	1	2	3	4	5
Taking on a heavy workload	1	2	3	4	5	1	2	3	4	5
Selecting demanding courses	1	2	3	4	5	1	2	3	4	5

37. From your experience, rate the following statements:

	Very true for me			Not at all true for me
Some students find it hard to make friends	1	2	3	4
Some students feel there are a lot of things about themselves they would change if they could	1	2	3	4
Some students have a lot of friends	1	2	3	4
Some students are pretty sure of themselves	1	2	3	4
Some students don't think they are a very important member of their group	1	2	3	4
Some students feel good about the way they act	1	2	3	4
Some students are always doing things with a lot of kids	1	2	3	4
Some students think maybe they are not a very good person	1	2	3	4
Some students wish more people liked them				
Some people are very happy being the way they are	1	2	3	4
Some students are popular with their classmates	1	2	3	4
Some people aren't very happy with the way they do a lot of things	1	2	3	4
Some people are really easy to like	1	2	3	4
Some people are usually sure that what they are doing is the right thing	1	2	3	4

IV. CAREER PROSPECTS

38. Indicate briefly but as specifically as possible the professional career which you are most likely to pursue:

_____

_____

39. How set are these career goals?

             very   not at all
             determined   determined

              1   2   3   4   5

40. Do you presently anticipate that your career will involve
(MULTIPLE REPLY POSSIBLE)

    ____Utilizing your particular expertise with regard to a specific
foreign country? Specify: _____

    ____Utilizing the general international experience you will obtain
as a consequence of overseas study?

    ____Considerable contact/cooperating with a specific foreign country
(regardless of where you are living and working)? Specify: _____

    ____Considerable international contact/cooperation?

    ____Your living and working where you will study abroad?

    ____Your living and working in another foreign country?

V. LANGUAGE PROFICIENCY

41. Please check all the phases below, which describe what you can do quite easily
in a foreign language. MULTIPLE REPLY POSSIBLE!

             Specify language: _____

Count to 10 in the language   _____

Say the day of the week   _____

Give the current date (month, day, year)   _____

Order a simple meal in a restaurant   _____

Ask for directions on the street   _____

Buy clothes in a department store   _____

Introduce yourself in social situations and use appropriate
greetings and leave-taking expressions

____

Give simple biographical information about yourself (place of birth,
composition of family, early schooling, etc.)

____

Talk about your favorite hobby at some length, using appropriate
vocabulary

____

Describe your present job, studies, or other major life activities
accurately and in detail

____

Tell what you plan to be doing five years from now, using appropriate
vocabulary

____

Describe your country's educational system in some detail

____

State and support with examples and reasons a position on a
controversial topic (for example, birth control, nuclear safety,
environmental pollution)

____

Describe the system of government of your country

____

Listening Comprehension

Understand very simple statements or questions in the language ("Hello,
How are You", "What is your name?", "Where do you live?", etc.)

____

In face-to-face conversation, understand a native speaker who is speaking
slowly and carefully (deliberately adapting his or her speech to suit you)

____

On the telephone, understand a native speaker who is speaking to you slowly
and carefully (deliberately adapting his or her speech to suit you)

____

In face-to-face conversation with a native speaker who is speaking slowly
and carefully, tell whether the speaker is referring to past, present, or
future events

____

In face-to-face conversation, understand a native speaker who is speaking
as quickly and is colloquially as he or she would to another native speaker

____

Understand movies without subtitles

____

Understand news broadcasts on the radio

____

From the radio, understand the words of a popular song you have
not heard before

____

Understand play-by-play descriptions of sports events (for example
a soccer match) on the radio

____

Understand two native speakers when they are talking rapidly with one another ____

On the telephone, understahd a native speaker who is talking as quickly
and as colloquially as he or she would to another native speaker   ____

Reading Proficiency

Read handwritten personal letters or notes written to you in which the
writer has deliberately used simple words and constructions   ____

Read on store fronts the type of store or the services provided (for
example, "dry cleaning," "book store," or "butcher")   ____

Understand newspaper headlines   ____

Read handwritten personal letters and notes written as they would be to a
native user of the language   ____

Read and understand magazine articles at a level similar to those found
in a publication such as _Time_, _Der Speigel_ or _Express_ without using a
dictionary   ____

Read technical material in a particular academic or professional field with
not use or only very infrequent use of a dictionary   ____

Read popular novels without using a dictionary   ____

Read newspaper "want ads" with comprehension, even when many abbreviations
are used   ____

42. Please assess the level of your writing ability in your language of
     proficiency. Check only the one paragraph which best describes your
     writing ability.

I cannot really communicate any information in writing.   ____

I can write a few sentences using very basic vocabulary and structures.   ____

I can write relatively simple items (such as a short note to a friend)
that communicate basic messages but usually contain a considerable number
of misspellings and/or grammatical errors.   ____

I can write fairly long personal letters as well as uncomplicated
business letters, which convey meaning accurately and which contain
relatively few errors, although they are not completely idiomatic
in expression.   ____

I can write complex personal and business letters, as well a s many other
kinds of documents (for example, a "letter to the editor" of the local
newspaper) using in each case that particular vocabulary and style of
expression appropriate to the particular writing situation. There is
only an occasional hint that I am not a native writer of the language.   ____

My writing, in all situations, cannot be distinguished from that of an educated native speaker of the language. ‾‾‾‾

43. What is your present knowledge of other foreign languages?

FOREIGN LANGUAGE	Fluent			Minimal	
_____ · _____	1	2	3	4	5
_____	1	2	3	4	5
_____	1	2	3	4	5

VI. MOTIVATION, CHOICE AND PREPARATION FOR THE STUDY ABROAD PROGRAM (SAP)

44. When were you informed about the SAP?

_____Prior to enrolling in the institution of higher education in which you enrolled

_____At some point during study at institution offering the SAP

45. How did you learn about the existence of the SAP in which you enrolled? MULTIPLE REPLY POSSIBLE.

_____ Part of written information on field of study/institution of higher education in which you enrolled

_____ Written information on the SAP itself (e.g. brochure, etc.)

_____ Poster

_____ Announcement by teaching staff or student counselors

_____ Special information meeting(s)

_____ Informal, "word of mouth": information from fellow students/friends

_____ Other, please specify:

46. Which of the following reasons influenced your decision to study abroad?

	very important				not at all important
To become acquainted with subject matter not offered at your institution	1	2	3	4	5
You expected you would get better marks/ examination results after your return from SAP	1	2	3	4	5
To become acquainted with teaching methods other than those adopted at your institution	1	2	3	4	5
Desire to travel (e.g. SAP offered convenient/ cheap means of going abroad)	1	2	3	4	5
You expected the SAP would improve your career prospects	1	2	3	4	5
Desire to live in/make acquaintances from another country	1	2	3	4	5
Desire to use/improve a foreign language	1	2	3	4	5
Other friends were going	1	2	3	4	5
To gain another perspective on your home country	1	2	3	4	5
To enhance your understanding of the particular SAP host country	1	2	3	4	5
SAP afforded opportunity to establish ties with your family/ethnic heritage	1	2	3	4	5
Break from routine	1	2	3	4	5

Other, please specify: _____

What is the most important reason? _____

47. Who most influenced your desire to study abroad? Indicate only the two most influential. Place a "1" next to the most influential; a "2" next to the second most influential.

_____ It was primarily your own idea

_____ Brother/sister

_____ Parents

_____ Friends in home country

_____ Friends in SAP host country

_____ Teachers/professors

_____ Study abroad advisor

_____ Other, please specify: _____

ADDITIONAL COMMENTS:

THANK YOU FOR YOUR ASSISTANCE!

C: POSTMEASURE COMPARISON GROUP QUESTIONNAIRE

Name _____ Year of birth _____ Sex _____

Home University _____

Major academic field _____

I. Background

1. Upon reflection, to what extent were (are) you interested in other countries, European and/or international affairs (a) prior to your junior year; and (b) now?

   Prior to Junior Year   Now
   1   2   3   4   5   1   2   3   4   5

   __   __   __   __   __   __   __   __   __   __

2. To what extent were (are) you interested in current events relating to your own country: (a) prior to junior year; and (b) now?

	Extremely interested				Not at all interested
	1	2	3	4	5
Prior to Junior Year	__	__	__	__	__
Now	__	__	__	__	__

3. List the aspects of American society for which you have developed fresh or deepened interest since your sophomore year.

   _____

   _____

   _____

   _____

4. During your Junior Year period, did you (MULTIPLE RESPONSE POSSIBLE)

   ____ Take courses to broaden your academic and cultural background (i.e., courses not related to your field of study and not required by your campus)?

   ____ Develop a new area of interest?

   ____ Change an earlier chosen major?

   ____ Take foreign language courses?

5. What is your grade point average? _____

6. How have you financed your studies in higher education? Please
    estimate percentages.

    Cash or other contributions from parents   _____%
    (e.g., rent-free while living with them*)

    Income from your own work   _____%

    Grants, scholarships, loans   _____%

    Other (please specify below)   _____%

    TOTAL   100 %

    * If you live with your family rent-free, please consider this a
      contribution of 30%

7. What are your major sources of information about other countries?
    MULTIPLE RESPONSE POSSIBLE. Check only the 3 most frequently consulted
    sources.

    ____ Books published in your own country

    ____ Newspapers/magazines published in your own country

    ____ Foreign newspapers/magazines

    ____ Books published in foreign countries

    ____ Television, radio news

    ____ Family/relatives

    ____ Friends, contacts from your own country

    ____ Friends, contacts from other countries

8. Please indicate the frequency with which you spend time in each
    category of activity.

	Very Frequently 1	2	3	4	Never 5
Participating in sports	—	—	—	—	—
Performing in music, arts, etc.	—	—	—	—	—
Participating in clubs (e.g., social, political or religious organizations)	—	—	—	—	—
Working (i.e., employment during academic years such as giving private lessons, work study or off-campus job)	—	—	—	—	—

	Very Frequently				Never
	1	2	3	4	5
Visiting museums, attending concerts, theater, film, etc.	—	—	—	—	—
Attending sports events (e.g., spectator sports)	—	—	—	—	—
Traveling	—	—	—	—	—
Reading (i.e., literature other than coursework)	—	—	—	—	—
Watching TV	—	—	—	—	—
Other, please specify _____	—	—	—	—	—

9. To what extent did you have significant problems in any of the following areas during your junior year?

	Very Serious Problems			No Problems At all	
	1	2	3	4	5
Academic level of courses too advanced	—	—	—	—	—
Academic level of courses too elementary	—	—	—	—	—
Differences in teaching/learning methods	—	—	—	—	—
Readiness on part of teaching staff to meet and/or help students	—	—	—	—	—
Differences in class or student project group size	—	—	—	—	—
Administrative matters	—	—	—	—	—
Financial matters	—	—	—	—	—
Guidance concerning academic program	—	—	—	—	—
Guidance concerning nonacademic matters	—	—	—	—	—
Finding a place to concentrate on studies, outside the classroom	—	—	—	—	—
Accommodation	—	—	—	—	—
Climate, food, health, etc.	—	—	—	—	—
Interaction among/with students	—	—	—	—	—
Other, please specify _ _____	—	—	—	—	—

10. On the basis of your experiences over the last academic year, which of the teaching, learning and assessment characteristics do you <u>especially like or appreciate in your home institution</u>?

_____

_____

_____

_____

11. On the basis of your experiences over the last academic year, which of the teaching, learning and assessment characteristics are you <u>most critical of regarding your home institution</u>?

_____

_____

_____

_____

12. Rate the following statements by indicating how true each statement is for <u>you</u>, as compared with the hypothetical "some".

	Very True For Me				Not At All True For Me
	1	2	3	4	5
Some students find it hard to make friends	—	—	—	—	—
Some students feel there are a lot of things about themselves they would change if they could	—	—	—	—	—
Some students have a lot of friends	—	—	—	—	—
Some students are pretty sure of themselves	—	—	—	—	—
Some students don't think they are a very important member of their group	—	—	—	—	—
Some students feel good about the way they act	—	—	—	—	—
Some students are always doing things with a lot of kids	—	—	—	—	—
Some students think maybe they are not a very good person	—	—	—	—	—

	Very True For Me				Not At All True For Me
Some students wish more people liked them	___	___	___	___	___
Some people are very happy being the way they are	___	___	___	___	___
Some students are popular with their classmates	___	___	___	___	___
Some people aren't very happy with the way they do a lot of things	___	___	___	___	___
Some people are really easy to like	___	___	___	___	___
Some people are usually sure that what they are doing is the right thing	___	___	___	___	___

II. __Knowledge and Views of Other Countries and International Affairs__

13. What is the degree of your overall satisfaction with your junior year?

Very
Satisfied

Very
Dissatisfied

1   2   3   4   5

14. Please indicate your current _opinion_ about each of the following in the foreign country which you feel you know best. Indicate the country:

_____

	Highly Positive 1 2		Highly Negative 3 4		Do Not Know 5 6	
Post-secondary or higher education	___	___	___	___	___	___
Governmental foreign policies in general	___	___	___	___	___	___
Television, radio, newspapers, magazines	___	___	___	___	___	___
Cultural life (e.g. art, music, theater, cinema, literature)	___	___	___	___	___	___
Customs, traditions	___	___	___	___	___	___
Treatment of recently arrived immigrant groups	___	___	___	___	___	___
Social structure (e.g. family, class system)	___	___	___	___	___	___

	Highly Positive		Highly Negative		Do Not Know	
Urban life	—	—	—	—	—	—
Government domestic policies in general	—	—	—	—	—	—
Quality of civic life	—	—	—	—	—	—

15. Please indicate your current <u>opinion</u> about each of the following in the United States.

	Highly Positive		Highly Negative			Do Not Know
	1	2	3	4	5	6
Post-secondary or higher education	—	—	—	—	—	—
Governmental foreign policies in general	—	—	—	—	—	—
Television, radio, newspapers, magazines	—	—	—	—	—	—
Cultural life (e.g. art, music, theater, cinema, literature)	—	—	—	—	—	—
Customs, traditions	—	—	—	—	—	—
Treatment of recently arrived immigrant groups	—	—	—	—	—	—
Social structure (e.g. family, class system)	—	—	—	—	—	—
Urban life	—	—	—	—	—	—
Government domestic policies in general	—	—	—	—	—	—
Quality of civic life	—	—	—	—	—	—

16. How would you describe your position on the following?

	Ex- tensive	Con- siderable	Fair	Slight		Non- Existent
	1	2	3	4	5	6	7
Awareness of problems common to many nations	—	—	—	—	—	—	—
Concern with problems of Third World countries	—	—	—	—	—	—	—

	Ex-tensive 1	Con-siderable 2	3	Fair 4	Slight 5	6	Non-Existent 7
Desire for international peace	—	—	—	—	—	—	—
Wish to help find solutions to global problems such as hunger, disease, etc.	—	—	—	—	—	—	—
Respect for historical, cultural, etc. traditions and achievement of nations other than your own	—	—	—	—	—	—	—
Need for closer cooperation among nations	—	—	—	—	—	—	—
Desire to meet and interact with persons not from USA	—	—	—	—	—	—	—
Actual or desired travel to foreign nations	—	—	—	—	—	—	—
Actual participation in activities aimed at effecting greater international understanding	—	—	—	—	—	—	—
Negative feelings about foreigners	—	—	—	—	—	—	—
Critical views of your own country	—	—	—	—	—	—	—
View that values of your own society are not universal and that values of other societies are just as valid	—	—	—	—	—	—	—
Respect for traditions, culture, way of life, etc. of other cultures	—	—	—	—	—	—	—
Belief that problems of developing nations should be of no concern to the developing ones	—	—	—	—	—	—	—
Interest in learning more languages	—	—	—	—	—	—	—
Membership in organizations concerned with international issues and problems	—	—	—	—	—	—	—

17. For the following statements, please decide whether or not you agree.
     After you have read each statement, please circle the number in the
     line below to indicate your response.

Strongly Disagree	Moderately Disagree	Slightly Disagree	Indifferent	Slightly Agree	Moderately Agree	Strongly Agree
1	2	3	4	5	6	7

Pacific demonstrations--picketing missile bases, peace walks, etc.--are harmful to
the best interest of the U.S.

    1   2   3   4   5   6   7

I believe that my country should send food and materials to any country that needs
them.

    1   2   3   4   5   6   7

The immigration of foreigners to my country should be kept down so that we can
provide for our own people first.

    1   2   3   4   5   6   7

Since the world's supplies of essential minerals are limited, the mining and
distribution of mineral resources should be controlled by an international authority.

    1   2   3   4   5   6   7

We should not allow foreign business enterprises to have substantial holdings in our
country.

    1   2   3   4   5   6   7

Patriotism and loyalty are the first and most important requirements of a good
citizen.

    1   2   3   4   5   6   7

Immigrants should not be permitted to come into our country if they compete with our
own workers.

    1   2   3   4   5   6   7

We should have a World Government with the power to make laws that would be binding
to all its member nations.

    1   2   3   4   5   6   7

An international authority should be established and given direct control over the
production of nuclear energy in all countries.

    1   2   3   4   5   6   7

Strongly Disagree	Moderately Disagree	Slightly Disagree	Indifferent	Slightly Agree	Moderately Agree	Strongly Agree
1	2	3	4	5	6	7

It is our responsibility to do everything possible to prevent people from starving anywhere in the world.

| 1 | 2 | 3 | 4 | 5 | 6 | 7 |

It is none of our business if other governments restrict the personal freedom of their citizens.

| 1 | 2 | 3 | 4 | 5 | 6 | 7 |

No duties are more important than duties towards one's country.

| 1 | 2 | 3 | 4 | 5 | 6 | 7 |

I prefer to be a citizen of the world rather than of any country.

| 1 | 2 | 3 | 4 | 5 | 6 | 7 |

18. How would you rate your level of knowledge concerning the attitudes and values of persons living in the foreign country which you know best? Please indicate the country: _____

	Extensive			Moderate		Minimal	
	1	2	3	4	5	6	7
Human rights	—	—	—	—	—	—	—
Significance of education	—	—	—	—	—	—	—
Foreigners	—	—	—	—	—	—	—
International (regional) cooperation	—	—	—	—	—	—	—
Your home country	—	—	—	—	—	—	—
The Third World	—	—	—	—	—	—	—
International Affairs	—	—	—	—	—	—	—
East-West relations	—	—	—	—	—	—	—
Nationals of your home country	—	—	—	—	—	—	—
Recent immigrant groups	—	—	—	—	—	—	—
Social welfare	—	—	—	—	—	—	—

	Extensive			Moderate		Minimal	
	1	2	3	4	5	6	7
International peace	—	—	—	—	—	—	—
Business as a career	—	—	—	—	—	—	—
International cooperation in business and finance	—	—	—	—	—	—	—

III. <u>Assessment of Learning Styles, Abilities, and Accomplishments</u>

19. To what extent did/do you feel integrated into the academic life of your home institution BEFORE your sophomore year and NOW?

	To a great Extent			Not at all	
	1	2	3	4	5
Before sophomore year	—	—	—	—	—
Now	—	—	—	—	—

20. If there is a change, please indicate briefly why the change has occurred.

_____

_____

_____

_____

21. If you reflect on your own ways of thinking and learning, how important in your judgment are the following for your learning and intellectual development?

	Very Important			Not At All Important	
	1	2	3	4	5
Learning facts	—	—	—	—	—
Understanding theories	—	—	—	—	—
Applying knowledge to practical areas	—	—	—	—	—
Systematic thinking	—	—	—	—	—
Methodology (research methodology, computer programming, etc.)	—	—	—	—	—
Familiarity with different schools of thought	—	—	—	—	—

	Very Important			Not At All Important	
	1	2	3	4	5
Examining relations between facts/observations/hypothesis/concepts	—	—	—	—	—
Obtaining comparative (e.g., international/European) intercultural perspectives	—	—	—	—	—
Utilizing publications in foreign languages	—	—	—	—	—
Obtaining knowledge from different disciplines interdisciplinary approach)	—	—	—	—	—
Regular class attendance	—	—	—	—	—
Developing one's own point of view	—	—	—	—	—
Freedom to choose own areas of study	—	—	—	—	—
Active participation in class discussions	—	—	—	—	—
Out-of-class communication between students and teaching staff	—	—	—	—	—
Independent work (e.g., writing papers), project work	—	—	—	—	—
Obtaining regular feedback from teachers	—	—	—	—	—
Studying to get good grades, good marks on examinations	—	—	—	—	—
Taking a heavy workload	—	—	—	—	—
Selecting demanding courses	—	—	—	—	—
Regarding the teacher as the main source of information	—	—	—	—	—

22. How would you assess your CURRENT academic/learning abilities accomplishments?

	Very Strong			Very Weak	
	1	2	3	4	5
Working consistently (e.g., rather than leaving everything to the last minute)	—	—	—	—	—
Discipline in learning (e.g., not easily distracted from your studies)	—	—	—	—	—
Assuming a heavy workload	—	—	—	—	—

	Very Strong 1	2	3	4	Very Weak 5
Working under time pressure	—	—	—	—	—
Figuring out what is most significant to learn	—	—	—	—	—
Accepting criticism as a stimulus for further learning	—	—	—	—	—
Developing your own points of view	—	—	—	—	—
Cooperating with others in academic work	—	—	—	—	—
Good memory	—	—	—	—	—
Applying theories or abstract knowledge to practical issues	—	—	—	—	—
Quick understanding	—	—	—	—	—
Tackling abstract problems, working with theories	—	—	—	—	—
Motivating other people	—	—	—	—	—
Articulating your own thoughts/views	—	—	—	—	—
Planning and following through accordingly	—	—	—	—	—
Formulating hypotheses and using them in analysis	—	—	—	—	—
Imagination	—	—	—	—	—
Knowledge of your field	—	—	—	—	—
Choosing tasks commensurate with your abilities	—	—	—	—	—
Coping with ambiguity	—	—	—	—	—
Developing comparative perspectives	—	—	—	—	—
Understanding approaches from several disciplines	—	—	—	—	—
Knowledge of research conducted abroad in your field	—	—	—	—	—
Knowledge of other cultures, countries, international and/or European affairs	—	—	—	—	—

IV. Career Prospects

23. Do you presently anticipate that you will enter post-graduate studies?

Most probably 1	2	3	4	Not likely 5

24. Indicate briefly but as specifically as possible the professional career which you are most likely to pursue: _____

_____

25. How set are these career goals?

Very Determined				Not At All Determined
1	2	3	4	5

26. Do you presently anticipate that your career will involve (MULTIPLE REPLY POSSIBLE)

____Utilizing your particular expertise with regard to a specific foreign country?

____Utilizing the general international experience you will obtain as a consequence of overseas study?

____Considerable contact/cooperation with a specific foreign country (regardless of where you are living and working)?

____Considerable international contact/cooperation?

____Your living and working in another foreign country?

V. Foreign Language Proficiency

If you are a foreign language major, how many quarters have you studied the foreign language? _____

27. Please check all the phases below which describe what you can do quite easily in a foreign language. MULTIPLE REPLY POSSIBLE.
Specify language: _____
If you are not a foreign language major, indicate the language you know best.
_____

Speaking

Count to ten in the language.   _____

Say the day of the week.   _____

Give the current date (month, day, year).   _____

Order a simple meal in a restaurant.   _____

Ask for directions on a street.   _____

Buy clothes in a department store.   _____

Introduce yourself in social situations and use appropriate
greetings and leave-taking expressions.   _____

Give simple biographical information about yourself (place of birth,
composition of family, early schooling, etc.).   _____

Talk about your favorite hobby at some length, using appropriate
vocabulary.   _____

Describe your present job, studies, or other major life activities
accurately and in detail.   _____

Tell what you plan to be doing five years from now, using appropriate
vocabulary.   _____

Describe your country's educational system in some detail.   _____

State and support with examples and reasons a position on a
controversial topic (for example, birth control, nuclear safety,
environmental pollution).   _____

Describe the system of government of your country.   _____

Listening Comprehension

Understand very simple statements or questions in the language ("Hello,
How are You", "What is your name?", "Where do you live?", etc.).   _____

In face-to-face conversation, understand a native speaker who is speaking
slowly and carefully (deliberately adapting his or her speech to suit you). _____

On the telephone, understand a native speaker who is speaking to you slowly
and carefully (deliberately adapting his or her speech to suit you).   _____

In face-to-face conversation with a native speaker who is speaking slowly
and carefully, tell whether the speaker is referring to past, present, or
future events.   _____

In face-to-face conversation, understand a native speaker who is speaking
as quickly and is colloquially as he or she would to another native speaker. _____

Understand movies without subtitles.   _____

Understand news broadcasts on the radio.   _____

From the radio, understand the words of a popular song you have
not heard before.   _____

Understand play-by-play descriptions of sports events (for example,
a soccer match) on the radio.   _____

Understand two native speakers when they are talking rapidly with one another._____

On the telephone, understand a native speaker who is talking as quickly and as colloquially as he or she would to another native speaker.   _____

Reading Proficiency

Read handwritten personal letters or notes written to you in which the writer has deliberately used simple words and constructions.   _____

Read on store fronts the type of store or the services provided (for example, "dry cleaning", "bookstore", or "butcher").   _____

Understand newspaper headlines.   _____

Read handwritten personal letters and notes written as they would be to a native user of the language.   _____

Read and understand magazine articles at a level similar to those found in a publication such as Time, Der Speigel, or Express without using a dictionary.   _____

Read technical material in a particular academic or professional field with no use or only very infrequent use of a dictionary.   _____

Read popular novels without using a dictionary.   _____

Read newspaper "want ads" with comprehension, even when many abbreviations are used.   _____

28. Please assess the level of your writing ability in your language of proficiency. Check only the one paragraph which best describes your writing ability.

I cannot really communicate any information in writing.   _____

I can write a few sentences using very basic vocabulary and structures.   _____

I can write relatively simple items (such as a short note to a friend) that communicate basic messages but usually contain a considerable number of misspellings and/or grammatical errors.   _____

I can write fairly long personal letters as well as uncomplicated business letters, which convey meaning accurately and which contain relatively few errors, although they are not completely idiomatic in expression.   _____

I can write complex personal and business letters, as well a s many other kinds of documents (for example a "letter to the editor" of the local newspaper) using in each case the particular vocabulary and style of expression appropriate to the particular writing situation. There is only an occasional hint that I am not a native writer of the language.   _____

My writing, in all situations, cannot be distinguished from that of an educated native speaker of the language.

_____

29. If you would like to receive summary information of the results of this questionnaire, please give us your permanent mailing address:

_____ (Name)
_____ (Address)
_____ (City, State, Zip Code)

D: Postmeasure Study Abroad Group Questionnaire

Name _____ Year of birth _____ Sex _____

Home
Institution_____ Host
Institution_____

Major academic field _____ Date arrival back in U.S._____

1. Where did you live during the period you spent abroad while in the study abroad program (SAP)?

    ___ University dormitory/hall of residence

    ___ Apartment/house

    ___ Room in private home (with another family)

    ___ Other. Please specify: _____

    Of the people with whom you lived what percent were:

    (a) other Americans _____%

    (b) host country nationals _____%

    (c) other foreign country nationals _____%

2. How have you financed your SAP?

    Cash or other contributions from parents   _____%

    Income from your own work   _____%

    Income from working spouse   _____%

    Financial aid, grant, scholarship, loan   _____%

    Special study abroad scholarship.
    Please specify source(s): _____   _____%

    Other sources. Please specify: _____

    _____   _____%

3. To what extent were (are) you interested in other countries, European and/or international affairs: (a) prior to study abroad; and (b) now?

        Prior to SAP   Now
    1   2   3   4   5   1   2   3   4   5

    __   __   __   __   __   __   __   __   __   __

4. To what extent were (are) you interested in current events relating to your own country: (a) <u>prior</u> to study abroad; and (b) <u>now</u>?

	Extremely interested				Not at all interested
	1	2	3	4	5
PRIOR TO STUDY ABROAD	—	—	—	—	—
NOW	—	—	—	—	—

5. List the aspects of American society for which you have developed fresh or deepened interest since you studied abroad:

_____

_____

6. Are you satisfied with the courses/other activities offered by your home institution that prepared students for the SAP?

	Entirely satisfied				Not at all satisfied
	1	2	3	4	5
Academic preparation	—	—	—	—	—
Linguistic preparation (if applicable)	—	—	—	—	—
General orientation to SAP country, society, etc.	—	—	—	—	—

If you marked "X" in boxes 4 or 5 above, please indicate the reasons for your dissatisfaction. (MULTIPLE REPLY POSSIBLE)

	ACADEMIC PREPARATION	LINGUISTIC PREPARATION	GENERAL ORIENTATION
No/not enough preparation provided	___	___	___
Preparation provided was irrelevant	___	___	___
Preparation provided was of poor quality	___	___	___
Preparation provided was wrongly timed	___	___	___
Other. Please specify: _____			
_____ ___		___	___

7. How long were you abroad in your SAP, and at what stage of studies in your home institution did you go abroad?

    (a) Length of period abroad (number of months)   _____

    (b) Dates of period abroad (e.g., 3/84 - 6/84)   _____

    (c) At what stage of your studies at your home institution did you go abroad (e.g., 3rd year of undergraduate)?   _____

8. Do you believe the time you spent abroad was:

    _____ too long   _____ too short   _____ just about right

9. During your study abroad period, did you: (MULTIPLE RESPONSE POSSIBLE)

    ___ Take courses involving content/topics not available at your home institution?

    ___ Take courses involving teaching methods not practiced or available at your home institution?

    ___ Utilize laboratories or other facilities (e.g., computerized data analysis) not available or of lesser quality at your home institution?

    ___ Take courses to broaden your academic and cultural background (i.e., courses not related to your field of study and not required by your home or host institution)?

    ___ Develop a new area of interest?

    ___ Change an earlier chosen major?

    ___ Take language courses in the language of the SAP host country, other than any intensive language program, possibly arranged as part of the SAP?

    ___ Take language courses in a language other than that of the SAP host country?

    ___ Take courses outside of your major which you would not ordinarily have taken at your home institution? Please indicate:

    _____

    _____

10. According to your experience, to what extent are each of the following
    emphasized at your host institution, as compared with your home institution?

	HOST INSTITUTION					HOME INSTITUTION				
	Strongly Empha-Sized				Not at All Empha-Sized	Strongly Empha-Sized				Not at All Empha-Sized
EMPHASIS ON:	1	2	3	4	5	1	2	3	4	5
Acquiring facts (including learning equations and formulas, where applicable)	—	—	—	—	—	—	—	—	—	—
Understanding theories, concepts, paradigms	—	—	—	—	—	—	—	—	—	—
Development of applied knowledge and personal skills for practical problem-solving and/or future employment opportunities (e.g., computer, urban planning)	—	—	—	—	—	—	—	—	—	—
Methodology of inquiry in discipline areas and field methods	—	—	—	—	—	—	—	—	—	—
Providing views from different school af thought	—	—	—	—	—	—	—	—	—	—
Providing comparative (e.g., inter-national/ European, intercultural) perspectives	—	—	—	—	—	—	—	—	—	—
Using publications in foreign language(s)	—	—	—	—	—	—	—	—	—	—
Interdisciplinary approaches	—	—	—	—	—	—	—	—	—	—
Instructor-assigned text books/reading lists	—	—	—	—	—	—	—	—	—	—
Regular class attendance	—	—	—	—	—	—	—	—	—	—
Students developing their own points of view	—	—	—	—	—	—	—	—	—	—
Student-written papers and project work	—	—	—	—	—	—	—	—	—	—
Teachers as the main source of information	—	—	—	—	—	—	—	—	—	—
Students stimulating and challenging each other academically	—	—	—	—	—	—	—	—	—	—

EMPHASIS ON:	HOST INSTITUTION					HOME INSTITUTION				
	Strongly Empha-Sized				Not at All Empha-Sized	Strongly Empha-Sized				Not at All Empha-Sized
	1	2	3	4	5	1	2	3	4	5
Students' freedom to choose specific areas of study within general subject fields	—	—	—	—	—	—	—	—	—	—
Active participation in class discussion	—	—	—	—	—	—	—	—	—	—
Out of class communication between students and teaching staff	—	—	—	—	—	—	—	—	—	—
Academic credit given for applied/ practical experience	—	—	—	—	—	—	—	—	—	—
Use of the library as a learning resource	—	—	—	—	—	—	—	—	—	—
Use of the laboratory facilities as a learning resource	—	—	—	—	—	—	—	—	—	—
Adherence to deadlines	—	—	—	—	—	—	—	—	—	—
Independent work	—	—	—	—	—	—	—	—	—	—
Instructors regularly monitoring students' achievements	—	—	—	—	—	—	—	—	—	—
Grades	—	—	—	—	—	—	—	—	—	—
High standard, quality courses	—	—	—	—	—	—	—	—	—	—
Writing and communication skills	—	—	—	—	—	—	—	—	—	—

11. According to your experience, to what extent are each of the following methods of assessing student performance emphasized at your host institution, as compared with your home institution?

EMPHASIS ON:	HOST INSTITUTION					HOME INSTITUTION				
	Strongly Emphasized				Not at All Emphasized	Strongly Emphasized				Not at All Emphasized
	1	2	3	4	5	1	2	3	4	5
Oral examinations	—	—	—	—	—	—	—	—	—	—
Written essay examinations	—	—	—	—	—	—	—	—	—	—
Multiple choice tests	—	—	—	—	—	—	—	—	—	—
Evaluation of class participation	—	—	—	—	—	—	—	—	—	—

	HOST INSTITUTION					HOME INSTITUTION				
	Strongly Emphasized			Not at All Emphasized		Strongly Emphasized			Not at All Emphasized	
EMPHASIS ON:	1	2	3	4	5	1	2	3	4	5
Evaluation of papers submitted (written independently or as a product of group work)	__	__	__	__	__	__	__	__	__	__
Other. Please specify: _____										
	__	__	__	__	__	__	__	__	__	__

12. According to your experience, to what extent are each of the following types of courses and learning modes emphasized at your host institution, as compared with your home institution?

	HOST INSTITUTION					HOME INSTITUTION				
	Strongly Emphasized			Not at All Emphasized		Strongly Emphasized			Not at All Emphasized	
EMPHASIS ON:	1	2	3	4	5	1	2	3	4	5
Lectures	__	__	__	__	__	__	__	__	__	__
Seminars	__	__	__	__	__	__	__	__	__	__
Tutorials	__	__	__	__	__	__	__	__	__	__
Group projects or other forms of group study	__	__	__	__	__	__	__	__	__	__
Individual projects or other forms of independent study	__	__	__	__	__	__	__	__	__	__
Laboratory work	__	__	__	__	__	__	__	__	__	__

13. How would you compare with your home institution the standard(s) of academic performance expected of you while at your host institution?

Much lower		About the same		Much greater
____	____	____	____	____

14. How would you compare the academic standard(s) expected of you in contrast to host country students at your host institution?

Much lower		About the same		Much greater
____	____	____	____	____

15. In your judgment were <u>you</u> graded more easily than host nationals?

   Yes _____   No _____

16. In your judgment were <u>you</u> graded more easily than foreign exchange students?

   Yes _____   No _____

17. On the basis of your experiences in the SAP country, which of the teaching, learning and assessment characteristics do you <u>especially like or appreciate in your home institution</u>?

   _____

   _____

   _____

   _____

   _____

   _____

18. On the basis of your experiences in the SAP country, which of the teaching, learning and assessment characteristics are you <u>most critical of your home institution</u>?

   _____

   _____

   _____

   _____

   _____

   _____

19. How would you rate your general academic accomplishment and intellectual development during your study period abroad, compared with what you would have expected had you stayed at your home institution?

Abroad Much less				Abroad Much greater
1	2	3	4	5
____	____	____	____	____

Please explain: _____

_____

_____

_____

_____

20. Please indicate the frequency with which you spend time in each category of activity DURING your study period abroad?

	Very Frequently 1	2	3	4	Never 5
Participating in sports	—	—	—	—	—
Performing in music, arts, etc.	—	—	—	—	—
Doing hobby or craftwork (e.g., electronics, gardening, photography, knitting)	—	—	—	—	—
Participating in clubs (e.g., social, political or religious organizations	—	—	—	—	—
Working (i.e., employment during academic year such as giving private lessons, working as a graduate assistant)	—	—	—	—	—
Visiting museums, attending concerts, theater, cinema, etc.	—	—	—	—	—
Going to parties, being with friends, playing chess, bridge, etc.					
Attending sports events, (e.g., spectator sports)	—	—	—	—	—
Traveling	—	—	—	—	—
Reading (literature other than coursework	—	—	—	—	—
Watching Television	—	—	—	—	—
Other. Please specify _____	—	—	—	—	—

21. Indicate activities done abroad that you would have been less likely to pursue at home:

_____

_____

_____

22. While abroad, approximately how many days did you travel outside the immediate area in which the SAP host institution was located (include weekends and vacations)?

Days Spent in Travel	Immediately Prior to Formal SAP Period	During Formal SAP Period	After End of Course in Host Country
None at all	1. _____	1. _____	1. _____
Up to 10 days	2. _____	2. _____	2. _____
11 - 20 days	3. _____	3. _____	3. _____
21 - 30 days	4. _____	4. _____	4. _____
More than 30 days	5. _____	5. _____	5. _____

23. What were your most rewarding travel experiences? Why?

24. Of what importance was personal contact with the following people in shaping your overall experience while abroad?

	Very important			Not at all important		No contact
	1	2	3	4	5	6
Students of the SAP host country	—	—	—	—	—	—
Teaching staff of the SAP host country	—	—	—	—	—	—
Other people from the SAP host country (i.e., people outside the university)	—	—	—	—	—	—
Students from your home country	—	—	—	—	—	—
Administrative representatives from your home country	—	—	—	—	—	—
Instructors, researchers from your home country	—	—	—	—	—	—
Other people from your home country	—	—	—	—	—	—

	Very impor- tant			Not at all impor- tant	No con- tact
	1	2	3	4 5	6
Students from foreign countries other than you own	—	—	—	— —	—

Other. Please specify: _____

_____   — — — — —   —

25. Indicate the two _most_ important personal contacts listed above in shaping your overall experiences while abroad. Why were they important?

_____

_____

_____

26. During your study abroad, how extensively did you use the following methods to become informed about the host country?

	Exten- sively				Not At All
	1	2	3	4	5
Host country newspapers	—	—	—	—	—
Host country magazines	—	—	—	—	—
Host country fiction books	—	—	—	—	—
Host country non-fiction books	—	—	—	—	—
Host country professional journals and books	—	—	—	—	—
Host country radio programs	—	—	—	—	—
Host country television programs	—	—	—	—	—
Other media	—	—	—	—	—
Lectures	—	—	—	—	—
Discussion groups	—	—	—	—	—
Talking with host country nationals	—	—	—	—	—
Talking with fellow nationals	—	—	—	—	—
Talking with other foreign students	—	—	—	—	—

27. Below, you will find a list of areas in which assistance and/or guidance may have been offered to you by the SAP host institution. If assistance and/or guidance was <u>not</u> offered in one or more of the following areas, place an "X" in the appropriate box in the column "Not Provided." For each of the areas in which assistance and/or guidance <u>was</u> offered, indicate the degree to which you were satisfied and, if applicable, the reasons for your dissatisfaction.

WITH REGARD TO ASSISTANCE AND/OR GUIDANCE ON	Not Pro-vided	Entire-ly Sat-isfied 1	2	3	Not At All Satis-fied 4	5	Too Limited 1	Irrel-evant 2	Poor Quality 3	Wrongly Timed 4	Other 5
Living accommodation	—	—	—	—	—	—	—	—	—	—	—
Language training	—	—	—	—	—	—	—	—	—	—	—
Academic matters	—	—	—	—	—	—	—	—	—	—	—
Learning about the host country (history, economy, etc.)	—	—	—	—	—	—	—	—	—	—	—
Personal matters	—	—	—	—	—	—	—	—	—	—	—
Practical matters (e.g., insurance, registration with civil authorities)	—	—	—	—	—	—	—	—	—	—	—
Cultural, sports, other recreational activities	—	—	—	—	—	—	—	—	—	—	—
Social contacts in host country	—	—	—	—	—	—	—	—	—	—	—
Matters regarding students' financial support	—	—	—	—	—	—	—	—	—	—	—
Understanding the character of higher educational institutions in the host country	—	—	—	—	—	—	—	—	—	—	—
Orientation to the local community in which SAP host institution is located	—	—	—	—	—	—	—	—	—	—	—

Column group headings: DEGREE OF SATISFACTION WITH ASSISTANCE AND/OR GUIDANCE; REASONS FOR DISSATISFACTION (Multiple reply possible in each horizontal line)

28. Please check <u>all</u> the phrases below, which describe what you can presently do quite easily in the language of the SAP host country. (MULTIPLE REPLY POSSIBLE.)

<u>SPEAKING</u>

Count to 10 in the language   ____

Say the days of the week   ____

Give the current date (month, day, year)   ____

Order a simple meal in a restaurant

Ask for directions on the street   ____

Buy clothes in a department store   ____

Introduce yourself in social situations and use appropriate greetings and leave-taking expressions   ____

Give simple biographical information about yourself (place of birth, composition of family, early schooling, etc.)   ____

Talk about your favorite hobby at some length, using appropriate vocabulary   ____

Describe your present job, studies, or other major life activities accurately and in detail   ____

Tell what you plan to be doing five years from now, using appropriate vocabulary   ____

Describe your country's educational system in some detail   ____

State and support with examples and reasons a position on a controversial topic (for example, birth control, nuclear safety, environmental pollution)   ____

Describe the system of government of your country   ____

Discuss your coursework, ask for guidance, etc. in conversation with your teacher   ____

Ask for assistance in the library   ____

Participate actively in small group discussion, project or laboratory work, with other students who are native speakers of the SAP host country language   ____

Ask questions or participate in discussion in a large class setting   ____

Present a paper, results of laboratory experiments, etc. by yourself in front of a large group of students and teacher(s)   ____

Lead a small group seminar   ____
LISTENING COMPREHENSION

Understand very simple statements or questions in the language ("Hello.
   How are You", "What is your name?", "Where do you live?", etc.)   ____

In face-to-face conversation, understand a native speaker who is speaking
   slowly and carefully (deliberately adapting his or her speech to suit you) ____

On the telephone, understand a native speaker who is speaking to you slowly
   and carefully (deliberately adapting his or her speech to suit you)   ____

In face-to-face conversation with a native speaker who is speaking slowly
   and carefully, tell whether the speaker is referring to past, present, or
   future events   ____

In face-to-face conversation, understand a native speaker who is speaking
   as quickly and is colloquially as he or she would to another native speaker ____

Understand movies without subtitles   ____

Understand news broadcasts on the radio   ____

From the radio, understand the words of a popular song you have
   not heard before   ____

Understand play-by-play descriptions of sports events (for example,
   a soccer match) on the radio   ____

Understand two native speakers when they are talking rapidly with one another ____

On the telephone, understand a native speaker who is talking as quickly
   and as colloquially as he or she would to another native speaker   ____

Understand a lecture in your field(s)   ____

Understand students and teachers in a discussion, seminar situation, etc.,
   concerning topics in your field(s)   ____

Understand other non-natives of the SAP country, speaking the language of that
   country   ____

READING PROFICIENCY

Read handwritten, personal letters or notes written to you in which the
   writer has deliberately used simple words and constructions   ____

Read handwritten notes on the blackboard, viewgraphs, etc. whereby the
   writer has deliberately used simple words and constructions   ____

Read on store fronts the type of store or the services provided (for
   example, "dry cleaning", "bookstore", or "butcher")   ____

Understand newspaper headlines   ____

Read signboards at the university which explain, e.g., procedures for registering in courses, buy meal tickets in the cafeteria, loaning materials from the library, etc.

_____

Read handwritten personal letters and notes written as they would be to a native user of the language

_____

Read and understand magazine articles at a level similar to those found in _Time_ or _Newsweek_, without using a dictionary

_____

Read technical material in a particular academic or professional field with no use or only very infrequent use of a dictionary

_____

Read popular novels without using a dictionary.

_____

Read newspaper "want ads" with comprehension, even when many abbreviations are used.

_____

29. Please assess the level of your writing ability in your language of the SAP host country. Check only the one paragraph which best describes your writing ability.

I cannot really communicate any information in the language of the SAP host country through writing

_____

I can write a few sentences in the language of the SAP host country, using very basic very basic vocabulary and structures

_____

I can write relatively simple items (such as a short note to a friend) that communicate basic messages but usually contain a considerable number of misspellings and/or grammatical errors

_____

I can write fairly long personal letters as well as uncomplicated business letters, which convey meaning accurately and which contain relatively few errors, although they are not completely idiomatic in expression

_____

I can write complex personal and business letters, as well a s many other kinds of documents (for example, a "letter to the editor" of the local newspaper) using in each case the particular vocabulary and style of expression appropriate to the particular writing situation. There is only an occasional hint that I am not a native writer of the language

_____

My writing, in all situations, cannot be distinguished from that of an educated native speaker of the language of the SAP host country

_____

30. To what extent did you feel restrained with regard to language proficiency under the following circumstances, at the BEGINNING of your study abroad and at the END?

	AT BEGINNING OF SAP					AT THE END OF SAP				
	Very Restrained			Not at All Restrained		Very Restrained			Not at All Re- strained	
	1	2	3	4	5	1	2	3	4	5
Entering into conversations with host country students	__	__	__	__	__	__	__	__	__	__
Entering into academic conversations with instructors	__	__	__	__	__	__	__	__	__	__
Meeting the language requirements of daily life	__	__	__	__	__	__	__	__	__	__

31. To what extent did you have significant problems in any of the following areas during your study period abroad?

	Very Serious Problems			No Problems At All	
	1	2	3	4	5
Taking courses/examinations in a foreign language (if applicable)	__	__	__	__	__
Academic level of courses too advanced	__	__	__	__	__
Academic level of courses too elementary	__	__	__	__	__
Differences in teaching/learning methods (between home and host institutions)	__	__	__	__	__
Readiness on part of teaching staff to meet and/or help foreign students	__	__	__	__	__
Differences in class or student project group size	__	__	__	__	__
Administrative matters	__	__	__	__	__
Financial matters	__	__	__	__	__
Guidance concerning academic program	__	__	__	__	__
Guidance concerning nonacademic matters	__	__	__	__	__
Finding a place to concentrate on studies, outside the classroom	__	__	__	__	__
Accommodation	__	__	__	__	__

	Very Serious Problems		No Problems At All	
	1	2	3	4	5
Climate, food, health, etc.	—	—	—	—	—
Lifestyles of nationals in SAP host country Interaction among/with host country students	—	—	—	—	—
Not enough contact with people from your own country	—	—	—	—	—
Too much contact with people from your own country	—	—	—	—	—
Communicating in a foreign language outside the classroom (if applicable)	—	—	—	—	—
Time available for travel	—	—	—	—	—
Other. Please specify: _____					
_____	—	—	—	—	—

32. How would you assess your CURRENT academic/learning abilities accomplishments?

	Very Strong				Very Weak
	1	2	3	4	5
Working consistently (e.g., rather than leaving everything to the last minute)	—	—	—	—	—
Discipline in learning (e.g., not easily distracted from your studies)	—	—	—	—	—
Assuming a heavy workload	—	—	—	—	—
Working under time pressure	—	—	—	—	—
Figuring out what is most significant to learn	—	—	—	—	—
Accepting criticism as a stimulus for further learning	—	—	—	—	—
Developing your own points of view	—	—	—	—	—
Cooperating with others in academic work	—	—	—	—	—
Good memory	—	—	—	—	—
Applying theories or abstract knowledge to practical issues	—	—	—	—	—
Quick understanding	—	—	—	—	—
Tackling abstract problems, working with theories	—	—	—	—	—

	Very Strong				Very Weak
	1	2	3	4	5
Motivating other people	__	__	__	__	__
Articulating your own thoughts/views	__	__	__	__	__
Planning and following through accordingly	__	__	__	__	__
Formulating hypotheses and using them in analysis	__	__	__	__	__
Imagination	__	__	__	__	__
Knowledge of your field	__	__	__	__	__
Choosing tasks commensurate with your abilities	__	__	__	__	__
Coping with ambiguity	__	__	__	__	__
Developing comparative perspectives	__	__	__	__	__
Understanding approaches from several disciplines	__	__	__	__	__
Knowledge of research conducted abroad in your field	__	__	__	__	__
Knowledge of other cultures, countries, international and/or European affairs	__	__	__	__	__

33. Rate the following statements by indicating how true each statement is for you, as compared with the hypothetical "some":

	Very true for me			Not at all true for me	
	1	2	3	4	5
Some students find it hard to make friends	__	__	__	__	__
Some students feel there are a lot of things about themselves they would change if they could	__	__	__	__	__
Some students have a lot of friends	__	__	__	__	__
Some students are pretty sure of themselves	__	__	__	__	__
Some students don't think they are a very important member of their group	__	__	__	__	__
Some students feel good about the way they act	__	__	__	__	__
Some students are always doing things with a lot of students	__	__	__	__	__
Some students think maybe they are not a very good person	__	__	__	__	__

	Very true for me				Not at all true for me
Some students wish more people liked them	—	—	—	—	—
Some people are very happy being the way they are	—	—	—	—	—
Some students are popular with their classmates	—	—	—	—	—
Some people aren't very happy with the way they do a lot of things	—	—	—	—	—
Some people are really easy to like	—	—	—	—	—
Some people are usually sure that what they are doing is the right thing	—	—	—	—	—

34. How would you rate your current level of knowledge with regard to the following aspects of the SAP country?

	Extensive Knowledge 1	2	3	4	Minimal Knowledge 5
Political system and institutions	—	—	—	—	—
Dominant political issues	—	—	—	—	—
Government foreign policy in general	—	—	—	—	—
Government policy toward your own country	—	—	—	—	—
System of post-secondary or higher education	—	—	—	—	—
Cultural life (e.g., art, music, theater, cinema literature)	—	—	—	—	—
Dominant social issues	—	—	—	—	—
Economic system	—	—	—	—	—
The country's geography	—	—	—	—	—
Social structure (e.g., family, class system, etc.)	—	—	—	—	—
Customs, traditions (including religious)	—	—	—	—	—
Treatment of recently arrived immigrant groups	—	—	—	—	—
Sports, leisure/recreational activities	—	—	—	—	—

35. Please list in order of significance the main areas in which you gained the most significant knowledge about the SAP host country:

1. _____

2. _____

3. _____

4. _____

5. _____

36. What is your current <u>opinion</u> about each of the following aspects of the <u>SAP host country</u>?

	Highly positive opinion			Highly negative opinion		Do Not know
	1	2	3	4	5	6
Post-secondary or higher education	__	__	__	__	__	__
Governmental foreign policies in general	__	__	__	__	__	__
Cultural life (e.g. art, music, theater, cinema, literature)	__	__	__	__	__	__
Television, radio, newspapers, magazines	__	__	__	__	__	__
Customs, traditions	__	__	__	__	__	__
Treatment of recently arrived immigrant groups	__	__	__	__	__	__
Social structure (e.g. family, class system)	__	__	__	__	__	__
Urban life	__	__	__	__	__	__
Government domestic policies	__	__	__	__	__	__
Quality of civic life	__	__	__	__	__	__

37. What is your current <u>opinion</u> about each of the following in your <u>home country</u>?

	Highly positive opinion			Highly negative opinion		Do not know
	1	2	3	4	5	6
Post-secondary or higher education	__	__	__	__	__	__
Governmental foreign policies in general	__	__	__	__	__	__

	Highly positive opinion 1	2	3	Highly negative opinion 4	5	Do not know 6
Cultural life (e.g. art, music, theater, cinema, literature)	___	___	___	___	___	___
Television, radio, newspapers, magazines	___	___	___	___	___	___
Customs, traditions	___	___	___	___	___	___
Treatment of recently arrived immigrant groups	___	___	___	___	___	___
Social structure (e.g. family, class system)	___	___	___	___	___	___
Urban life	___	___	___	___	___	___
Government domestic policies	___	___	___	___	___	___
Quality of civic life	___	___	___	___	___	___

38. How would you describe your position on the following?

	Ex- tensive 1	Consider- able 2	3	Fair 4	Slight 5	6	Non- Existent 7
Awareness of problems common to many nations	___	___	___	___	___	___	___
Concern with problems of Third World countries	___	___	___	___	___	___	___
Desire for international peace	___	___	___	___	___	___	___
Wish to help find solutions to global problems such as hunger, disease, etc.	___	___	___	___	___	___	___
Respect for historical, cultural, etc. traditions and achievement of nations other than your own	___	___	___	___	___	___	___
Need for closer cooperation among nations	___	___	___	___	___	___	___
Desire to meet and interact with persons not from your home country	___	___	___	___	___	___	___
Actual or desired travel to foreign nations	___	___	___	___	___	___	___
Actual participation in activities aimed at effecting greater international understanding	___	___	___	___	___	___	___
Negative feelings about foreigners	___	___	___	___	___	___	___

	Ex- tensive 1	Consider- able 2	3	Fair 4	Slight 5	6	Non- Existent 7
Critical views of your own country	—	—	—	—	—	—	—
View that values of your own society are not universal and that values of other societies are just as valid	—	—	—	—	—	—	—
Respect for traditions, culture, way of life, etc. of other cultures	—	—	—	—	—	—	—
Belief that problems of developing nations should be of no concern to the developing ones	—	—	—	—	—	—	—
Belief that conflicts among particular national do not affect the rest of the world	—	—	—	—	—	—	—
Interest in learning more languages	—	—	—	—	—	—	—
Membership in organizations concerned with international issues and problem	—	—	—	—	—	—	—

39. For the following statements please decide whether or not you agree. After you
have read each statement, please circle the number in the line below to indicate
your response:

Strongly Disagree 1	Moderately Disagree 2	Slightly Disagree 3	Indifferent 4	Slightly Agree 5	Moderately Agree 6	Strongly Agree 7

Pacific demonstrations--picketing missile bases, peace walks, etc.--are harmful to
the best interests of my home country.

    1   2   3   4   5   6   7

I believe that my country should send food and materials to any country that needs
them.

    1   2   3   4   5   6   7

The immigration of foreigners to my country should be kept down so that we can
provide for our own people first.

    1   2   3   4   5   6   7

Since the world's supplies of essential minerals are limited, the mining and
distribution of mineral resources should be controlled by an international authority.

    1   2   3   4   5   6   7

We should not allow foreign business enterprises to have substantial holdings in our
country.

Strongly Disagree	Moderately Disagree	Slightly Disagree	Indifferent	Slightly Agree	Moderately Agree	Strong Agree
1	2	3	4	5	6	7

Patriotism and loyalty are the first and most important requirements of a good citizen.

| 1 | 2 | 3 | 4 | 5 | 6 | 7 |

Immigrants should not be permitted to come into our country if they compete with our own workers.

| 1 | 2 | 3 | 4 | 5 | 6 | 7 |

We should have a World Government with the power to make laws that would be binding to all its member nations.

| 1 | 2 | 3 | 4 | 5 | 6 | 7 |

An international authority should be established and given direct control over the production of nuclear energy in all countries.

| 1 | 2 | 3 | 4 | 5 | 6 | 7 |

It is our responsibility to do everything possible to prevent people from starving anywhere in the world.

| 1 | 2 | 3 | 4 | 5 | 6 | 7 |

It is none of our business if other governments restrict the personal freedom of their citizens.

| 1 | 2 | 3 | 4 | 5 | 6 | 7 |

No duties are more important than duties towards one's country.

| 1 | 2 | 3 | 4 | 5 | 6 | 7 |

I prefer to be a citizen of the world rather than of any country.

| 1 | 2 | 3 | 4 | 5 | 6 | 7 |

40. How would you rate your level of <u>knowledge</u> concerning the attitudes and values of persons living in the foreign country which you know best?

	Extensive			Moderate		Minimal	
	1	2	3	4	5	6	7
Human rights	—	—	—	—	—	—	—
Significance of education	—	—	—	—	—	—	—
Foreigners	—	—	—	—	—	—	—
International (regional) cooperation	—	—	—	—	—	—	—

	Extensive			Moderate		Minimal	
	1	2	3	4	5	6	7
Your home country	—	—	—	—	—	—	—
The Third World	—	—	—	—	—	—	—
International affairs	—	—	—	—	—	—	—
East-West relations	—	—	—	—	—	—	—
Nationals of your home country	—	—	—	—	—	—	—
Recent immigrant groups	—	—	—	—	—	—	—
Social welfare	—	—	—	—	—	—	—
International peace	—	—	—	—	—	—	—
Business as a career	—	—	—	—	—	—	—
International cooperation in business and finance	—	—	—	—	—	—	—

41. Please indicate the extent to which you agree or disagree with the following statements:

	Strongly Agree				Strongly Disagree
	1	2	3	4	5
The E.E.C. should be strengthened	—	—	—	—	—
Closer European cooperation is an essential prerequisite to economic progress	—	—	—	—	—
Only European cooperation can help Europe catch up with the technological advance of the U.S. and Japan	—	—	—	—	—
The goal of European political union is not important	—	—	—	—	—
European cooperation is less important than worldwide international cooperation	—	—	—	—	—
More emphasis should be placed on European cooperation in the fields of education and culture	—	—	—	—	—

42. Did you stay abroad over and above the period originally envisioned for your SAP?

_____ NO

_____ YES. If "YES" please describe briefly what you did during that additional time:

_____

_____

43. Would you have liked to remain at your host institution abroad to complete your overall degree program there?

_____ NO

_____ YES

44. If you did not remain at the host institution, why? (MULTIPLE REPLY POSSIBLE)

_____ Lack of financial support

_____ Family/personal reasons

_____ Regulations of home and/or host institution made it difficult

_____ Other. Please specify: _____

_____

45. To what extent did you feel integrated into the academic life of your SAP host institution while you were abroad?

To a great Extent				Not at all
1	2	3	4	5
—	—	—	—	—

46. To what extent did/do you feel integrated into the academic life of your home institution BEFORE your study abroad and NOW?

	To a great Extent				Not at all
	1	2	3	4	5
BEFORE SAP	—	—	—	—	—
NOW	—	—	—	—	—

47. If there is a change, please indicate briefly why the change has occurred.

_____

_____

_____

_____

48. Did you return to the same field of study/major which you had chosen prior to going abroad?

_____ YES

_____ YES, but I am interested in courses or areas of study I did not consider before.

_____ NO, I changed my field of study/major. Field of study prior to going abroad: _____

_____ I had not chosen a field of study/major prior to going abroad.

49. How much of the academic study you carried out at the SAP host institution is granted credit at your home institution?

_____ The entire program

_____ Part of the program, and you wanted to receive credit for more than this

_____ Part of the program, because you wanted credit for only part of it

_____ None of the program, although you wanted to receive credit for work done abroad

_____ None of the program because you did not want to receive credit

_____ Degree of credit/recognition not yet determined

50. Is your study abroad likely to prolong the total duration of your undergraduate studies?

_____ NO

_____ YES, by up to one semester/term

_____ YES, by more than one semester/term

_____ DO NOT KNOW

51. Did you make use of the measures provided by your home institution to assist in your re-integration within that institution?

_____ N/AP (i.e., because you have not returned to your former home institution or because no reintegration assistance was provided)

_____ NO

_____ YES. If yes, please indicate your degree of satisfaction with the measures provided:

Extremely Satisfied				Extremely Dissatisfied
1	2	3	4	5
—	—	—	—	—

52. List the main activities offered by your home institution to assist in your reintegration:

_____

_____

_____

_____

_____

53. How have you maintained contact/interest in the SAP host country since your return home?

	To a Consid- erable Extent				Not At All
	1	2	3	4	5
Reading or watching media of your own country	—	—	—	—	—
Communicating with persons in your own country who are knowledgeable about the SAP host country	—	—	—	—	—
Corresponding with persons living in the host country	—	—	—	—	—
Communicating with persons at your home institution who come from the SAP host country	—	—	—	—	—
Reading journals and popular literature from the SAP host country	—	—	—	—	—
Reading professional journals and books on or about the host country	—	—	—	—	—

	To a Consid- erable Extent				Not At All
	1	2	3	4	5
Attending conferences, seminars, lectures, etc. dealing with the host country	—	—	—	—	—
Joining organization(s) involved with the host country	—	—	—	—	—
Attending art exhibits, concerts, films, and other cultural events related to the host country	—	—	—	—	—
Returning to the SAP host country	—	—	—	—	—
By meeting with persons like yourself who have studied in the host country	—	—	—	—	—
By speaking the language of the host country	—	—	—	—	—
By taking courses in the language of the host country	—	—	—	—	—
By giving presentations in your home town on the SAP host country	—	—	—	—	—
Other. Please specify: _____	—	—	—	—	—
_____	—	—	—	—	—
_____	—	—	—	—	—

54. List the most significant things that could help you maintain contact with the host country:

_____

_____

_____

_____

55. In which way(s) have you informed your home institution about your study period abroad and/or aspects of the SAP host country (MULTIPLE REPLY POSSIBLE)?

___ Discussion paper(s) designed specifically to prepare future cohorts of students going abroad.
___ Oral or written report(s) requested by SAP program director or other member(s) of teaching/administrative staff, not necessarily for use in preparing next cohort of students for going abroad
___ Participation in evaluation of study abroad (e.g., answering questionnaire) OTHER THAN THE CURRENT INVESTIGATION
___ Other. Please specify:_____
___ Not at all.

56. If you reflect on your own ways of thinking and learning before your study period abroad and after you returned home, how important in your judgment are the following for your learning and intellectual development?

	IMPORTANCE BEFORE SAP					IMPORTANCE NOW				
	Very Impor- tant				Not Impor- tant At All	Very Impor- tant				Not Impor- tant At All
	1	2	3	4	5	1	2	3	4	5
Learning facts	—	—	—	—	—	—	—	—	—	—
Understanding theories	—	—	—	—	—	—	—	—	—	—
Applying knowledge to practical areas	—	—	—	—	—	—	—	—	—	—
Systematic thinking	—	—	—	—	—	—	—	—	—	—
Methodology (research methodology, computer programming, etc.)	—	—	—	—	—	—	—	—	—	—
Familiarity with different schools of thought	—	—	—	—	—	—	—	—	—	—
Examining relations between observations/hypothesis/facts/ concepts	—	—	—	—	—	—	—	—	—	—
Obtaining comparative (e.g., international/European, inter- cultural perspectives)	—	—	—	—	—	—	—	—	—	—
Utilizing publications in foreign languages	—	—	—	—	—	—	—	—	—	—
Obtaining knowledge from different disciplines (interdisciplinary approach)	—	—	—	—	—	—	—	—	—	—
Regular class attendance	—	—	—	—	—	—	—	—	—	—
Developing one's own point of view	—	—	—	—	—	—	—	—	—	—
Freedom to choose own areas of study	—	—	—	—	—	—	—	—	—	—
Active participation in class discussions	—	—	—	—	—	—	—	—	—	—
Out-of-class communication between students and teaching staff	—	—	—	—	—	—	—	—	—	—
Independent work (e.g., writing papers), project work	—	—	—	—	—	—	—	—	—	—

	IMPORTANCE BEFORE SAP					IMPORTANCE NOW				
	Very Impor- tant				Not Impor- tant At All	Very Impor- tant				Not Impor- tant At All
	1	2	3	4	5	1	2	3	4	5
Obtaining regular feedback from teachers	—	—	—	—	—	—	—	—	—	—
Studying to get good grades, good marks on examinations	—	—	—	—	—	—	—	—	—	—
Taking a heavy workload	—	—	—	—	—	—	—	—	—	—
Selecting demanding courses	—	—	—	—	—	—	—	—	—	—
Regarding the teachers as the main source of information	—	—	—	—	—	—	—	—	—	—

57. What is the degree of your overall satisfaction with the study period abroad?

Very Satisfied				Very Dissatisfied
1	2	3	4	5
——	——	——	——	——

58. What was the worst thing that happened to you while you were abroad?

_____

_____

_____

59. What was the best thing that happened to you while you were abroad?

_____

_____

_____

60. What are the most difficult things you successfully accomplished while you were abroad?

_____

_____

_____

61. To what extent was it worthwhile for you to study abroad with respect to the following?

	Extremely Worth-while 1	2	3	4	Not At All Worth-while 5	Not Appli-cable 6
Exposure to teaching methods other than those adopted at your home institution	—	—	—	—	—	—
Exposure to subject matter not offered at your institution	—	—	—	—	—	—
Your marks/examination results after return from SAP	—	—	—	—	—	—
Opportunity to travel	—	—	—	—	—	—
Career prospects	—	—	—	—	—	—
Acquaintance with people in another country	—	—	—	—	—	—
Foreign language proficiency	—	—	—	—	—	—
Perspective on your home country	—	—	—	—	—	—
Knowledge and understanding of the SAP host country	—	—	—	—	—	—
Acquaintance with your family/ethnic heritage	—	—	—	—	—	—
Break from your usual surroundings	—	—	—	—	—	—
Exposure to other intellectual perspectives in your field	—	—	—	—	—	—
Perspectives gained on your own future life	—	—	—	—	—	—

Other. Please specify: _____

_____   — — — — — —

62. What specific changes would you propose for the SAP? (Consider preparation and follow-up in your home country, as well as the actual time spent abroad.)

_____

_____

_____

_____

_____

63. Do you presently anticipate that you will enter postgraduate studies?

I have already registered/am already
Most probably   Not likely   involved in postgraduate studies
  1   2   3   4   5   6

__   __   __   __   __   __

64. How set are your career goals?

Very   Not at all
determined   determined
  1   2   3   4   5

65. Please indicate briefly and as specifically as possible your present career plans:

_____

_____

_____

66. How does the SAP relate to your present career plans?

_____

_____

_____

67. Do you presently anticipate that your future career or work-related activities will involve: (MULTIPLE REPLY POSSIBLE)

____Utilizing your particular expertise with regard to the SAP host country?

____Utilizing the general international experience you obtained as a consequence of your SAP?

____Considerable contact/cooperation with the SAP host country (regardless of where you are living and working)?

____Considerable international contact/cooperation?

____Your living and working in the SAP host country?

____Your living and working in another foreign country?

68. Do you feel that your SAP experience will help you in achieving your professional and/or work-related goals?

<u>Most
Probably</u>   <u>Not likely
At all</u>
    1   2   3   4   5

    ___   ___   ___   ___   ___

69. ADDITIONAL COMMENTS: _____

_____

_____

_____

_____

_____

_____

_____

_____

THANK YOU FOR YOUR COOPERATION!

E: ALUMNA/US PROFILE

Name: _____

Current Address: _____

_____ zip _____

Best telephone number at which you can be reached for interview:
(   ) _____

Location of your study abroad program (city, country):

Year spent studying abroad: 19 _____ - _____

Major field of study (undergraduate & graduate):

Degrees earned and dates of degrees:

Brief list of jobs held since you completed your studies (use reverse side if necessary):

Current occupation (dates):

Volunteer (civic, religious, etc.) activities (use reverse side if necessary):

Approximate family income (please check):

_____ $0-10,000	_____ $35-50,000
_____ $10-20,000	_____ $50-100,000
_____ $20-35,000	_____ above $100.000

Present Marital Status:

Number and ages of children:

Have you travelled or lived abroad since your study abroad experience?
___yes ___no

___Check here if you wish to receive a summary of research findings when they become available.
9/86

F: ALUMNI/AE FOCUSED-INTERVIEW QUESTIONNAIRE

NAME:

DATE:

PROGRAM:

YEAR:

I. CAREER/VOLUNTEER/WORK EXPERIENCE.

A. Have you lived, traveled, or studied abroad since your study abroad experience If yes, where have you been, for what purpose, and what duration?

B. Would you say that you have an international or intercultural dimension in your work activities?

C. Secondly, do you have an international or intercultural dimension in your volunteer activities?

D. Thirdly, do you have an international or intercultural dimension in your social or religious activities?

E. Has your study abroad experience ever been a drawback to thinks you've wanted to do?

F. Has it been a plus?

G. Do you have occasion to use a foreign language?
    (Elaborate)

H. Do you ever interpret or explain to other Americans the people, customs, or institutions of the country in which you studied?

II. INTERNATIONALIZATION OF HOME AND LIFESTYLE.

A. Are any foreign languages spoken in your home? If so, which ones?

B. What eye-openers or major impressions did you have during your experience in your host country concerning social issues facing that country?

C. What were the biggest problems that you personally faced in that country?

D. What people did you get to know best?

E. Do you still keep in touch with people you met during that year?

F. What especially impressed you about family life in that country?

G. Where did you meet your spouse?

H. Has your spouse had a foreign experience, speak a foreign language, come from a foreign country?

I. In what ways do your spouse and children share your international interests?

J. In terms of American children today, would you

    1) encourage or provide international experiences?

    2) encourage studying foreign languages? Why?

K. What are the main things that Americans should be getting from a study abroad experience?

L. Do you think that any aspects of your lifestyles have been affected by your study abroad experience (i.e., reading materials, interaction with people from other cultures, etc.)?

M. Are these international interests focussed primarily on the country in which you studied, Europe as a whole, or do they include other areas as well?

N. Do you have any strong interest in following important events in the country in which you studied?

III. WORLD PERSPECTIVE.

A. What effect, if any, did study abroad have on shaping and influencing how you evaluate world issues?

B. In what ways has your foreign experience made you reassess your outlook on your life in the U.S.?

IV. GENERAL REFLECTIONS ON STUDY ABROAD.

A. Was there anything that you consider to be especially great, or not so great, about your academic experience abroad? (i.e., class size, independence, research, etc.)?

B. Was there anything that you consider to have been especially great, or not so great, about your personal living experience abroad?

C. Many people who have studied abroad have felt that when they returned they were out of sync with life in the U.S. Did this happen to you?

D. Do you still feel changed in any way?

E. What did you get out of your study abroad experience that was lasting?

F. What impact has study abroad had on your political perspective on the United States?

G. Looking back now, how do you feel about what you've done so far in your education and work, particularly as it pertains to your international interests?

V. The time we have is over, but is there anything else you would like to add?

REFERENCES

Abbott, A. (1988). *The systems of professions: An essay on the division of expert labor.* Chicago: University of Chicago Press.

Abrams, I. (1960). *Study abroad. New dimensions in higher education: Some newer developments.* New York: McGraw-Hill.

Ad Hoc Committee on Global Education. (1987). Global education: In bounds or out? A report submitted to the board of directors, National Council for the Social Studies. *Social Education,* April/May, 242–249.

Adler, P. S. (1975). The transitional experience: An alternative view of culture shock. *Journal of Humanistic Psychology,* 15, 13–23.

Affifi, A. A. & Clark, V. (1984). *Computer aided multivariate analysis.* Belmont, CA: Wadsworth.

Allport, G. (1955). *Theories of perception and the concept of structure.* New York: Wiley.

Astin, A. (1985). *Achieving educational excellence.* San Francisco: Jossey-Bass.

Astin, A., Green, E. C., & Korn, W. S. (1987). *The American freshman: Twenty year trends: 1966–1985.* Los Angeles: University of California Higher Education Research Institute.

Bandura, A. (1982). Self-efficacy in human agency. *American Psychologist,* 37, 122–147.

Barber, E. & Ilchman, W. (1980). The preservation of the cosmopolitan research university in the United States. In R. D. Lambert (Ed.), *New directions in international education: The Annals of the American Academy of Political and Social Science,* 449, May 1980.

Barrows, T., Ager, S. M., Bennett, M. F., Brown, H. I., Clark, J.L.D., Harris, L. G., & Klein, S. F. (1981). *College students' knowledge and beliefs: A survey of global understanding.* New Rochelle, NY: Change Magazine Press.

Becker, J. (Ed.). (1979). *Schooling for a global age.* New York: McGraw-Hill.

Bell, D. (1973). *The post industrial society.* New York: Basic Books.

Bianchi, S. M. & Spain, D. (1986). *American women in transition.* New York: Russell Sage.

Bledstein, B. J. (1976). *The culture of professionalism: The middle class and the development of higher education in America.* New York: Oxford University Press.

Block, J. (1982). Assimilation, accommodation, and the dynamics of personality development. *Child Development, 53,* 281–295.

Bowen, H. R. with Clecak, P., Doud, J. P., & Douglass, G. E. (1977). *Investment in learning: The individual and social value of higher education.* San Francisco: Jossey-Bass.

Brislin, R. W. (1981). *Cross-cultural encounters.* New York: Pergamon.

Burn, B. (1980). *Expanding the international dimension of higher education.* San Francisco: Jossey-Bass.

Burn, B. (1985). Higher education is international. In W. H. Allaway & H. C. Shorrock (Eds.), *Dimensions of international higher education.* Boulder, CO: Westview.

Burn, B. & Briggs, A. (1985). *Study abroad: A European and American perspective on organization and impact of study abroad.* Amsterdam: European Institute of Education and Policy Study.

Campbell, D. T. (1967). Stereotypes and the perception of group differences. *American Psychologist, 22,* 817–829.

Campbell, D. T. & Fiske, D. W. (1959). Convergent and discriminant validation by the multitrait-multimethod matrix. *Psychological Bulletin, 56,* 81–105.

Campbell, D. T. & Stanley, J. C. (1963). *Experimental and quasi-experimental designs for research.* Chicago: Rand McNally.

Campbell, R. & Schnell, S. (1987). Language conservation. *Annals of the American Academy,* 177–185.

Carlson, J. S. & Widaman, K. F. (1988). The effects of study abroad during college on attitudes toward other cultures. *International Journal of Intercultural Relations, 12,* 1–17.

Carlson, J. S. & Yachimowicz, D. (1986). *Evaluation of the University of California's Education Abroad Program: The 1985–86 Participant Questionnaire.* Santa Barbara: University of California.

Carlson, J. S. & Yachimowicz, D. (1987). *Evaluation of the University of California's Education Abroad Program: The 1986–87 Participant Questionnaire.* Santa Barbara: University of California.

Carsello, C. & Greiser, J. (1976). How college students change during study abroad. *College Student Journal, 10,* 276–278.

Church, A. T. (1982). Sojourner adjustment. *Psychological Bulletin, 91,* 540–572.

Coelho, M. (1962). Personal growth and educational development through working and studying abroad. *Journal of Social Issues, 18,* 55–67.

Coelho-Oudegeest, M. (1971). Cross-cultural counseling: A study of some variables in the counseling of foreign students. (Doctoral dissertation, University of Wisconsin, Madison.) *Dissertation Abstracts, 31,* 6340A.

David, K. H. (1971). Culture shock and the development of self-awareness. *Journal of Contemporary Psychotherapy, 4,* 44–48.

Davis, J. A. (1964). *Great aspirations: The graduate school plans of America's college seniors.* Chicago: Aldine.

Davis-Van Atta, D., Carrier, S. C., & Frankfort, F. (1985). *Educating America's scientists: The role of research colleges.* Oberlin, Ohio: Oberlin College.

Deutsch, S. E. (1970). *International education and exchange: A sociological analysis.* Cleveland: Case Western Reserve University Press.

Eagley, A. H. & Himmelfarb, S. (1978). Attitudes and opinions. In M. F. Rosenzweig & H. L. Porter (Eds.), *Annual Review of Psychology, 29,* 517–555.

Erikson, E. H. (1975). *Life history and the historical moment.* New York: Norton.

Festinger, L. (1957). *A theory of cognitive dissonance.* Evanston, IL: Row-Peterson.

Furnham, A. & Bochner, S. (1982). Social difficulty in a foreign culture: An empirical analysis of culture shock. In S. Bochner (Ed.), *Culture in contact.* New York: Pergamon.

Geiger, R. L. (1986). *To advance knowledge: The growth of American research universities, 1900–1940.* New York: Oxford University Press.

German Academic Exchange Service (DAAD). (1980). *Research on exchanges: Proceeding of the German-American conference at the Wissenschaftszentrum.* Bonn: DAAD.

Gitlin, T. (1987). *The sixties: Years of hope, days of rage.* New York: Bantam.

Goodrich, H. B., Knapp, R. H., & Boehm, G.A.W. (1951). The origin of U.S. scientists. *Scientific American, 185,* no. 1, 15–17.

Goodsell, C. T. & Dunbar, U. F. (1933). *Centennial history of Kalamazoo College.* Kalamazoo, MI: Kalamazoo College.

Goodwin, C. & Nacht, M. (1988). *Abroad and beyond.* New York: Cambridge University Press.

Grant, W. V. & Snyder, T. D. (1984). *Digest of education statistics 1983–84.* Washington, DC: National Center for Education Statistics.

Haber, S. (1974). The professions and higher education in America: A historical view. In M. S. Gordon (Ed.), *Higher education and the labor market.* New York: McGraw-Hill.

Harter, S. (1978). Effectance motivation reconsidered: Toward a comprehensive model of self-worth. In R. Leaky (Ed.), *The development of self.* New York: Academic Press.

Hull, F. (1978). *Foreign students in the United States of America: Coping behavior within the education environment.* New York: Praeger.

Hunt, J. McV. (1961). *Intelligence and experience.* New York: Ronald.

Jencks, C. & Riesman, D. (1968). *The academic revolution.* Garden City, NY: Doubleday.

Kelman, H. (1975). Intercultural interchanges: Some contributions from theories of attitude change. In W. Coplin & J. M. Rochester (Eds.), *A multimethod introduction to international politics.* Chicago: Markham.

Klineberg, O. (1981). The role of international university exchanges. In S. Bochner (Ed.), *The mediating person.* Cambridge, MA: Shenkman.

Klineberg, O. & Hull, W. F. (1979). *At a foreign university: An international study of adaptation and coping.* New York: Praeger.

Lachman, M. E. (1986). Personal control in later life: Stability, change, and cognitive correlates. In M. M. Baltes & P. B. Baltes (Eds.), *The psychology and control of aging.* Hillsdale, NJ: Erlbaum.

Levine, D. O. (1986). *The American college and the culture of aspiration, 1915–1940.* Ithaca, NY: Cornell University Press.

Levy, F. *Dollars and dreams: The changing American income distribution.* New York: Russell Sage Foundation.

Luria, A. R. (1976). *Cognitive development: Its cultural and social foundation* (Trans. by M. Cole). Cambridge, MA: Harvard.

McGuigan, F. J. (1984). Psychological changes related to intercultural experiences. *Psychological Reports,* 4, 55–60.

Mills, C. W. (1956). *White collar.* New York: Oxford University Press.

Morris, R. T. (1960). *The two-way mirror: National status in foreign students' adjustment.* Minneapolis: University of Minnesota Press.

Mulder, A. (1958). *The Kalamazoo College story: The first quarter of the second century of progress 1933–1958.* Kalamazoo, MI: Kalamazoo College.

OECD. (1988). *Financing and external debt in developing countries: 1987 survey.* Washington, DC: Organization for Economic Co-Operation and Development.

Oleson, A. & Voss, J. (1976). *The organization of knowledge in modern America: The middle class and the development of higher education in America.* New York: W. W. Norton.

Piaget, J. (1950). *The psychology of intelligence* (Trans. by M. Piercy & D. E. Barlyne). London: Routledge & Kegan Paul.

Pool, I. (1965). Effects of cross-national contact on national and international images. In H. C. Kelman (Ed.), *International behavior: A social psychological analysis.* New York: Holt, Rinehart & Winston.

Prater, C. H., Barutia, R., Larkin, B. D., & Weaver, H. D. (1980). *Final report of the foreign-language review committee.* Santa Barbara: University of California.

President's Commission on Foreign Language and International Studies. (1980a). *A report to the president from the President's Commission.* Washington, DC: Government Printing Office.

President's Commission on Foreign Language and International Studies. (1980b). *Background papers and studies.* Washington, DC: U.S. Government Printing Office.

Rosenthal, R. & Rosnow, R. L. (1975). *The volunteer subject.* New York: Wiley.

Rosenthal, R. & Rubin, D. B. (1982). A simple general purpose display of magnitude of experimental effect. *Journal of Educational Psychology,* 74, 166–169.

Sanders, I. T. & Ward, J. C. (1970). *Bridges to understanding: International programs of American colleges and universities.* New York: McGraw-Hill.

Sanford, N. (1962). Higher education as a field of study. In N. Sanford (Ed.), *The American college.* New York: Wiley.

Sell, D. K. (1983). Attitude change in foreign study participants. *International Journal of Intercultural Relations,* 7, 131–147.

Smith, H. D. (1955). Do intercultural experiences affect attitudes? *Journal of Abnormal and Social Psychology,* 51, 469–477.

Solomon, B. M. (1985). *In the company of educated women: A history of women and higher education in America.* New Haven: Yale University Press.

Spaeth, J. L. & Greeley, A. M. (1970). *Recent alumni and higher education: A survey of college graduates.* New York: McGraw-Hill.

Spaulding, S. & Flack, M. J. (1976). *The world's students in the United States: A review and evaluation of research on foreign students.* New York: Praeger.

Stassen, M. (1985). Objective and cognitive dimensions of study abroad. In W. H. Allaway & H. C. Shorrock (Eds.), *Dimensions of international higher education.* Boulder, CO: Westview.

Tilly, C. (1986). *The contentious French: Four centuries of popular struggles.* Cambridge, MA: Belknap Press of Harvard University Press.

U.S. Department of Commerce, Bureau of the Census. (1987). *Statistical abstract of the United States*. Washington, DC: Government Printing Office.

U.S. Department of Education, Office of Educational Research and Improvement for Education Statistics. (1980, 1987, 1988). *Digest of education statistics*. Washington, DC: Government Printing Office.

U.S. Department of Labor, Bureau of Labor Statistics. (1984). *Educational attainment of workers (March 1982–1983)*. Washington, DC: Government Printing Office.

Useem, J., Donoghue, J. D., & Useem, R. H. (1963). Men in the middle of the third culture: The roles of American and non-Western people in cross-cultural administration. *Human Organization, 22,* 169–179.

Vanneman, R. & Cannon, L. W. (1987). *The American perception of class*. Philadelphia: Temple University Press.

Walton, B. J. (1968). Foreign student exchange in perspective: What the research tells us. *International Education and Cultural Exchange, 3,* 1–14.

Weaver, H., Martin, J., Burn, B., Useem, J., & Carlson, J. S. (1987). *A researcher's guide to international educational exchange*. Santa Barbara: University of California.

Westkott, M. (1986). *The feminist legacy of Karen Horney*. New Haven: Yale University Press.

Yachimowicz, D. J. (1987). "The effect of study abroad during college on international understanding and attitudes toward the homeland and other cultures." Doctoral dissertation, University of California, Riverside.

Zajonc, R. B. (1981). Attitudinal effects of mere exposure. *Journal of Personality and Social Psychology, 9,* 1–27.

INDEX

About the Authors

JERRY S. CARLSON is Professor of Education and Cooperating Member of the Department of Psychology at the University of California, Riverside. He is the recipient of awards from the Alexander von Humbolt Foundation for research on mental abilities and from the Council on International Educational Exchange for research in the area of international education.

BARBARA B. BURN is Associate Provost for International Programs, Adjunct Professor, and teaches comparative higher education at the University of Massachusetts at Amherst. She is the author of *Expanding the International Dimension of Higher Education.*

JOHN USEEM is Professor Emeritus of Sociology at Michigan State University. He is the author of numerous articles, books and monographs and has been awarded Michigan State University's "Distinguished Faculty Award," the Society for the Study of Social Problems' Lee Founders Award for "Significant Achievement Over a Distinguished Career," as well as other scholarly awards.

DAVID YACHIMOWICZ is Professor of Education and Cooperating Member of the Department of Psychology at the University of California, Riverside.